WHY SOME WARS NEVER END

Text © 2010 by Joseph Cummins

First published in the USA in 2010 by
Fair Winds Press, a member of
Quayside Publishing Group
100 Cummings Center
Suite 406-L
Beverly, MA 01915-6101
www.fairwindspress.com

12 11 10 09 08   1 2 3 4 5

ISBN-13: 978-1-59233-431-5
ISBN-10: 1-59233-431-8

Library of Congress Cataloging-in-Publication Data
Cummins, Joseph.
  Why some wars never end : the stories of the longest conflicts in history / Joseph Cummins.
     p. cm.
  Includes bibliographical references and index.
  ISBN-13: 978-1-59233-431-5
  ISBN-10: 1-59233-431-8
  1. Military history. 2. War—History. I. Title.

  D25.5.C86 2010
  355.0209—dc22

                                                              2010018229

Cover design: Peter Long
Book design: Sheila Hart Design, Inc.
Book layout: Sheila Hart Design, Inc.
Cover image: Getty Images
Page 8: © The Art Gallery Collection/Alamy
Page 82: The Bridgeman Art Library International
Page 134: Getty Images

Printed and bound in Singapore

Contributing writers: Alan Axelrod (chapters 13 and 14) and Cormac O'Brien (chapter 11)

WHY SOME WARS NEVER END

THE STORIES OF THE LONGEST CONFLICTS IN HISTORY

JOSEPH CUMMINS

FAIR WINDS
PRESS
BEVERLY, MASSACHUSETTS

CONTENTS

INTRODUCTION

Why Some Wars Never End: The Stories of the Longest Conflicts in History focuses on an underexamined phenomenon: the frequency of "never-ending" wars that run counter to the expectation that war takes off from a point of political or diplomatic impasse and has a relatively predictable duration.

The fourteen wars discussed in this volume went on for decades, some for generations—the Punic Wars went on for 120 years, the Ottoman Wars lasted centuries, the modern-day wars in Vietnam continued for a total of fifty years. It is important to note that my definition of long war does not mean continuous fighting for the noted period of time—though sometimes it does—but that an unresolved state of enmity existed between the warring parties for at least two generations, a condition that can and does erupt again and again into violence.

Many people think that long wars are irrational—a conflict in which both a great-grandfather and his great-grandson can fight runs counter to normal human impulses toward sanity and self-preservation. The problem with this thinking is that it presupposes that it is in the best interests of a combatant to actually end the war. Many times, it is not.

The chapters in *Why Some Wars Never End* are grouped into sections indicating the main reasons wars go on forever—wars of empire, religious wars, guerilla wars, nationalist struggles, and wars of chaos (where events spin out of control, proving historian Carl von Clausewitz's maxim that "war is the province of chance. In no other sphere of human activity must such a margin be left for this intruder").

LIVING TO FIGHT ANOTHER DAY

Long wars such as the Vietnam struggle against France and the United States, the nineteenth-century British battles in Afghanistan, or the U.S. attempt to crush the Seminoles in Florida go on for years because the weaker combatant (militarily) uses guerilla tactics and the advantages of local landscape to wear its opponent down. Fighting, then running away to fight another day, takes time.

Another reason wars never end is because peacemaking can be so imperfect and unfair. Every truce called during the Hundred Years' War was not so much a real peace as a breathing space for exhausted combatants to rest their weary sword-arms before leaping at each other's throats again. Peace can be unworkable because—as was the case with Carthage, defeated in the First Punic War by Rome—one party is still ready to go on fighting, or feels that the victors are exacting unduly harsh penalties.

Long wars are made long by fearless and charismatic leaders such as Hannibal, Ho Chi Minh, and David Ben-Gurion—generals and politicians who decided (generally speaking against conventional wisdom and to the surprise of their enemies) to keep on fighting, no matter what the cost. A powerful factor in a long war is a leader's estimation that his people have more to lose by conceding than by fighting on.

Perhaps some of the primary reasons for never-ending warfare are ethnic and religious tensions, both of which run like fast-moving currents throughout the millennia spanned by *Why Some Wars Never End*. Territory can be negotiated, as can monetary losses, even the destruction of entire cities—but religion cuts too close to the bone. The Balkan Wars, the Arab-Israeli conflicts, the Ottoman Wars, and the Troubles in Northern Ireland are wars that have lasted an interminable amount of time because religion entered the argument. The mujahideen fighting U.S. and allied forces today in Afghanistan are descendants of the holy warriors who battled the British more than a century before. When Slobodan Milošević stirred up Serbian nationalism in 1989 at a famous speech in Kosovo, his main rallying point was a battle in which the Christian Serbs had been defeated by Muslim Ottomans six hundred years before.

In an age of worldwide jihad, never-ending war may well be the future of conflict. The administration of George W. Bush formally put forth this concept in 2006, when a Defense Department report titled *Fighting the Long War* claimed that "the United States is a nation engaged in what will be a long war" against terror in Iraq, Afghanistan, and throughout a so-called "arc of instability" that includes the Middle East and parts of Africa and Central and South Asia. Then-Secretary of Defense Donald Rumsfeld said that the war on terrorism was "a generational conflict akin to the Cold War." If this happens, if long wars become the norm and not the exception, then real and lasting peace will be something even more precious than it is now.

"CARTHAGE MUST BE DESTROYED!"

WARS OF EMPIRE

Great struggles that were long because
the future of empires were at stake.

CHAPTER I

THE GRECO-PERSIAN WARS

"REMEMBER THE ATHENIANS"

500–449 BCE

The overweaning ambitions of a vast aristocracy
and the stubborn independence of a young people led to
a fifty-year-long war that opened the way to the flowering
of the Greek golden age.

In a time when the average man lived, at most, thirty-five years, a half-century of war was an eternity. The Greco-Persian Wars, one of the most important wars in history, lasted for fifty years in part because it featured an epic struggle between two very different ways of life. On the one side was the Persian Empire, a vast autocracy ruled by a godlike king who believed that all the peoples of the world were essentially his subjects. On the other were the Greek city-states, which, despite the disputes that often flared between them, shared a common Hellenic identity, as well as a democratic spirit that allowed for open political debate and favored representative forms of government.

The Greco-Persian Wars was the first clash of empires in history that had a direct effect on the Western world, because the survival of the Greeks would translate into a Golden Age of art, literature, culture, and thought that influences us to this day. It was a clash between an old world and a new one. The old world of the Persians featured demigods, magic, high priests, the wealth of the East, and the sense that the world was there to be conquered. The new world of the Greeks was one based on independent thought, majority rule, and individual striving—all of which would result in the democracies of the West.

The wars fought between the Greeks and the Persians—fought really between two different ways of life—lasted for fifty years because there could be no compromise solution between such differing world philosophies. In heroic battlefields like Marathon, Thermopylae, and Salamis, the arrogant armies of the god-kings met the sturdy stubbornness and independent tactical thinking of the Greeks, particularly in the form of three Greek commanders, each iconoclastic and flawed, yet willing to take chances. Because of these three men, the Greeks lived to fight another day—until an eternity of war had passed and the Greeks, and eventually Western civilization, were triumphant.

"THAT I MAY PUNISH THE ATHENIANS"

In 500 BCE, the Persian Empire was reaching its peak. It began sixty years earlier when Cyrus the Great's armies had swept out of the grasslands of what is now Iran to destroy the Medes and Babylonians. After Cyrus died in battle in 529, a usurper named Darius became king and by 500 presided over an empire that extended from modern-day Pakistan in the east to Macedonia in the north to Egypt in the south.

The Persians were probably the world's first real empire, in the sense that they established roads, developed humankind's first large-scale coinage system, and sought to colonize. Yet they were a highly rigid autocracy in the ancient mode: Darius was considered a near-god, referred to as the "One King" or "the Great King," and his administration was monolithic. He tolerated little political opposition. Persian *satraps*, or governors, often ruled newly acquired territories with leniency—until the faintest whiff of rebellion was detected, at which time disloyal citizens were ruthlessly slaughtered or enslaved.

The Greek city-states, on the other hand, were too disorganized to set out to conquer the world, but they were, as the Greek playwright Aeschylus would write in his play, *The Persians*, "no man's slaves or dependents." However, the Persians had already conquered the Greek cities of Ionia, across the Aegean in what is now western Turkey. In 500 BCE, they revolted, and Darius sent an army to destroy them. It took the Persians six years to bloodily put down this revolt, and Darius was furious that Athens had the temerity to send soldiers to aid the rebellious Ionian cities.

Darius was particularly affronted because Athenian forces had set fire to the Persian-held town of Sardis, sacking it and burning it to the ground. When the Great King heard about it, according to the Greek historian Herodotus, he did not even know who the Athenians were. When he learned that this obscure Greek city-state had dared to confront him, he commanded that his bow be brought to him. He took it and fired an arrow up into the air, shouting, "Grant, O God, that I may punish the Athenians!" Then Darius told his steward to repeat to him the words "Master, remember the Athenians!" three times whenever he sat down to dinner.

Having made this vow, Darius set about destroying the rebellious Ionians. In 494, the Persians sank almost the entire Ionian fleet during a massive sea battle near the island of Lade. By 494, the rebellion was over, and thousands of enslaved Ionians were sent back to the cities of Persia, while destitute refugees fled to mainland Greece, and even as far as Sicily and Italy.

> DARIUS WAS CERTAIN HIS MASSIVE ARMY
> COULD MAKE QUICK WORK OF THE GREEKS,
> BUT HE HAD UNDERESTIMATED THE POWERFUL SPIRIT
> OF HIS ENEMY, AND THEIR HATRED OF THE PERSIANS—
> TWO ELEMENTS THAT WOULD LEAD
> TO A VERY LONG WAR INDEED.

The stage was now set for the invasion of Greece, for Darius to fulfill his vow. He was certain his massive army could make quick work of the Greeks, but he had underestimated the powerful spirit of his enemy, and their hatred of the Persians—two elements that would lead to a very long war indeed. And the Persians were about to meet the first of the Greek commanders who would turn what should have been a quick invasion of an annoying enemy into a humiliating defeat that would lead to ever-greater warfare.

MILTIADES AND THE BATTLE OF MARATHON

In the spring of 492, Darius placed his nephew and son-in-law Mardonius in command of a huge fleet and instructed him to conquer Greece and revenge the Persians for the Athenian destruction of Sardis. Mardonius was easily able to subdue the northern provinces of Thrace and Macedonia; however, a storm destroyed his fleet near Cape Athos and he was forced to return to Persia. In 490, a still-angry Darius sent another commander, Datis, with an even larger invading army to land on the shores of Attica and march on Athens. Datis had with him Hippias, the former tyrant of Athens whom the Athenians had ousted; Darius hoped to rally the Athenians around Hippias and install him as puppet ruler.

Herodotus writes that Datis's orders were "to reduce Athens ... to slavery and to bring the slaves before the King." Datis moved through the Aegean, capturing island after island and sending alarms sounding all through Greece. The Persians captured Eretria, another city-state that had fought them during the Ionian revolt. Their fleet numbered about 400 merchant ships, with 200 fighting triremes, the ubiquitous three-tiered oared warships of the Greco-Persian Wars, and their army and cavalry combined were 25,000 strong. Added to this were thousands of conscripts Datis had taken from the Greek islands along the way.

Darius I, the Persian god-king, vowed to destroy the upstart Athenians after they sacked and burned the Persian-held town of Sardis. However, his underestimation of his enemy and Greek hatred of the Persians were two elements that prolonged the war. Darius is shown being waited on by attendants in this 1881 chromolithograph of a frieze in the citadel at Susa, the capital of Persia.

In early August, the Persian fleet entered the Bay of Marathon, about 24 miles (38.6 km) northeast of the city of Athens. The Marathon plains were a long, flat strip of land between the mountains and the sea. The beach was wide, made of firm sand, an easy place for Datis to draw up his ships. The single main road to Athens led through a narrow gap in the mountains; there was no way Datis could be attacked from his flanks, and the wide plain gave excellent maneuvering to his fine cavalry forces.

The moment Datis landed, signal fires flared on mountaintops, and the news quickly spread to Athens. A runner was sent to Sparta, some 140 miles (225.3 km) away, begging the Spartans to help the Athenians fight the Persians, but the Spartans claimed that a religious festival dedicated to Apollo made it a sacrilege for them to take up arms until after the full moon. When this news reached the Athenians, many thought it a convenient excuse not to fight. However, there was nothing they could do. The choice of strategies argued in the Assembly came down to two: either fortify Athens against a Persian siege and hope the Spartans would indeed attack after the full moon (roughly August 12) or sally forth to meet the enemy.

Miltiades, one of ten Greek *strategos*, or generals, elected to fight the Persians, was for meeting the enemy in battle, and it was his strategy that carried the day. Miltiades's name comes from the word *miltos*, which was a red ochre clay used as paint; it was a name given to those with red hair and fiery dispositions. At the time of the Persian invasion he was fairly well advanced in age, about sixty, and had had a checkered history. He had been a vassal of King Darius in Asia Minor but had joined the Ionian Revolt. After it failed, he fled to Athens, where he was nearly imprisoned for collaboration with the Persians, but he managed to convince the Athenians that he had turned against Darius and now wanted nothing more than to help lead the Athenians to victory.

"A DESTRUCTIVE MADNESS"

Having decided to fight, the Athenians immediately sent 10,000 heavily armed citizen-soldiers—mostly small landowners, men who could afford their own spears and armor—to meet the Persians. They were joined by some 600 to 1,000 men from the town of Plataea, the only other Greeks willing to help the Athenians. The Athenian warriors were known as *hoplites*, from the large circular shield they carried, the *hoplon*. They wore extraordinarily heavy armor—at 50 to 60 pounds (22.7 to 27.2 kg), not including the weight of the hoplon, the heaviest that would be seen until the advent of the medieval knight—and they fought in phalanx formations, tightly packed groups of men standing shield to shield, thrusting out their long spears.

The Athenians arrived at Marathon around August 7 and arrayed themselves with the ocean on their right and low foothills on their left. And then they waited. The Persian army, including cavalry and archers (the Greeks had neither), was probably about 2 miles (3.2 km) away, down the beach. The two armies faced each other for three or four days without action. The Greeks knew they would be at a disadvantage if they came out and met the Persians in the open area where they could be flanked by the swift Persian cavalry, and so they stayed put.

Why the Persians delayed is a little less clear. They may have simply been waiting for the Greeks to make a move. There is also a story, which numerous modern historians believe, that Datis was in league with Greek traitors in Athens, who had told him they would flash a shield from a mountaintop when they were ready to mount a coup and take over Athens, at which point he would begin the attack.

But nothing happened—there was no shield flash, and the Greek army did not expose itself by making a rash move. However, dissension continued in the ranks of the Greek high command. Five of the commanders wanted to retreat in the face of a Persian army that outnumbered them by more than two to one, while the other five, spurred on by Miltiades, insisted on standing their ground. The decision was taken out of their hands on August 12. Although he had still not received a signal from Greek traitors, Datis decided to disembark from Marathon with most of his cavalry on the night of August 11–12 and sail to Phaleron Bay to attack Athens while the Greek army waited at Marathon.

This was a bold end-around move and might have worked, but some Ionian Greek soldiers, conscripted into the Persian army, passed a message to the Greeks at Marathon that "the cavalry are away." Miltiades quickly understood that the one chance that Athens had for survival was for the Greeks to attack the remaining Persian forces at Marathon, defeat them, and then race back the 24 miles (38.6 km) to Athens to face Datis's fleet, which would take perhaps twelve hours to reach Athens.

Thus, at about six o'clock that morning of August 12, the Greeks began to advance toward the Persian army, whose commanders were astonished to see them on the move, having been certain that the Greeks would not dare attack in the open because they had no archers or cavalry.

But the Greeks were desperate and willing to risk all when fighting for their homeland—the kind of stubbornness that makes long wars last even longer. When the phalanxes marched to within 150 yards (137.2 m) of the Persian line and the expert Persian archers opened up with a deadly shower of arrows, the Greeks surprised their enemy by running straight at them. This move not only helped take the Greeks out of danger from the barbed arrow points, but it also gave them momentum. Thousands of Greeks wearing heavy armor running for 150 yards (137 m; not the mile that some accounts would have it, however) crashed into the Persian ranks with the weight of a squadron of tanks. The lightly armored Persians, fighting with scimitars and short spears, were no match for the Greeks, who drove them back on their camp.

So bloodthirsty were the Athenians that the Persians—in their first ever major battle on the Greek homeland—were sure that "a destructive madness" had taken possession of the Greeks, according to historian Victor Davis Hanson. They raced for the ships and departed as fast as they could, leaving more than 6,000 dead behind. The whole affair lasted probably no more than three hours. "Up until that time," wrote

Herodotus, speaking of Marathon, "the mere name of the Persians brought on fear among the Greeks."

But no longer.

"A FAR GREATER STRUGGLE"

Miltiades now led his victorious men on a determined forced march back to Athens, where they arrived mid-afternoon, just as Datis's fleet was entering Phaleron Bay. Seeing that his army had been defeated, Datis waffled, and finally decided to sail away.

The Greeks had won a great victory, but the war was far from over. Losing at Marathon made the Persians even more determined to destroy the Athenians—more evidence that lengthy wars are fought because of vendetta. After the death of Darius in 486, his son Xerxes, the new ruler of the Persian Empire, began to make preparations for the greatest invasion force the world had ever known. At the same time, however, Athens had let down its guard. As the Roman historian Plutarch later wrote: "Now …the Athenians supposed that the Persian defeat at Marathon meant the end of the war." However, according to Plutarch, one man named Themistocles "believed that [the Greek victory at Marathon] was only the prelude to a far greater struggle."

Themistocles would be the second of the Greek commanders who were prepared to wage war in perpetuity against the Persian invaders. He was born in 525 BCE to an aristocratic family and probably spent much of his life as a lawyer and a sort of political boss in the tangled alleyways of Athenian democracy. Ancient Greek sources generally portray him as brilliant, gregarious, and perhaps none too trustworthy—similar to Miltiades. But, though he fought as a strategos at Marathon and took part in that glorious victory, he understood that the Persians had by no means been defeated.

Therefore, he lobbied vigorously to use the proceeds from a state-owned silver mine to build a much larger Athenian navy of triremes to at least come close to matching

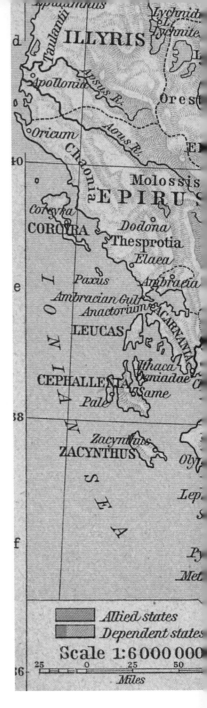

The arrogance of the Persian leaders prevented them from taking the Greeks seriously—they considered the Greek states, shown here, mere stepping stones on the way to a larger invasion of the West.

the vast Persian fleet. Themistocles also pushed to fortify the harbor at Piraeus, crucial to Greek seagoing fortune.

His efforts met with resistance. As with the Romans in the Punic Wars (see page 28), many Greeks thought that the navy was not the most honorable profession, one that was home to drunks and rabble-rousers. But Themistocles understood that a change in

tactics was needed—that the Greek army could not defeat the much larger Persian force that was coming.

And what a force it was. By 480, Xerxes had completed his own preparations for invasion, and they were astonishing ones. King for six years when he invaded Greece, the thirty-eight-year-old Xerxes had assembled what, Herodotus would write, brought together "all the nations of Asia." There were Assyrians with iron-studded war clubs; Scythians with their trademark short, curved bows; Indians in cotton dhotis; Caspian tribesmen with scimitars; and Ethiopians who covered themselves with red war paint and wore the scalps of horses—with the ears and mane still attached—as headdresses.

This is not even to mention the heart of the army, the 10,000 Immortals, crack Persian soldiers who were the king's own personal guard and the most fearsome troops in the army. Herodotus put the number of Xerxes's army (which was led personally by the king) at one million, but modern historians estimate that Xerxes had about 210,000 soldiers, including 170,000 infantry, 8,000 cavalry, 2,000 charioteers and camel corps, and 30,000 turncoat Greeks. In all, a far greater and more formidable force than that which had been stopped at Marathon a decade before.

THE PERSIAN INVASION

Despite the events at Marathon, the Greeks were still small change to an empire on the scale of Persia. Xerxes was an intelligent man, but his arrogance would not allow him to truly take the Greeks seriously. He wanted to punish the Athenians, and would, but they were merely a stepping-stone for a larger invasion of the West that would include a push to the Italian peninsula (in fact, almost simultaneous with Xerxes's attack on Greece, Carthage, a Persian ally, was attacking Greek settlements on Sicily).

> DESPITE THE EVENTS AT MARATHON, THE GREEKS WERE STILL SMALL CHANGE TO AN EMPIRE ON THE SCALE OF PERSIA. XERXES WANTED TO PUNISH THE ATHENIANS, AND WOULD, BUT THEY WERE MERELY A STEPPING-STONE FOR A LARGER INVASION OF THE WEST.

Xerxes began the hostilities of this second stage of the Greco-Persian Wars by sending emissaries to Sparta and Athens, the two most powerful Greek states, demanding that they give Xerxes water and earth, tokens of surrender in the ancient

Spartan King Leonidas, the third of the great Greek leaders, fights at the Battle of Thermopylae in this 1814 painting by Jacques-Louis David. Leonidas's sacrifice bought time for the rest of the Greeks to escape and also gave new life and hope to the Greek side in the war against the Persians.

Bridgeman Art Library / SuperStock

world. The Spartans threw the Persian messengers into a well, telling them that they could get all the water they needed there. The Athenians shoved their Persians emissaries into a pit.

War was now inevitable. Determined to destroy the Greeks, Xerxes performed the unprecedented feat of actually bridging the Hellespont. In an extraordinary demonstration of ancient engineering, about fifty triremes were lashed together, anchored, and connected with a cable that was winched tight by huge pulleys on each shore, and then a bridge of dirt and wood was laid across them and fenced on the sides. This allowed his troops to safely cross that stormy strait leading into the Black Sea, although at least one bridge was destroyed during a storm, causing Xerxes to order that the water of the Hellespont be lashed 300 times while curses were shouted at it ("You salt and bitter stream, your master lays this punishment on you for injuring him!" was just one of them).

After the Hellespont cooperated enough to let his army across, probably around March of 480, Xerxes led his army down through Thrace and Macedonia into northeastern Greece. His destination was the central plains of Attica, and Athens. To oppose him, the Greeks banded together to form an organization of city-states called the Hellenic League. While Themistocles gathered a Greek navy consisting of perhaps 370 triremes, an army led by the Spartan King Leonidas marched north to a narrow pass between the mountains and the sea, the only place where Xerxes and his army could enter central Greece from the northern mountains, arriving there in late August or early September.

About 85 miles (136.8 km) northwest of Athens, this place was called Thermopylae —a word that means "hot gates," because there were numerous sulfurous springs in the area. Leonidas was the third great Greek commander to fight the Persians. Born roughly around 540, Leonidas—whose name means "lionlike" and who was supposedly descended from Hercules—was raised in what is still among the most famous warrior cultures in history: Sparta. There, at the age of seven, boys were taken from their parents and raised in a large barracks. They were given a deliberately sparse diet, so that they would learn how to forage and steal; however, if they were caught doing either of these things, they were beaten mercilessly, which taught them to be wily when they scavenged. By the time they were in their teens, Spartan men were the most hardened fighters in the world. Seeing the way they were brought up, one Greek visitor to Sparta said: "Now I understand why the Spartans do not fear death."

"IF THESE MEN CAN BE DEFEATED"

Leonidas had with him at Thermopylae 300 Spartan warriors and 8,000 other Greek fighters. This force was a mere handful when one considers the size of the Persian army, but the Greeks did have topography on their side. The pass at Thermopylae was perhaps 4 miles (6.4 km) long. Leonidas had chosen to place his front lines at a place called the Middle Gate, which was perhaps 20 yards (18.3 m) across and spanned by an ancient wall. As Leonidas's men rebuilt the wall, the rest of the Greeks prepared to make their stand. On their left were the towering walls of Mount Kallidromon. On their right was the Gulf of Maliakós, off the Aegean Sea, which in that era lapped right up against the pass.

Although they were not guerilla fighters, Leonidas and his men functioned in that way by using terrain to hold off a much larger enemy and thus buy time—a tactic favored by fighters like the Jewish zealots (see page 118) and the Seminoles (see page 136) as a way of extending war and wearying their enemy. Like any good commander, Leonidas also scouted the area, and he realized that there was a track that ran across the ridges of Mount Kallidromon west of his position, emerging 6 miles (9.7 km) behind his lines. He sent a thousand of the local Greek fighters—the Phocians—to guard this pass.

SPARTAN FIGHTERS WERE STANDING, NOT BEHIND, BUT IN FRONT OF THEIR DEFENSES, CASUALLY COMBING THEIR HAIR. THE ASTONISHED PERSIAN KING WAS INFORMED BY A GREEK TRAITOR WHO ACCOMPANIED HIM THAT IT WAS NORMAL FOR THE SPARTANS TO CAREFULLY GROOM THEMSELVES WHEN THEY EXPECTED TO DIE.

A day after Leonidas had finished setting up his defenses, the Great King and his massive army arrived. When he had finished setting up his pavilion tent, Xerxes went forward to observe the Greeks and could not believe his eyes. Spartan fighters were standing, not behind, but in front of their defenses, casually combing their hair. The astonished Great King was informed by a Greek traitor who accompanied him that it was normal for the Spartans to carefully groom themselves when they expected to die. "If these men can be defeated," he told the king, "then there is no one else in the world who will dare lift a hand, or stand against you."

After a few days of waiting for his fleet to catch up to him—it had been caught in a storm and did not make it to Thermopylae before the battle was over—Xerxes decided to attack. First he sent in a wave of Medes, fierce fighters from what is now northwestern Iran, who were known as excellent bowmen. They rained showers of arrows down on the Spartans, who protected themselves with their broad shields and then spitted the Medes on their long lances when the Medes came charging toward them. Xerxes then sent in the first of his Immortals, but they were unable to move the Spartans. At the end of the first day's fighting, piles of dead lay in front of the Spartan position, yet their line held.

"WITH THEIR HANDS AND TEETH"

The fighting resumed at dawn the next day, with wave after wave of Immortals attacking the Spartans and being cut down. Soon even these toughened soldiers were so afraid to attack that they had to be driven forward with whips, according to Herodotus. The evening of that second day, Xerxes sat down and pondered his situation. His ships, delayed by storms and harried by Greek triremes, were still not able to move in and resupply him, and the Spartan line appeared impregnable. But then the fortunes of war smiled upon the Great King. A Greek traitor named Ephialtes was brought before him. For a large sum of money, Ephialtes promised to guide the Persians across the mountain trail that ran across the ridges behind Mount Kallidromon.

Immediately seeing his chance, Xerxes sent 1,000 Immortals to follow the traitor through the night across the trail. Arriving at Leonidas's rear just as dawn was breaking, the Immortals easily swept aside the Phocians guarding the trail and, turning north, headed for Leonidas's line, 6 miles (9.7 km) distant. Hearing of this, Leonidas made a split-second decision—he sent almost his entire force heading back into Greece, keeping with him his 300 Spartans, their 900 Helots (infantrymen who worked as servants for the Spartans), 700 Thespians, and about 400 Thebans.

Within a few hours, the Persians renewed their attacks on the Spartans at the Middle Gate. The fighting was ferocious, with the Persians attacking from the front finally able to push their way into the Spartan lines, knocking off their spear points with their swords, slashing and stabbing at them. Four times the Spartans fought them off, killing hundreds, including two half-brothers of Xerxes. It was at this point that Leonidas was killed.

Finally, the Immortals who had broken through at the rear arrived, and the Spartans were hemmed in on two sides. They managed a fighting retreat to a small hillock, where, Herodotus wrote, "they defended themselves to the last, with their swords, if they still had them, and, if not, with their hands and teeth."

Even down to their last few wounded men, the Spartans were so fearsome that the Persians were afraid to approach them. Instead, they stood off from the hillock, picking off their foes one by one. The Spartans died, one by one, and the Battle of Thermopylae was over.

Thermopylae has justly come down in history as a turning point battle. Not only did the Spartan stand buy time for the rest of the Greek soldiers to make their way to safety, but also the Spartan example was extraordinarily fraught with meaning. It was immediately understood that the Spartans had chosen to die, not just for Sparta, but for all of Greece, and, as the Persians swept into the plains of Attica, that example was the only thing that kept the Greeks from capitulation.

IN DESPERATE STRAITS

Leonidas's stand had given the Greco-Persian Wars—a conflict that should have been over a decade before—new life, but the Greeks were still in desperate straits. There was no one to oppose Xerxes as his armies swept down from the mountains and headed southeast for the plains of Attica and Athens.

Themistocles ordered 150,000 people evacuated from the path of the Persian army, including the entire city of Athens, in what was one of the greatest evacuations of its time. The Athenian navy managed to fight a holding action against the Persian navy at the Artemisium Straits, off the island of Euboea, but was forced to retreat once the Greek loss at Thermopylae rendered their supply position untenable. Themistocles led the navy to the island of Salamis, shaped like a horseshoe, with about 60 miles (96.6 km) of coastline, which is separated from the mainland of Attica by a strait just over 1 mile (1.6 km) wide. Themistocles also told all able-bodied male refugees to make their way to Salamis, where he was preparing for the naval battle that would decide the fate of Greece.

In the meantime, Xerxes had easily swept through Greece and his forces had taken Athens, murdering the few Greeks who had remained and burning the old wooden Acropolis to the ground. The Greeks on Salamis could see the black smoke rising and could have taken it as the funeral pyre of their civilization—in fact, some did, wanting to surrender to the Persians then and there. But Themistocles argued persuasively against it.

It was now late September. He had about 370 triremes at Salamis, crewed by members from most of the twenty-two-nation Hellenic League—Sparta, Corinth, Chalcis, Eretria, Naxos, and Melos, among others. The Greek armies—including the full army of the Spartans—prepared to make a last stand on the Isthmus of Corinth, the narrow land bridge that connects the Peloponnesian peninsula to the Greek mainland. Themistocles knew that for the navy to retreat there would be seen as capitulation by the Persians and the Greeks themselves. One of the reasons Themistocles was such a profound leader is that he knew that symbolism, during this last stage of an epic war, was the only thing that was keeping the Greek people going.

The Persian fleet, numbering more than 700 triremes, twice as many as the Greeks, now lay at anchor in the harbor at Phaleron Bay, southwest of Athens. On the afternoon of September 24, it ventured out into the straits off Salamis, inviting the Greeks to do battle, but the Greeks refused to sally forth, and the Persians returned slowly to Phaleron, daring the Greek triremes to come out and fight.

Themistocles knew he did not have much time before his fragile alliance of Greeks broke apart—many were already talking about retreating to Corinth to make a last stand there with the rest of the Greeks. Things weren't helped any by the fact that Xerxes had elements of his massive army march up and down the coastline, raising large clouds of dust designed to intimidate the Greeks on Salamis.

THE RUSE

Themistocles was one of the few who realized that, in fact, Salamis represented an opportunity for the Greeks. Because of the very narrowness of the straits, the Persians would be unable to maneuver, outflank, and surround the Greek triremes. What the Greeks needed to do, Themistocles realized, was force the Persians to do battle within the straits. If Xerxes simply decided to wait the Greeks out, blockading Salamis, they would starve to death in short order. So Themistocles secretly plotted a daring ruse. He decided to give the Persians what is these days called "disinformation"—false intelligence. Not only that, but he also gave this information directly to the Great King himself.

While his nervous commanders bickered, Themistocles sent his personal slave Sicinnus—a trusted retainer who had tutored Themistocles's children—by a small boat to Persian headquarters on the mainland. He gave Sicinnus instructions to tell Xerxes that Themistocles wanted to defect (for a price, of course) and, as token of his sincerity, wanted Xerxes to know that the Greeks were getting ready to flee. Through Sicinnus, Themistocles urged the Great King to mobilize his forces immediately, at night, to bottle up the Greeks at Salamis. When morning came and the Greek triremes tried to flee, they could be destroyed.

This would have been an extremely dangerous mission for Sicinnus to undertake—it was quite likely that he would have been killed the moment he set foot on shore. It was also possible that the Persians would torture him to find out whether his information was true, so some historians believe that Themistocles actually convinced Sicinnus that he really wanted to defect. However it happened, Xerxes, perhaps influenced by the fact that his forces had successfully employed a Greek traitor at Thermopylae, brought the story. He ordered his triremes to deploy and had his chariot taken to the high hill overlooking Salamis, where he would be able to oversee his triumph at first light.

Themistocles, seeing the dark shapes of the Persian triremes move out into the night, must have been satisfied that his ruse had worked. Now, the Greeks were indeed bottled in, and those who had been recalcitrant would be forced to fight. There was nothing else for them to do.

"THEY BONED THEM LIKE TUNA"

Just before eight o'clock on the morning of September 25, the Persian fleet—the triremes manned mostly by Phoenicians, who had been rowing in place all night—heard a huge shout echo out from Salamis. It was the paean, part shout, part song, a battle cry uttered by thousands of Greek voices at once: *Ie, ie Paian! Ie, ie Paian!*, meaning "Hail, hail, healing Lord!"

This was not the straggling, panicked, fleeing mob that the Persians expected, but instead an organized, spirited navy, ready to do battle. Hundreds of brightly painted triremes, white water foaming about them, an eye of polished, painted marble on either side of the prow, raced toward the Persians. Below decks, the rowers in their three tiers, their backs to the action, rowed and chanted with all their might. Above, Greek archers and marines made ready for the moment when their ship's brass ram would catch and hold a Persian vessel, and they could board and fight.

Despite the fact that they were exhausted from rowing all night, the Persians set out to do battle with equal fervor, not wanting to be seen lacking in the eyes of the Great King, who was watching from high on his hilltop. The two fleets neared each other, each struggling to keep formation—for when a formation of triremes was scattered, the enemy could destroy individual boats. First blood went to the Greeks, to an Athenian captain named Ameienas, who rammed a Phoenician ship (one of the many nationalities fighting for the Persians) so hard that his ram sheared off its stern section. Most of the battles between individual ships were not that quick, however. Ships would ram, catch in the enemy hull, and arrows would fly between each ship's archers, before Persian and Greek marines would meet on shipboard for pitched combat.

Although many Persian captains fought bravely, Themistocles had foreseen correctly that the Persian triremes were simply too numerous to all enter the strait at once. Many milled around outside the channel, waiting for an opportunity to enter the fray. The skilled Greek oarsmen and captains, fighting on home waters, were able to meet the Persians without being at such a disadvantage of numbers, and gradually their skill and ferociousness in combat began to tell. By early afternoon, the Persian formations began to

In the Battle of Marathon in 490 BCE, the Persians met the first of the Greek commanders who would turn what should have been a quick invasion of an annoying enemy into a humiliating defeat that would lead to ever-greater warfare. Led by Miltiades, the outnumbered Greeks slaughtered their Persian enemies; the Greeks lost fewer than 200 men, the Persians more than 6,000. The battle is depicted in this 1902 engraving by German-French illustrator Hermann Vogel from the book *Spamers, Illustrierte Weltgeschichte.*

break up, the triremes fleeing, most to the southeast, seeking the shelter of the harbor at Phaleron. The combat became that of individual Greek ships seeking out and destroying fleeing Persians, ramming them without mercy—as the playwright Aeschylus (who fought there that day) later wrote, "They boned them like tuna or some catch of fish."

Soon thousands of Persian corpses littered the straits—20,000 Persians in all died that day, drowned, killed by Greek soldiers in battle, or speared by Greek civilians as they attempted to crawl ashore. The next morning, the Great King withdrew from Attica.

AN END TO HEROES

The war that had lasted since 500 BCE was not yet over. Although the Persian king had seen with his own eyes the destruction of a great portion of his navy, he believed—with the kind of ignorance that often keeps long wars going even longer—that he could still best the Greeks. He left behind his commander Mardonius with about 70,000 Persian soldiers, but in August 479, Mardonius was killed and his army defeated by a united Greek army at Plataea. Around the same time, a Greek navy force destroyed what was left of the Persian fleet near the island of Samos.

Xerxes, the Great King, was assassinated during a palace coup in 466, but even then the war continued, intermittently. The Athenians founded and led the Delian League, an alliance of 150 Greek city-states, which eventually drove the Persians from all Greek territory, including the Greek states in Asia Minor. The Peace of Callas in 449 finally ended the great conflict and obliged the Persians to stay out of the Aegean. The long war was finally at an end.

The Greco-Persian conflict had major consequences for the world and for history. After the Greek victory and the creation of the Delian League, what is called the Golden Age of Athens began, spawning Greek literature with such major figures as Aeschylus, Aristophanes, Euripides, and Sophocles; philosophers including Plato and Socrates; and historians like Thucydides and Herodotus. Ironically, the great war with the Persians would lead to another war—the Peloponnesian War, which was fought against Athens by Sparta and other Greek city-states bankrupted by helping finance the Delian League. The war lasted from 431 to 404 BCE and ended the Athenian dominance in the region.

As for the heroes who had helped Athens stave off Persian domination for so long? The Greeks, it turns out, don't treat their heroes well, unless they're dead. Leonidas was lionized for his role at Thermopylae, but Miltiades died in prison the year after Marathon, charged with treason by political opponents when he bungled an expedition against a Greek island that had conspired with the Persians. Themistocles was driven out of Athens by charges that he took bribes (probably true) and was an agent of the Persians (doubtful). He ended up in exile, ironically spending his remaining years as the governor of a Persian city.

CHAPTER 2

THE PUNIC WARS

THE END OF CARTHAGE

264–146 BCE

A devastating war made long by virulent
hatred gutted one Mediterranean civilization
even as it gave rise to another.

I magine the entire world swept by a tidal wave of war, more horrible than any in human memory, and then imagine that this same war lasts for 120 years—to put it in contemporary context, let's say from 1890 to 2010—so that a foot soldier fighting at the end of this war could say that his great-great-grandfather battled in the same conflict.

Imagine this and you begin to imagine the Punic Wars, the longest-running conflict in ancient history. The combatants were Rome and Carthage and the battleground was the Mediterranean basin. The Punic Wars lasted as long as they did not just because they were wars for empire, with two aggressors seeking to dominate and exploit the same territory—the rich lands of Sicily, the Iberian Peninsula, and North Africa. The main reason the Punic Wars went on for more than a century was the sheer hatred each side had for the other. There would be no armistice, when all was said and done. One civilization would triumph; the other would be destroyed as completely as if it had never existed.

"SO FEROCIOUS WERE THE ROMANS"

Carthage was founded around 800 BCE on the coast of what is present-day Tunisia. Its founders were that ancient race of wide-ranging seafarers, the Phoenicians (the word "Punic" comes from the Latin word *Punicus*, which derives in turn from a Greek word meaning "Phoenicians"). Carthage was originally an outlying colony of the great Phoenician commerce center of Tyre, on the coast of what is now Lebanon, but by the third century BCE, Carthage had far surpassed the Phoenicians in mercantile ambition.

The Carthaginians were traders and merchants, ambitious and smart, seekers after "commercial adventure," as one historian has written. Their trading adventures led them to establish colonies in North Africa, Spain, Sardinia, Cyprus, Corsica, Malta, and the west coast of Sicily, where they clashed with colonizing Greeks who had settled on the island.

Rome was founded in about 750 BCE on the spot where several important trade routes converged on the Tiber River. It was at first controlled by kings and later became a republic. By about 350 BCE, it had expanded, defeating Etruscans and then Gauls to the north and Samnite tribes to the south, before clashing with Greek colonists at the very tip of the Italian boot.

THE MAIN REASON THE PUNIC WARS WENT ON FOR MORE THAN A CENTURY WAS THE SHEER HATRED EACH SIDE HAD FOR THE OTHER.

This expansion was steady but incremental, and to a certain extent opportunistic. While Carthage increased its influence via trade, Rome enlarged itself by warfare when a neighboring state seemed weak enough to be taken. Unlike the Carthaginians, who had a relatively small population of about 700,000 men, women, and children, and fought with hired mercenaries officered by native Carthaginians, the Romans, with perhaps 3 million to 4 million men, women, and children, built up a warrior class of some 400,000 that valued honor, courage, and, above all, sheer reckless aggression over everything else. "So ferocious were the Romans of the later first millenium BCE," the historian John Keegan writes, "that, in broad perspective, their behavior bears comparison only with that of the Mongols or the Timurids 1,500 years later."

At this stage in its development, Rome was a young state, the inhabitants of which shared conservative values, a warrior ethos, and a strong sense of family. The Romans were about to clash with an older and wealthier civilization with far different values. The result would define the course of Western civilization for thousands of years to come.

CHANGING TACTICS

The Punic Wars began in 264 BCE in Sicily, where Carthaginian and Roman forces had moved closer to each other since the beginning of the third century. Taking advantage of a clash between local groups, Carthage attempted to seize the strategically important town of Messana (current-day Messina), where a natural harbor faced across the Straits of Messana to Italy. Rome opposed this, and the two great powers came to blows for the first time. What followed was an escalation of a small-scale conflict into an increasingly larger war, as each side built up its forces.

The Romans easily defeated the Carthaginians in several battles, ultimately forcing them to retreat to the sea after the Battle of Agrigentum off the southwest coast in 262 BCE. The Romans entered the city, slaughtered or enslaved its entire population, and, drunk with victory, decided that their goal—which at first had been merely to check the Carthaginians in Messana—would now be to drive all Carthaginians from Sicily.

This was far easier said than done, but it shows how wars with limited objectives—

THE CARTHAGINIANS HAD BEEN SURPRISED AT THE FEROCITY OF THE ROMAN ASSAULTS, THE WILLPOWER AND DISCIPLINE OF THE ROMAN SOLDIER, AND THE SHEER NUMBER OF LEGIONARIES THEY FACED. AND SO THE CARTHAGINIANS CHANGED TACTICS.

wars such as the Anglo-Afghan Wars (see chapter 9) and those in Vietnam in the mid-twentieth century (see chapter 10)—can escalate into longer conflicts. Success breeds confidence that is often misplaced. And failure can be educational. This was so in the case of both the Carthaginians and the Romans. The Carthaginians had been surprised at the ferocity of the Roman assaults, the willpower and discipline of the Roman soldier, and the sheer number of legionaries they faced.

And so the Carthaginians changed tactics. They stationed their Sicilian army in several heavily fortified coastal cities that could be supplied from the sea by the superior Carthaginian navy. The navy would also carry troops around the countryside and land forces behind Roman lines, to harass isolated garrisons and cut off supply lines. Much later in the war, in 247 BCE, a master at this tactic would appear in the form of Hamilcar Barca, whose last name probably means "lightning flash" (possibly "sword flash"), who would become one of the fiercest opponents the Romans had and who would father their deadliest enemy, Hannibal Barca. Hamilcar would not beat the Romans, but he would fight them to a standstill.

Around 260 BCE, the Romans realized that a stalemate was forming in Sicily because of the change in Carthaginian tactics and sought for a way to bring the war home to Carthage on the North African mainland. The chief problem the Romans had

The Roman quinquireme, shown, was the chief fighting vessel in the Punic Wars. Note the moveable bridge, or corvus, held by pulleys attached to a mast. The Romans would drop the corvus on the bridge of an enemy ship and pour across to attack.

was they had almost no navy to speak of and what few ships they did possess were vastly outclassed by the Carthaginians and their quinqueremes, single-deck ships with fifty or sixty oars and five men to an oar. (Some sources, however, cite a double-deck with two sets of oars, but the name comes from the number of men on each oar, not the numbers of rows of oars.) The quinquereme would become the standard warship of the Punic Wars, just as the trireme was the basic vessel of the Greco-Persian conflicts. The quinquereme was slow but very stable and extremely powerful, equipped with a copper-sheathed ram that could rip an enemy hull asunder.

The Romans had nothing like it, but in 260 BCE they had a stroke of luck. Roman soldiers came upon a Carthaginian quinquereme that had run aground and been abandoned on the shores of northern Sicily. The industrious Romans took it apart, plank by plank, brought it back to Italy, and used it as a model from which to construct their own quinqueremes. A fleet of 100 of them was ready within two months, an extraordinary feat that supposedly took the labor of 35,000 men. The Romans then hired Greeks to teach them how to row and maneuver the boats. Even so, they were at first clumsy at handling the large and unwieldy vessels—on the first outing of the fleet, a Roman admiral found himself trapped in the Straits of Messina by a large squadron of Carthaginian quinqueremes and was forced to abandon several ships.

However, the Romans had a technological innovation up their sleeves that would even the odds between the two powers and lengthen the course of the war. Some quick-thinker, whose name is now lost, came up with the idea of the *corvus*, or raven, which was a moveable wooden bridge, 4 feet (1.2 m) wide and about 36 feet (11 m) long, with railings on the sides, which was attached by pulleys to a long mast at the front of each warship. At its tip was a large, hooked spike that looked like a raven's beak, hence the name. When a Roman warship got close enough to a Carthaginian vessel, it would drop the corvus onto the opposing ship. The spike would embed itself in the wooden deck and Roman soldiers would pour across the bridge.

It was another brilliant response to an enemy's superiority. The Romans had taken a naval vessel and turned it into a battlefield where their infantry, their legionaries, could once again reign supreme. The first time the Romans employed it, toward the end of 260 BCE, the Carthaginian sailors watched in horror as the corvus rammed down on their ship, holding them fast, while Roman legionaries swarmed onto their vessels, swinging their dreaded short swords. The Roman admiral was honored at home for his feat; his Carthaginian counterpart was chastised for bringing ignominy on the fleet and was, a short time later, crucified by his own officers at the Carthaginian naval base in Sardinia.

AN UNJUST PEACE, A LONGER WAR

With their own fleet, the Romans now decided to carry the war home to Carthage. In 256 BCE, they gathered together 330 ships, set sail from Italy, and landed on the southern shores of Sicily, 75 miles (120 km) away, where they picked up an invasion force of Roman legionaries and marines (the latter trained especially for shipboard fighting).

The second-century BCE historian Polybius—the main source for much of what we know about the Punic Wars, a near contemporary who was present at the fall of Carthage—claims that the Roman forces numbered 140,000 crew, infantry, and marines.

To face this force, the Carthaginians, once again according to Polybius, sallied forth with a fleet of 350 ships and 150,000 men, and these two massive forces met within sight of the southern Sicilian shore, near Mount Economus. If Polybius is to be believed—some historians subtract about 100 ships from his estimate for both navies, but others feel his numbers are accurate—this was the largest naval battle in the history of the world.

Oared ships won battles by smashing into opposing vessels with the 7-foot (2.1 m)-long rams attached to their ships at the bow just above the keel, or, in the case of corvus-equipped Roman quinqueremes, dropping the spike down and boarding for hand-to-hand combat. Ramming was an art. Warships avoided a bow-to-bow ram because the shock could be as disastrous to attacker as attackee. Most vessels attempted to hit opponents from the side at a shallow angle, tearing a long gash in the hull before pulling away.

In the Battle of Economus, these two huge fleets clashed in a whitecap-filled seas with the rugged coast of Sicily providing a dramatic backdrop. Creating a diversion, the Carthaginian forces went straight for the Roman transport ships, attempting to ram them and drown the troops aboard. But the Romans countered with their corvuses, which the Carthaginians had yet to effectively develop a strategy against, and after a lengthy battle, drove off the main Carthaginian fleet before trapping those who had attacked the transports and capturing them.

It is possible that, with the sheer number of ships on the water, the Carthaginians were unable to use their still superior seamanship to maneuver properly to ram their opponents. In any event, they lost eighty ships, sunk or captured, and fled back to Carthage, leaving the way open for an invasion of North Africa.

However, the Romans were unable to press their advantage. A year later, in 255 BCE, Carthaginian forces led by a Greek mercenary general stymied an invasion of North Africa. At sea, the Romans were unable to use the advantage the corvus gave them because the Carthaginians, still better sailors, had learned to dodge the device by maneuvering their ships away at the last moment; also, the weight of the contraption overbalanced Roman quinqueremes during storms at sea, causing many of them to sink.

Meanwhile, Hamilcar Barca began his long campaign in Sicily, managing to keep the Roman army there, away from Carthage, and even strike with guerilla raids against the Italian mainland. Any guerilla warfare—whether it is that of the Seminoles against U.S. authorities (see chapter 8) or the Guatemalan leftists during the Guatemala Civil Wars (see chapter 13)—always lengthens warfare.

But it was Carthage, not Rome, that blinked first. Prominent Carthaginians and members of the Council of Thirty, a group of nobles to whom most real power in Carthage had been delegated by the ruling oligarchy, wanted the war to end because it was costly and interfering with business, which included expanding the Carthaginian Empire in Africa and Spain. By 241 BCE, they were ready to seek peace, despite the fact that generals such as Hamilcar Barca considered themselves undefeated. The peace made with the Romans forced the Carthaginian evacuation of Sicily, enraging Barca, and made Carthage pay an indemnity to Rome for twenty years.

Shortly after the fighting ended, Carthage faced a grim, three-year struggle against an army of rebellious mercenaries that had not been paid. This army was finally cornered and slaughtered by Hamilcar Barca, using repeated elephant charges. Those who survived, some of whom had served under Barca in Sicily, were publicly crucified. Rome took advantage of this distraction to seize the islands of Sardinia and Corsica, even though this had not been part of the agreed-upon treaty. But Carthage was powerless to stop them.

The map shows Rome and Carthage at the beginning of the Second Punic War in 218 BCE. The two powers vied for the rich and fertile territory surrounding the Mediterranean. The areas in pink are those controlled by Rome, those in brown by Carthage.

Courtesy of the University of Texas Libraries, The University of Texas at Austin

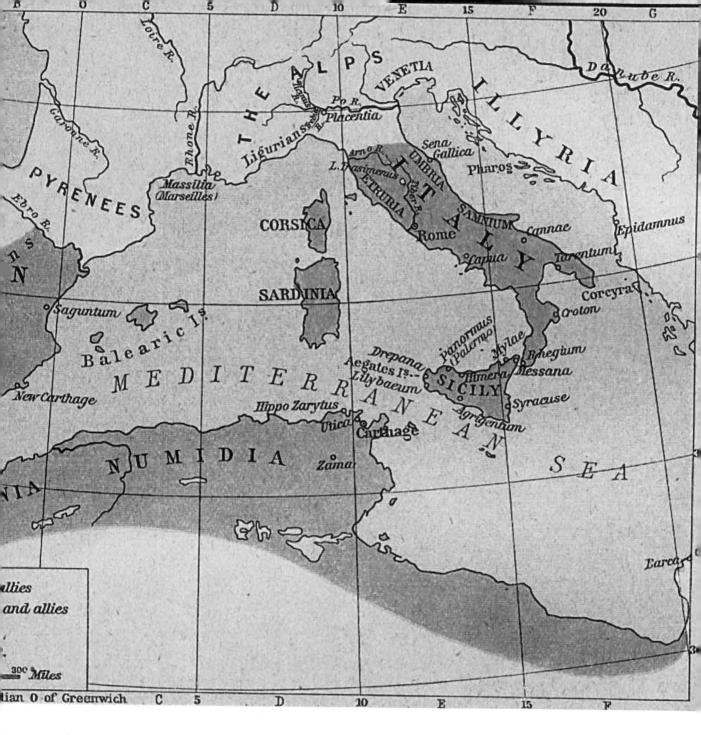

So the First Punic War ended in 241 BCE in a way guaranteed to keep hostilities
going, with the Carthaginians feeling resentful and bitter in defeat, and the Romans,
perhaps, making too much of a victory that was far from complete. The Romans usually

expected their wars to end with the utter annihilation or absorption of the enemy, but Carthage was still too large, powerful, and physically distant for this to happen, and so a long war became even longer.

HANNIBAL'S HATRED

Perhaps surprisingly, hatred is not always present in warfare. Many combatants in major wars speak not of hating their opponent, but of simply trying to kill the enemy or force him to surrender to "get the job done" and get home. In the Second Punic War, beginning in 218 BCE, the two sides, cultures that were poles apart, shared an overwhelming hatred for each other, which led to extreme casualties and the extended duration of the war.

Nowhere is that hatred more personified than in the person of Hannibal Barca, the one major figure of the war who remains a part of our military culture, and thus popular imagination, thousands of years later. We don't know what he looked like, but his shadow looms large. He is the man of a thousand legends, whose very name was used to frighten Roman children. He led elephants across the Alps, fought courageously for a corrupt regime, and was hounded into suicide by his enemies years after the Second Punic War ended. Most of all, he is one of the reasons why the Punic Wars continued as long as they did.

Hannibal was born in 247 BCE, the son of Hamilcar Barca, a man who had good reason to hate the Romans. Hannibal was thus only six years old when the First Punic War ended, but he grew up filled with the same hatred his father felt for his enemies. One of four boys—Hannibal was the oldest, followed by Hanno, Mago, and Hasdrubal, all of whom would fight against the Romans—Hannibal was raised among the ranks of the privileged in Carthaginian society, but he never allowed to forget his true mission in life: to defeat the Romans. Hannibal himself told the story that, when he was only nine years old, he had to swear an oath to his father that "as soon as [my] age will permit . . . I will use fire and steel to resolve the destiny of Rome."

Hamilcar Barca was already doing that. In 237 BCE, he led an expeditionary force to Iberia (modern-day Spain), where he spent the next nine years, and was soon joined by his sons. They subdued local tribes, either by force or treaty, and added to Carthaginian territory, something that the Romans, probably rightly, saw as a threat to what they considered their sovereignty in the Mediterranean. In 229 BCE, however, Hamilcar was killed during a skirmish with a local Celtiberian tribe. His son-in-law Hasdrubal the Fair (not to be confused with Hamilcar's son Hasdrubal) took over command and continued Carthaginian expansion until he was assassinated in 221 BCE by a Celt who may have been in the employ of the Romans. Thereafter, the Carthaginian army in Spain voted unanimously to make Hannibal, twenty-six years old, their new commander, a vote that was supported by the Carthaginian government.

> HANNIBAL WAS RAISED AMONG THE RANKS OF
> THE PRIVILEGED IN CARTHGINIAN SOCIETY, BUT HE NEVER
> ALLOWED TO FORGET HIS TRUE MISSION IN LIFE:
> TO DEFEAT THE ROMANS.

Hannibal immediately took up where his father and brother-in-law had left off, ranging far into central Spain and subduing tribes there. In 219 BCE, despite the fact that Hasdrubal had made an informal agreement with the Romans not to take his forces above the River Ebro, Hannibal led his men against the city of Saguntum, a Roman ally north of the Ebro. Despite a warning by a delegation of Romans, Hannibal continued to besiege the city, an action that took eight months and showed the young general's extraordinary persistence. When he finally managed to knock down a section of the city's wall, Hannibal sent his men in with permission to kill, rape, and steal. The slaughter was so great that many of the inhabitants of the city threw themselves into fires rather than face Hannibal's soldiers.

Although Iberians inhabited Saguntum, it was the Romans whom Hannibal was really striking at, revenging himself for humiliations the Barcas and Carthage had suffered at their hands. Enraged, the Romans sent a delegation to Carthage, brusquely demanding that Hannibal and his officers be delivered to Rome as war criminals. The Roman ambassador held his hands inside his toga and declared: "I hold here both peace and war. I will let fall from my hands whichever you choose."

The Carthaginian senate leader told him: "Let fall whichever you choose."

The Roman ambassador held out his hand. "I let fall war," he declared, at which point a great shout arose from the Carthaginians: "We accept it!"

Thus the Second Punic War began.

THE INVASION OF ITALY

From the beginning of the war, and probably well before that, Hannibal seemed to have resolved to defeat Rome on her own ground, or probably not at all. In studying the First Punic War, and perhaps in discussing it with his father, the young Carthaginian commander understood that the Romans could take heavy losses and replace them with relative ease. They had the will and resources to fight a long protracted war, but they had never been truly tested in Italy itself.

Hannibal intended to do just that. Even as Rome raised an army under the consul Publius Cornelius Scipio the Elder with the intention of invading Spain, Hannibal was preparing to invade Italy. But not by sea—the Carthaginian navy had been severely weakened in the First Punic War, while the Roman navy had gotten correspondingly stronger. Instead, Hannibal proposed to do something no one had ever done before—cross the Alps and attack Rome from the rear. He wasted no time.

In the spring of 218 BCE, he gathered 40,000 men around him, a classic army of Carthaginian mercenaries—Celtiberians in animal skins; slingers from the Balearic Islands (who took their pay in captured women rather than gold); Numidian horsemen, known for their expertise and ferocity; and, famously, forty elephants. While Cornelius

TWELVE THOUSAND MEN WOULD PERISH BEFORE HANNIBAL'S WEARY ARMY DESCENDED INTO THE FERTILE FARMLAND OF NORTHERN ITALY (AND ONLY ONE ELEPHANT WOULD SURVIVE), BUT THESE MEN, AFTER RESTING, WERE READY TO DESTROY ROME.

Scipio prepared to sail across the Mediterranean to attack Spain, Hannibal, leaving his brother Hasdrubal behind with 10,000 men, crossed the Pyrenees into Gaul, in what is now southern France, and fought his way through hostile Gallic tribes. By chance, Scipio's fleet landed to reprovision near the site of the modern city of Marseilles as Hannibal was passing nearby. Cavalry scouts from the two armies blundered into each other and both generals soon realized that an enemy army was near.

Hannibal hurried away from the coast, while Scipio, ordering his army to continue on toward Spain, hastened back to Italy to prepare a defense against Hannibal. But he was too slow. Hannibal's epic crossing of the Alps took place, probably in early November, probably through the 9,000-foot (2,745 m)-high Col de la Traversette. His army suffered terribly. Hannibal lost men to ambushes by hostile Celtic tribes and the terrain, with literally thousands of soldiers falling screaming to their deaths from the icy heights of the pass. Twelve thousand men would perish before Hannibal's weary army descended into the fertile farmland of northern Italy (and only one elephant would survive), but these men, after resting, were ready to destroy Rome.

Gathering allies from local Gallic tribes that had feuded with Rome, Hannibal fought a series of battles—at Ticino River, Trebia, and Lake Trasimene—as he made his way down the Italian peninsula. Hannibal, now riding the army's sole remaining elephant, Syrus, was to lose the sight in his right eye due to an infection from an illness he caught traversing the vast marshes near present-day Florence. Despite this, he had shown his men (and the Italian tribes he hoped would join him) that he could beat the Romans. Cornelius Scipio had been badly wounded at Ticino (his adopted son, Cornelius Scipio the Younger, had spurred his horse forward to save his father's life) and defeated, as had all the other Roman armies sent to impede Hannibal's march.

FABIUS MAXIMUS: THE DELAYER

At this point, critical in the history of Rome, Quintus Fabius Maximus, a Roman politician and general who had twice been consul, was named dictator, a role given to trusted politicians during times of severe crisis. The sixty-three-year-old Fabius, well aware of the strength of Hannibal's forces and how the Carthaginian general had bested the Romans three times in combat on the Italian peninsula, decided on a strategy of delay and avoidance for dealing with the enemy.

During much of 217 BCE, Fabius's army shadowed Hannibal's without doing battle, attempting to cut off his supply lines and deny his army sustenance. Every day without a fight was a day that the Carthaginians were further weakened by hunger.

The strategy worked, driving Hannibal farther south, away from Rome and through the modern-day southern provinces of Apulia and Campania. Every time Hannibal's forces turned on Fabius's Romans, the Romans fled, although they also harassed Hannibal's rear guard with small unit actions. Fabius's strategy of avoidance and harassment has been emulated numerous times in the course of history—the North Vietnamese fought a Fabian war for much of their conflict against the Americans during the 1960s. The strategy almost always favors weaker opponents for whom a prolonged war (but with little major combat) represents their best hope of survival.

The problem with Fabius's policy is that it was not glamorous, by definition took a long time, and also gave the impression to a Roman populace hungry for news of victory that Roman soldiers were running away from the Carthaginians.

For refusing to give battle, Fabius was mockingly called *Cunctator*, or "the Delayer." Finally, in the winter of 216 BCE, he was replaced by two consuls, Gaius Terentius Varro and Lucius Aemilius Paullus, who were determined to bring battle against Hannibal.

THE BLOODLETTING AT CANNAE

In the summer of 216 BCE, Hannibal and his army were in southern Italy near the small town of Cannae, which held a granary from which Hannibal wanted to feed his army. A Roman army of 80,000, led by Varro and Paullus, approached, confident that it had now cornered and could destroy Hannibal's 40,000 soldiers. One hot and dusty morning in early August, the two armies stood arrayed against each other on a narrow plain near the banks of the ancient Aufidus River (the modern-day Ofanto). The Romans stood on the east side of the plain, 5 miles (8 km) away from the Adriatic Sea, and the Carthaginians were on the west. Both armies were short of supplies—the area could not possibly feed 120,000 men and their animals—and needed to either fight or disengage. Disengaging would actually be the worst option for Hannibal, but fortunately the Romans chose to give battle.

Arrayed in their basic unit of *maniples* (meaning "handfuls"), with thirty maniples to a legion, each maniple consisting of 130 men, the Romans advanced, beating their swords and spears on their shields and shouting. These were heavy infantrymen, each equipped with the *gladius*, a short sword used mainly for stabbing; the *pilum*, the heavy Roman throwing spear; and the *scutum*, the oval shield 3 feet (1 m) high. The Roman right flank, almost flush against the river, consisted of cavalry led by consul Paullus (the two consuls took turns commanding, and so Varro was in overall command on this particular day).

The Roman center, consisting of thousands of massed heavy infantry, must have seemed an irresistible force, but Hannibal, in a strategy that would become famous, was about to use their mass and energy against them. He had stationed his Gauls—brave fighters, but

The Battle of Zama between Carthage and Rome in 202 BCE is depicted in this sixteenth-century oil painting. Unlike the scene in the painting, the Romans allowed the Carthaginian elephants to simply pass through their ranks, another example of Roman preparedness and adaptability, which allowed them to ultimately triumph in the Punic Wars.

not necessarily the most cohesive of his units—in the center of his line, pushing them out toward the advancing enemy, forming a convex bulge in his front. On either side, he stationed his heavier infantry and his famed Numidian horsemen.

When the Romans got to within 30 yards (27.4 m) of the Carthaginian line, they hurled their *pila* and then charged. The Gauls fought bravely, but were pushed slowly back, until Hannibal's line was concave, and nearly at the breaking point. The Romans, sensing victory, began shouting and pressing ahead, only to discover, on their flanks and at their rear, both heavier Carthaginian infantry and the Numidian cavalry, which, having dispersed the Roman horses, now charged into the packed mass of Roman soldiers.

Thousands of Roman soldiers were trapped, packed so tightly together they could barely move their swords, as Carthaginians waded in, killing them, their sword arms and shields dripping with blood. The Romans, blinded by dust, had little chance. Some of them dug holes in the earth and buried their heads, trying to suffocate themselves. Others organized desperate charges and escaped—one of these few was Cornelius Scipio the Younger, who managed to make it across the Aufidus and to safety. Still others merely lay there, waiting to be killed. The slaughter went on until the sun went down, when the exhausted Carthaginians withdrew temporarily to rest.

In the morning, they returned to finish the butchery. Thousands of corpses lay stacked up in an area a little over 3 square miles (7.8 square km). Some Roman soldiers begged to be killed, others attempted to crawl away, and others hid beneath piles of bodies. They were all slain—probably 50,000 dead—in a disaster that would haunt Rome for centuries. Did the sight of so many dead bodies, so many slaughtered young Roman men, assuage even Hannibal's hatred? We'll never know, but one is of reminded of the comment of General Robert E. Lee as he surveyed the thousands of Union dead who fell at the Battle of Fredericksburg: "It is well that war is so horrible, else we might grow too fond of it."

HANNIBAL'S DECISION

The tide was now turning against the Romans. Hundreds of their finest young men were killed at Cannae (Consul Varro died there as well), and their gold rings were gathered up by the Carthaginians and sent to Carthage, where they were tossed clattering to the floor in front of a delighted Carthaginian Senate. The victory convinced at least several tribes in southern Italy to join the Carthaginians. The panicked city of Rome closed its gates and even resorted to human sacrifice—a rare event for the Republic—to try to keep Hannibal away.

And perhaps it worked—for Hannibal did not come, at least not directly after Cannae. His decision not to immediately attack Rome has been second-guessed ever since. On the one hand, a successful assault on Rome would have ended the war. On the other, Hannibal had lost more than 10,000 men at Cannae, and the surviving troops needed to rest and regroup. Although he had destroyed a Roman army, there was another army near Rome, not nearly so skilled as the one he had killed, but strong enough to man city walls and make a powerful resistance.

So, in a decision that probably contributed greatly to the length of the Second Punic War, Hannibal did not attack Rome, but contented himself with campaigning in Italy, where he was to spend the next thirteen years trying to win a war that had become unwinnable. The Romans finally embraced the Fabian strategy of avoiding battle, and Hannibal's campaign became increasingly one of simply attempting to supply his army and keep it going. He did win victories—in 212 BCE, he completely destroyed two cornered Roman armies—but was never able to follow up on them because Roman armies simply avoided him afterward.

At last, unable to finally defeat the Romans and keep himself supplied, Hannibal retreated from Italy in 203 BCE to face a new threat: Cornelius Scipio the Younger, who, having neutralized the Carthaginians in Iberia, was now marching on Carthage. Scipio was the only Roman war leader of the Second Punic War—or any of the three conflicts—who could match Hannibal in military savvy. Scipio was a fighter. At the age of eighteen, having escaped Cannae, he led a group of young Romans who invaded the Senate at swordpoint as the senators were considering surrendering to Hannibal. There would be only death, no surrender, the senators were told. After this, Scipio had fought brilliantly to conquer Spain. He was a natural leader who was considered trustworthy, honest, and fair; his men also thought he possessed the gift of "second sight" and dreamed prescient dreams that could foretell the outcome of battles.

Whether he had one of these dreams before the September day in 202 BCE when his army faced Hannibal's on a broad plain about 100 miles (161 km) west of Carthage— near what would later become the Roman town of Zama—is not known. But fate was not on Hannibal's side at Zama. He sent eighty war elephants charging into the Roman lines to start the battle, but Scipio was prepared for this and had his men open ranks to let the trumpeting creatures harmlessly through. The two armies then clashed in a desperate melee that saw Hannibal's Carthaginian veterans more than holding their own—until, in an echo of Cannae, their flanks were attacked by Numidian horsemen in the employ of Masinissa, an ally of the Romans. Leaving behind 20,000 dead on the field, the Carthaginians, along with Hannibal, fled back to Carthage.

Scipio—soon to be dubbed Scipio Africanus by the triumphant Roman Senate—agreed to accept a peace delegation from the Carthaginians, but he imposed fairly harsh terms. Carthage must give up all her colonies, was forbidden to wage war without Roman permission, and had to pay annually for fifty years a heavy indemnity of 10,000 talents (a talent was a unit of weight equal to 75 to 100 modern pounds [34 to 45 kg]) over fifty years, the sum to be paid in annual installments in order to remind Carthage of the ignominy of defeat. As a final indignity, the entire Carthaginian navy—500 great quinqueremes—was towed out into the Bay of Tunis and set afire. A pall of smoke settled over the city—a dread harbinger of things to come.

"CARTHAGE MUST BE DESTROYED!"

The Punic War had already lasted for sixty-three years, both actual combat and tense cold war, and was still not finished, because the virulent hatred between the two cultures remained. The Romans despised and mistrusted Carthaginians with an almost racial hatred—for most Romans, the only good Carthaginian was presumed to be a dead one. And the same hatred smoldered within Carthaginians, who chafed at Rome's subjugation of their once proud empire.

However, the Carthaginians were resilient. They paid off their war debt by 152 BCE and began to prosper again, something not to the liking of the Roman elite. The senator Marcus Porcius Cato (Cato the Elder) returned from a visit to Carthage with his toga full of rich figs and grapes, which he threw on the Senate floor to underscore the prosperity of Rome's former enemy. "*Carthago est delenda!*" he shouted—"Carthage must be destroyed!" Thereafter, he ended every speech of his, no matter what the topic, with these same words. Shortly after this, Cato and his supporters found an excuse to declare war against Carthage when the Carthaginians defended themselves against the encroachments of Masinissa, Rome's Numidian ally—a technical breach of the promise never to go to war.

A Roman army and fleet arrived at Carthage in 149 BCE. The Carthaginians had no commander of the quality of Hannibal, who was long dead. (Having been hounded by the Romans throughout the Mediterranean, Hannibal had committed suicide in 183 BCE, at the age of sixty-five, trapped, as the Greek historian Plutarch wrote, "like a bird that has grown too old to fly.") When Roman forces approached Carthage, its inhabitants immediately surrendered. The Roman commander demanded hostages, which Carthage supplied. Then he demanded the surrender of all Carthaginian arms, and Carthage also complied. Then he told the Carthaginians to abandon their city and move somewhere else. At last, realizing that peace was impossible, the Carthaginians chose to fight.

The siege of the city took two years until finally, in early 146 BCE, Roman forces commanded by Scipio Aemilianus (grandson of Scipio Africanus) broke through the walls. The destruction was epic. Polybius, who was present, said that the Romans, leveling row upon row of houses to attack the Carthaginians holding out up in the Byrsa, Carthage's great citadel, literally used the dead and wounded as paving material, something borne out by recent archeological evidence. While a core of Roman deserters and Carthaginians fought on, 50,000 men, women, and children, gaunt and starving, were led away into slavery. Finally the Byrsa fell, and Scipio put the entire city to the torch and then tore it apart, stone by stone. There is a legend that salt was strewn upon the ground to render it infertile; this is probably an invention, but Carthage was well and truly obliterated, in an act of destruction quite similar to stepping on a bug and then grinding your shoe into the pavement.

After 120 years of war, Rome had triumphed. The year 146 BCE marked the end of an incredible period of expansion for the Republic, which was now in control of most of its known world. The Roman army had become the most feared fighting force alive, and the Roman way of life, its language, laws, and art, would eventually form the basis for the culture of the Western world. At the same time, however, the virulent hatred that culminated in the total destruction of Carthage in the Third Punic War—a war actively sought by Rome and engaged in under false pretenses—also marked the beginning of Rome's moral decline.

CHAPTER 3

THE HUNDRED YEARS' WAR

A PERFECT STORM OF WARFARE

1337–1453

The Hundred Years' War, fueled by outmoded notions of honor, a desire for profit, and the burgeoning of two soon-to-be nation-states that would fight for centuries over Europe and the New World, helped create the modern world.

The Hundred Years' War actually lasted 116 years and is the most famous long war in history. This is in part because of the name itself (which was not bestowed upon these conflicts between France and England until the nineteenth century) and in part because the Hundred Years' War contained a witch's brew of the conditions that lend themselves to endless warfare—everything from struggles over inherited land rights, always an intractable issue, to the enormous monetary motives involved in keeping the war going. The English, in particular, wanted to plunder the far richer land of France.

But the Hundred Years' War was also a classic war for empire, featuring two nations that, in the centuries to come, would battle to control Europe, and the world.

"A SINGLE COMMUNITY"

At its essence, the Hundred Years' War was a dynastic conflict between the two royal families that controlled France and England. Ever since the Norman Conquest of 1066, when William the Conqueror ended 500 years of Anglo-Saxon rule of England, the English kings had retained extensive land holdings in France. These were the source of conflict and acrimony. The situation came to a head in 1328, when the French king Charles IV died. The English monarch Edward III, who was the grandson of the former French king Philip IV (Charles's father) and ruler of the duchy of Guyenne in southwestern France, decided that he was the rightful heir to the French throne.

The French thought otherwise and an assembly of French nobles gave the crown to Philip, Count of Valois, who became Philip VI. In 1337, he declared Guyenne confiscated—he took it over from the English—which turned out to be the opening salvo of the Hundred Years' War. There is the sense, as the historian Jonathan Sumption has written, that the French and English were "a single community engaged in a civil war." There were powerful ties of blood and trade between the two countries, ties that would now be strained and broken.

Yet, if the French and English shared much, they were also very different. France was far more populous than England—20 million inhabitants to England's 4 or 5 million—and also much more prosperous. But England had by far the stronger central government (to be king in France was to constantly battle rival claimants) and a very popular and young king who had recently defeated a rebellion among the Scots and now strongly desired to fight France. With great civic pride, the English population was willing to follow him anywhere. And so, in 1340, Edward declared himself king of France, thus beginning the first segment of the war that historians generally divide into four phases.

"WHY ARE THE ENGLISH KNIGHTS MORE COWARDLY?"

The first major victory of this initial phase (1337–60) of the war took place at sea and was won by the English—this was a surprise because France had a much larger navy. For much of the first few years of the war, the only real action took place at sea. The French and English had raided each other's coastlines and burned towns, but the French had the upper hand, attacking the eastern and southern coasts of Britain, landing raiders to attack towns and castles, and destroying or carrying away a good deal of merchant shipping.

Not only was the French fleet larger, but also these oared galleys (which could operate under sail power as well) had the advantage of better-trained Castilian and Genoese seamen. England had not yet reached its status as the supreme seafaring nation in Europe and depended on round-hulled merchant ships to which it added "castles" (towers or platforms) at bow and stern to hold archers. Some of these ships had early cannon, but in the main the English vessels were unwieldy and far slower than the French fleet.

All of this was a major disadvantage for the English, for in order to attack France and press home his claims, Edward needed to be able to transport troops safely across the English Channel. In June 1340, Edward's 200 ships encountered the French fleet (along with their Spanish and Italian allies) off Sluys, near the current Dutch-Belgian border. The Flemish people were allies of the English because of their close interdependence in the woolen trade, and Edward was informed ahead of time that the

300-ship enemy fleet was anchored and in close formation.

On June 24, he attacked. The French were unable to maneuver in the tight space created by a close formation of too many ships anchored in a small and shallow area; thus, the English were able to attack with longbows and then board the French vessels, turning a sea battle into what one historian has called "a wooden battleground." The French admiral was killed and most of the Genoese ships were destroyed or driven off during a bloody, nine-hour battle, in which French and Castilian knights in full armor drowned or were clubbed to death in shallow water by the Flemish allies of the English.

After his great victory, Edward reembarked for England. He had not taken any French territory, but he had shown the French that their mastery of the sea was no longer assured. The news was considered so terrible that no one would break it to King Philip. Finally, only the king's fool would approach him, and he made the story into a riddle:

"Why are the English knights more cowardly than the French?"

"Because they did not jump in their armor into the sea, like our brave Frenchmen."

"RIDE DOWN THIS RABBLE!"

The fact that even a jester could have considered French knights drowning themselves rather than being captured a desirable trait underscores one of the reasons the Hundred Years' War lasted as long as it did: medieval notions of chivalry and honor died very hard, particularly with the French, who continued to fight as if the war were a series of sieges or battles between overlords, rather than the great conflagration it was becoming. The French assumed that their battles against the English would be decided knight against knight; instead, the peasant soldier came to the fore.

The ultimate test of medieval codes of honor against modern firepower came at the pivotal Battle of Crécy, in late August 1346. On July 12, King Edward had landed his latest invasion force at Caen on the north coast, sacked the town, and begun to march inland toward Paris, sending thousands of panicked refugees scurrying ahead of him (for the English attacking forces had acted with great brutality in Caen, murdering noncombatants, burning homes, and raping women).

King Philip responding by massing a force of approximately 30,000, including 20,000 men at arms, to meet Edward, whose roughly 11,000 fighters were arranged in a line of battle at the crest of a gentle slope in a valley located between the vast Crécy forest and the banks of the Maie River. Although the English were outnumbered, they had with them 7,000 archers armed with longbows, the great equalizing weapon of

The pivotal Battle of Crécy in 1346 pitted France's outmoded medieval codes of honor against the modern firepower of the English longbow. The French repeatedly and unsuccessfully charged the English, only to be slaughtered by their arrows, as shown in this nineteenth-century engraving from Froissart's *Chronicles*.

F. Strutt fec.

the Hundred Years' War. The longbow, which the English had adapted from a Welsh weapon, was made of strong but supple yew, and ranged in height from 5 1/2 to 6 1/2 feet (1.7 to 2 m) tall, depending on the size of the bowman. By the fourteenth century, English archers had become so adept at using it that they could kill accurately with it at 150 yards (137 m). It could penetrate church doors, and plate armor, at 60 yards (55 m), and a single archer could shoot a dozen arrows in the space of two minutes. Seven thousand archers could create an inferno of arrows that would blacken the sky, but the French and King Philip were not sufficiently aware of this at Crécy.

BY THE FOURTEENTH CENTURY, ENGLISH ARCHERS HAD
BECOME SO ADEPT AT USING THE LONGBOW THAT
THEY COULD KILL ACCURATELY WITH IT AT 150 YARDS (137 M).
THE LONGBOW COULD PENETRATE CHURCH DOORS, AND
PLATE ARMOR, AT 60 YARDS (55 M), AND A SINGLE ARCHER
COULD SHOOT A DOZEN ARROWS IN THE SPACE OF TWO MINUTES.

On the evening of August 26, Philip, who had to some extent lost control of his troops—they had mixed in with a crowd of angry refugees wanting revenge on the English—ordered a charge against the English positions. The French sent in Genoese crossbowmen first, through a brief but heavy downpour that turned the battlefield muddy. The longbow immediately proved its superiority to the slow and cumbersome weapons the Italian archers carried. Arrows rained down so quickly "it seemed as if it had snowed," one participant said later. After what was probably only a minute or two, the Genoese broke and ran, leaving hundreds dead behind them.

The French nobility were shocked by the timidity of their normally tough and brave crossbowmen. One count shouted: "Ride down this rabble who block our advance!" and led a charge against the English up the slopes of the muddy hill. The result was a horrible slaughter. The English archers fired their deadly weapons into horses and into the heads and limbs of the French knights, puncturing their armor as if it were made of tin. A French chronicler wrote: "A great outcry rose to the stars," horses and men screaming alike. Knights and their steeds fell into piles "like a litter of piglets." And still the awful arrows rained down.

The French, driven on by their notions of courage and honor, charged fifteen times, until almost midnight, and the long summer twilight was filled with carnage. When at last the French withdrew, the English slept in their positions, unable to

Edward the Black Prince receives the conquered French provinces from his father, King Edward III, in this nineteenth-century engraving. Since the time of William the Conqueror, the English kings had retained land holdings throughout France, one of the major factors behind the Hundred Years' War.

Getty Images

believe they had won such a great victory. As the next morning's fog slowly lifted from the battlefield, they saw before them a field littered with thousands of dead—perhaps 12,000, including 1,500 lords and knights.

Despite the fact that such tactics were not working, the French continued to battle the English with knightly courage against showers of deadly arrows—they would do the same at Agincourt, in 1415—extending the war by being unwilling or unable to change.

"THERE WAS NEVER SUCH A LOSS"

The first phase of the Hundred Years' War ended in 1360 with the Treaty of Brétigny. By this time, the English had captured the pivotal port of Calais and won other important battles with the French. King Philip had died in 1350, to be replaced by King John II, who was captured in battle in 1356 by King Edward's son, Edward Woodstock, who would become known to history as the Black Prince. The Treaty of Brétigny (initially signed in May and confirmed in Calais in October) forced the French to pay three million gold francs for the release of John II, and also cede territory amounting to half of France to King Edward, who in return agreed to give up his claim to the French throne.

THE SECOND PHASE OF THE HUNDRED YEARS' WAR WAS CHARACTERIZED BY SMALL-SCALE FIGHTING THAT NONETHELESS INFLICTED SERIOUS HARDSHIP ON FRENCH CITIZENS. BY THE END OF THE FOURTEENTH CENTURY, THE FRENCH HAD LEARNED TO BUILD ESCAPE TUNNELS AND UNDERGROUND SHELTERS NEAR THEIR HOMES TO EVADE RAIDS CONDUCTED BY THE ENGLISH AND THEIR ALLIES.

But the treaty—like the peace that ended the First Punic War—was satisfactory to neither party and thus eventually extended the war. Both England and France were exhausted from fighting and from the deadly Black Plague outbreak that spread through Europe from 1348 to 1450 and killed about a third of the people in Europe, and whose effects were still being felt, particularly in terms of each country's economy.

But neither side considered the conflict settled. The French resented giving up so much territory, while the English monarchy would ultimately never be happy without the French crown. As it happened, King John died in captivity with only a portion of his ransom paid, and the terms of the treaty were not fulfilled. The second phase of the war, lasting from 1369 to 1399, began when King John's son and successor, King Charles

V, a far more effective leader than his father, invaded Aquitaine, the inhabitants of which were being heavily taxed by the Black Prince, whose father had given him the province. By 1372, Charles had regained Poitiers, Poitou, and La Rochelle, and by 1374 had reconquered Aquitaine and Brittany, thus taking back all the land the English had received under the Treaty of Brétigny.

Except for major events such as Crécy, the second phase of the Hundred Years' War was characterized by small-scale fighting that nonetheless inflicted serious hardship on French citizens. By the end of the fourteenth century, the French had learned to build escape tunnels and underground shelters near their homes to evade raids known as *chevauchées*, from the French for "horse charge," conducted by the English and their allies. The English had learned the effectiveness of such armed sorties in force while fighting against the Scots and now made them a regular weapon of war against the French. Such raids had their advantages militarily. They used only about 3,000 soldiers at a time, gathered wealth and booty, and spread terror among the French.

That it was the French citizenry suffering rather than the French knights carried little weight with the English doing the raiding. In one classic chevauchée, the Black Prince led an army of 2,500 mounted men-at-arms and archers for two months through the French region of Languedoc, devastating the countryside. He captured the cities of Narbonne and Carcassone and burned down countless small towns and villages, killing peasants who desperately sought to escape the thundering hooves, flashing steel, and whizzing arrows of the English.

One of the Black Prince's secretaries, who accompanied the expedition and recorded the slaughter (and the booty taken), noted with some pride that "there was never such a loss nor destruction as hath been in this raid." A French priest wrote that roads were deserted, vineyards uncultivated, and starving wolves roamed everywhere: "The pleasant sound of bells was heard . . . not as a summons to divine worship but as a warning of hostile intention, so that men might seek out hiding places while the enemy was still on the way."

The region of Languedoc in southern France took decades to recover from the depredations wrought by the English. Chevauchées continued throughout the war, finally diminishing in effectiveness after the introduction of the cannon, which could be fired from castle walls to break up attacks. Ultimately, the chevauchées were a counterproductive tool of war. By not concentrating on major targets—such as the main French armies or population centers—and by killing ordinary citizens, they extended the war and increased hatred of the English among French people, who were now, for the first time, beginning to develop a sense of nationhood, a desire to join as one to fight off the invader.

MAKING MEN RICH

Another factor in lengthening the Hundred Years' War, one that was particularly prevalent during the middle years of the conflict, was the taking of hostages for ransom. Particularly on the English side, many of the battles became attempts by lower-ranking soldiers to disarm French knights and lead them away to the rear of English lines, where they would be held until ransom was paid for them. Hostage-taking was so prevalent that a class of entrepreneurs sprang up that would capture high-ranking hostages and then sell "shares" in them to the highest bidder. King Edward himself took part in this.

MOST NOBLE PRISONERS WERE TREATED WELL—IN FACT, KING JOHN MAY HAVE DIED IN ENGLISH CAPTIVITY AS A RESULT OF TOO MUCH FEASTING AND DRINKING—BUT THE PRACTICE HAD NUMEROUS ASPECTS TO IT THAT INCREASED THE LENGTH OF THE WAR. OFTEN ENGLISH SOLDIERS FOCUSED NOT ON WINNING, BUT ON SEIZING HOSTAGES OR BOOTY.

Ransoming prisoners was not always the easiest thing to do and was not without expense to the hostage-taker—one had to feed the hostage and keep him under guard, while at the same time contact a hostile enemy family and convince them to pay for their loved one's release. But because the king had the resources to do all this, his nobles would often turn to him with their captives.

According to English records, Sir Thomas Dagworth sold the French knight Charles of Blois to Edward for 25,000 gold crowns; Edward later sold Charles back to his family for 40,000, thus making a tidy profit. The biggest fish of all, of course, was the French King John, captured by Edward's son the Black Prince, in a battle outside of Poitiers in 1356. This English victory produced such a rich haul of hostages that even humble English archers had five or six of them—so many that they could not possibly all be guarded, and so they were released with a solemn promise that they would return by Christmas with their ransoms. One nobleman who was with the English at Poitiers wrote: "All such as were there with [the Black Prince] were made rich, as well as by ransoming prisoners as by winning of gold, silver, plate, [and] jewels."

Another English knight known as the Bascot (Bastard) of Mauléon related to the Belgian chronicler Jean de Froissart: "The first time I bore arms was at the battle of Poitiers . . . I had that day three prisoners, a knight and two squires, of whom I had one with another 400,000 francs." He had also captured an entire castle, he said, that he had ransomed back to the villages it protected in the surrounding countryside to the tune of 100,000 francs. And yet, Bascot told Friossart, he was so broke he could not now even afford his own horse.

Most noble prisoners were treated well—in fact, King John may have died in English captivity as a result of too much feasting and drinking—but the practice had numerous aspects to it that increased the length of the war. Often English soldiers focused not on winning, but on seizing hostages or booty. The war was a time, one English soldier remembered, "when we saw many poor men serving in the wars of France ennobled." But this goal let French armies live to fight on another day (with their redeemed hostages fighting with them). While taking hostages certainly did enrich some Englishmen and was not without its comic moments (the Archbishop of Paris was captured but only brought fifty gold crowns in ransom, embarrassing both the Archbishop and his captor), it was ultimately, like the chevauchées, a failed tactic.

"A FRENCH HEART"

The second phase of the war ended with almost total French victory. King Edward III had died in 1377, an old man of sixty-five (the Black Prince had died the year before). But King Charles—the best French leader of the entire war—had regained all of the ground that the French had lost, leaving the English with only Guyenne and Calais. Moreover, the war had finally grown unpopular among the English populace. The French were again resorting to attacks on the English mainland, which had largely gone unscathed during the war. These hit-and-run raids on places such as Winchelsea, Gravesend, Hastings, and other areas did not do the type of damage that a typical chevauchée might in France, but they terrified the English people.

The English were also beginning to suffer economically from the fighting. While certain soldiers enriched themselves, the English people back home paid heavy taxes to fund the endless warfare. When King Charles, who had been sickly for some time, died of a heart attack in 1380, the English were unable to take advantage of this, because they were barely able to finance an army into the field. However, the French, too, were nearly bankrupt. Reeling, both parties decided on another truce, the 1389 Truce of Leulinghen, which allowed them to rest and regroup and officially placed England's territory in France back where it had been in 1338. France, because of Charles V's expert leadership, had been successful during this phase of the war, but, once again, the truce merely afforded breathing space to the combatants. The war would be extended, its conflicts unresolved.

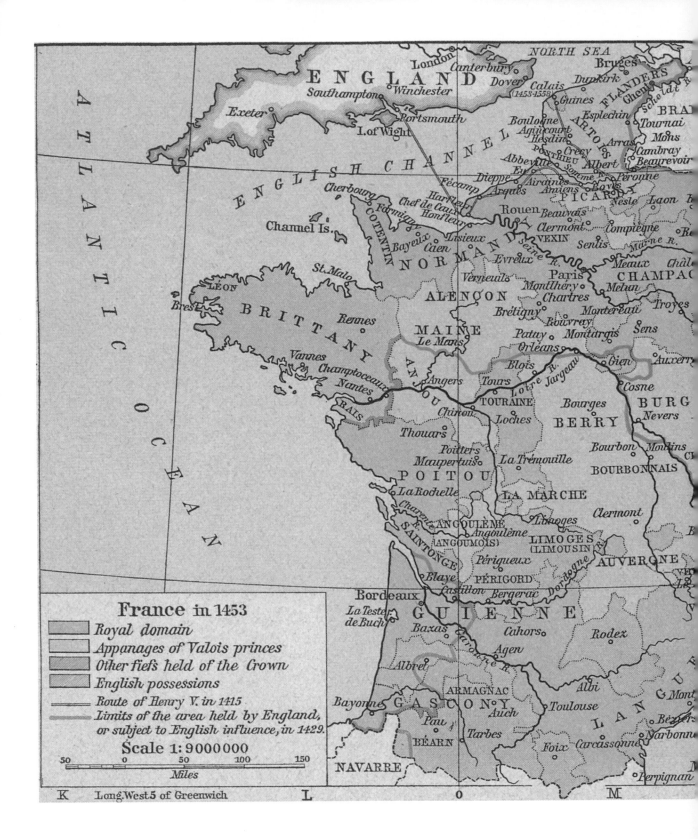

ATLANTIC OCEAN

ENGLAND

London · Canterbury
NORTH SEA
Dover · Calais · Bruges · Dunkirk
Southampton · Winchester (1458-1558) · Guines · FLANDERS
Exeter · Portsmouth · Boulogne · Esplechin · Scheldt · BRA
I. of Wight · Agincourt · Hesdin · Tournai · Mons
ENGLISH CHANNEL · Eu · Crecy · Albert · Cambray
Abbeville · Somme R. · Péronne · Beaurevoir
Fécamp · Dieppe · Airaines · Amiens · Boves
Harfleur · Arques · Nesle · Laon
Cherbourg · Chef de Caux · Honfleur · Rouen · Beauvais · PICARDY
Farmigny · Lisieux · Clermont · Compiègne · R
COTENTIN · Bayeux · Caen · VEXIN · Senlis · Marne R.
Channel Is. · NORMANDY · Evreux · Meaux · Châl
St. Malo · Verneuil · Paris · CHAMPA
ALENÇON · Montlhéry · Melun
LÉON · Rennes · BRITTANY · Chartres · Mortereau · Troyes
Brest · MAINE · Brétigny · Rouvray · Sens
Le Mans · Patay · Montargis
Vannes · ANJOU · Orleans
Champtoceaux · Angers · Blois · Loire R. · Gien · Auxerr
Nantes · Tours · Jargeau · Cosne
RAIS · TOURAINE · Bourges · BURG
Chinon · Loches · BERRY · Nevers
Thouars · Bourbon · Moulins
Poitiers · La Trémouille · BOURBONNAIS
Maupertuis · La Marche · Clermont
POITOU · LA MARCHE · B
La Rochelle · Limoges
Charente · ANGOULÊME · LIMOGES · AUVERGNE
SAINTONGE · Angoulême · (LIMOUSIN) · VE
(ANGOUMOIS) · Périgueux
Blaye · PÉRIGORD · Dordogne R.
Bordeaux · Castillon · Bergerac
La Teste de Buch · GUIENNE
Bazas · Cahors · Rodez
Agen
Albret · Garonne R. · Albi
ARMAGNAC · Mont
Bayonne · GASCONY · Toulouse · Béziers
Pau · Auch
BÉARN · Tarbes · Foix · Carcassonne · Narbonn
NAVARRE · Perpignan

France in 1453

- Royal domain
- Appanages of Valois princes
- Other fiefs held of the Crown
- English possessions
- Route of Henry V. in 1415
- Limits of the area held by England, or subject to English influence, in 1429.

Scale 1:9000000

50   0   50   100   150

Miles

K   Long.West 5 of Greenwich   L   0   M

After an uneasy peace of ten years, the conflict entered its third stage in 1399. In England, Richard II, the highly unpopular king who had succeeded Edward III, was seen by many as a French sympathizer, because he was actually trying to make peace with the French, even agreeing to marry the daughter of Charles VI, the new French king. The English whispered that he had "a French heart." A dictatorial figure made famous by William Shakespeare in *Richard II*, Richard was, as one biographer has written, "a mumbling neurotic sinking rapidly into a state of complete melancholia." He was deposed in 1399, succeeded by Henry IV, who was far more warlike than Richard when it came to France.

In France, civil war had broken out among French princes. The country had no strong central power because Charles VI had gone mad. In 1392, while out riding, he murdered four members of his own entourage and even tried to kill his own nephew. He was prone to running howling like a wolf through the halls of his castle and also believed that he was made out of glass and might shatter at any moment. He had moments of lucidity, but they were rare. In the meantime the French princes of Valois began to fight with each other over the provinces of Burgundy and Armagnac.

Such unstable conditions are a prime condition of endless war—stable governments manage to help keep wars short and focused—and Henry IV was desperate to take advantage of them. But he had his own problems, which included a shortage of money with which to fund an expensive war, and an uprising among the Welsh. While hostilities still simmered between France and England, the period from roughly 1399 to 1415 can be likened to a cold

The Hundred Years' War ended in 1453, the year depicted in this map of the two combatant countries. Battles over land rights, charismatic leaders such as King Henry V and Joan of Arc, and the ransoming of hostages all served to prolong the war.

war where both sides dealt with internal problems and readied themselves for the fight that was sure to lie ahead.

HENRY V

When war broke out again, however, it broke out in the most violent and bloody fashion imaginable—also a hallmark of endless war, where rage simmers below the surface for a while before exploding. This rage was personified in Henry V, another Shakespearean figure, of course, who ascended the throne after the death of Henry IV in 1413. Tall, thin, strangely ascetic looking (though known for his hard-partying ways), the twenty-eight-year-old Henry crossed the English Channel in August 1415 leading a fleet of 300 ships and a force of about 12,000 troops.

His swift and merciless attack caught the French by surprise. Henry's army and huge siege engines took the port of Harfleur in five weeks, after which Henry expelled all the French and planned on turning the city into a port of entry for English immigrants. However, during the siege dysentery ravaged Henry's men, costing 2,000 lives and severely weakening the army.

With his army in a decimated state, Henry abandoned plans to strike into the heart of France and instead decided to head north to winter at the English-held port of Calais. Leaving part of his army behind to fortify Harfleur, Henry set off with a force of about 900 men-at-arms and 5,000 longbowmen. The French had recovered by this time and brought together a force of roughly 25,000 men to shadow Henry during his travels. Henry, however, was not the type of leader to be easily alarmed. He had been fighting since he was sixteen years old and was a ferocious and often brutal warrior. The French, under the command of the constable of France, Charles d'Albret, stayed away from large encounters with Henry's force (the memories of the slaughter at Crécy in 1346 were still strong) but harassed them, keeping them away from favorable river crossings, picking off stragglers, and attempting to cut off their supply lines.

Henry stubbornly marched his men toward Calais, but he found himself finally, on October 24, blocked by the French near the village of Agincourt. The French thought they at last had enough advantage to risk a larger encounter with Henry's sick and exhausted army, but Henry was able to maneuver his men so that they were at the head of a long, narrow strip of land flanked on either side by thick forest. He was seriously outnumbered, but he knew that to allow himself to be outflanked would mean that his entire force would be engulfed and defeated—a disaster for England, because Henry would either be killed or captured and taken hostage, no doubt for a king's ransom that would bankrupt the nation and end the war.

LEOPARDS AND FLEUR-DE-LYS

A hallmark of any never-ending war is the one pivotal leader—such as Hannibal or Ho Chi Minh, to name just a couple—who can not only fight his way out of certain death but also can triumph and save his army and his country. Henry V was that person for the English at that moment in late October 1415. The night before the battle it rained hard. The French knights, certain of their victory the next day, drank hard and hurled taunts at the English, but Henry had ordered his men to keep completely quiet, which fooled many of the French into thinking that they faced a defeated army.

In Shakespeare's powerful drama *Henry V*, Henry made a stirring speech to his troops ("We few, we happy few, we band of brothers"), but in reality he probably had little time to make such a moving declamation. Instead, he did something even more powerful, and visible to thousands: he put on a royal coat over his armor that bore not only the three leopards that were symbols of England, but also the three gold fleur-de-lys that represented the throne of France. It was an act of extraordinary arrogance—thumbing his nose at his vastly superior enemy, on the enemy's home ground—but it was exactly the type of gesture the English needed. And he did one more thing. Although he rode out in front of his troops that morning on horseback, he wore no spurs—a sure sign he intended to fight on foot. The area was too narrow for cavalry maneuvering, and there would be no running away from the French knights.

All the English knights dismounted, armed with swords, battle-axes, and maces. As the morning light came up, the two forces faced each other without a move across the narrow, plowed field, which was quite muddy from the previous night's rainfall. The French, reluctant to charge, waited for the English to make the first move, and finally, around noon, Henry did, leading his men on a slow march toward the French forces about 600 yards (550 m) away.

When the English arrived within 200 yards (183 m) of the French, Henry gave an order and the English archers drove wooden stakes into the ground (to slow down French horsemen) and then loosed a volley of arrows into the air. Trying to avoid another Crécy, the French knights charged along the edges of the narrow field, near the woods, to come at the longbowmen from their flanks, but the field was too muddy for the horses to move quickly enough, and they were easy targets. When they got close to the English archers, the wooden stakes slowed them down, and now the deadly arrows sliced easily through their armor.

Those knights not killed fell to the ground and were either trampled or killed horribly by the English archers, who dropped their bows and rushed at the French knights with knives, axes, and heavy, long-handled mallets, with which they literally hammered the armored knights into the ground.

Now the main French force engaged the main English force, men-at-arms in innumerable single combat fighting away at each other with swords and battle-axes, seeking to find openings in their opponent's armor or club him to the ground. Many knights who fell in the muck could not rise again because of the weight of their armor and suffocated when others fell on them. Henry V was everywhere, racing all over the field with his bodyguards, doing personal battle with French knights. Eighteen of these swarmed around him, having sworn to kill him, and one got close enough to knock a floret off the king's helmet before being killed.

Gradually, the French retreated and it appeared that the English had won the day. Henry ordered that their 1,500 French prisoners be sent to the rear, but then heard that a French raiding party was behind his lines and sacking his baggage trains. Fearful that this might incite the main body of French to attack again, Henry ordered all 1,500 prisoners put to death, except for those who could bring a high ransom. No English man-at-arms would perform this deed; the job was left to longbowmen, who went at the butchery with mallet and knife. While combat of the day could be fierce, this was considered brutal, coldhearted slaughter in the extreme.

CHIVALRY DIED AT AGINCOURT THAT DAY, KILLED BY HENRY V.

Chivalry died at Agincourt that day, killed by Henry V. But when news of the slaughter reached the French force, it retreated, and Henry made his way, victorious, to Calais.

"TO BRING SUCCOR TO YOU"

Henry left France shortly after Agincourt to rest his army, but two years later invaded France again and won a series of victories against a French army weakened by serious internal difficulties. They were forced to sue for peace, and, in the 1420 Treaty of Troyes, Henry was able to have himself recognized as heir to the throne of France and

regent—King Charles VI having finally ceded the throne because of his mental illness. Henry even married the king's daughter, Catherine of Valois, in June 1420. But just as he was about to achieve the end to which England had aspired for eighty years—to have an Englishman as crowned head of both France and England—Henry died of dysentery, in 1422, at the age of thirty-four. Seven weeks later, Charles VI died.

In a very real sense, the French and English seemed back where they had started, so long ago. Each side had come close to winning the war, and each side had failed. And now the claims of both sides seemed equally strong. The English, with the Treaty of Troyes on their side, named Henry's son Henry VI as the new king of France, with John, Duke of Bedford, to rule as his regent until he came of age. However, the new English king was recognized only north of the Loire River; to the south, the French population supported Charles VI's son, Charles, who initially remained uncrowned, with the title dauphin. The English laid siege to the dauphin's stronghold in Orléans in 1428, to gain control of the rest of the kingdom of France. Decades of war had boiled down to one very simple fact: if Orléans fell, France would fall.

The slaughter on the field of Agincourt is shown in this engraving, artist unknown. Those French knights not killed fell to the ground and were either trampled or killed horribly by the English archers, who dropped their bows and rushed at the them with knives, axes, and heavy, long-handled mallets, with which they literally hammered the armored knights into the ground.

As the fourth phase of the war began, the conflict had become a desperate struggle for the French, who had already lost half their country to the English. As in all long wars, desperation has its uses in terms of making men fight as long and as hard as possible, but the French probably would not have been able to stem the English had it not been for a charismatic young woman named Joan of Arc. Although both sides were intensely Catholic in the years before the great Protestant Revolution of the sixteenth century, Joan of Arc brought a different, messianic fervor to the war. Fierce religious belief lengthens war because it places God firmly on the side of the believers, or so they believe. In fighting on, they are doing God's work. Dying, they find themselves in heaven.

Joan of Arc (Jeanne d'Arc) was born to a family of small landowners in the village of Domrémy, on the Meuse River, in 1412. Very early on, it was apparent that Joan was a pious child—she dropped whatever she was doing when she heard church bells and headed to the church to pray. By the time she was thirteen, however, her piety had taken a different turn. She was hearing voices from God. These voices (later accompanied by physical manifestations or apparitions) were mainly those of three saints: St. Michael, St. Catherine, and St. Margaret. Within a year or so, these voices were telling her she had to save France. More specifically, they were telling her to go and take Dauphin Charles to Reims, the city where French kings were traditionally crowned.

In 1428, at the age of perhaps sixteen, Joan journeyed to Chinon, where the dauphin had his court, and there convinced Charles—who seemed to have at first thought she was a witch—to allow her to lead a relief force against the English currently besieging Orléans. She told Charles: "Very noble Lord Dauphin, I am come and I am sent by God to bring succor to you and your kingdom."

Charles put aside his fears that she was a witch after he had her quizzed by a panel of theologians, and allowed her to lead a force of 5,000 against the English who were attacking Orléans. It was extraordinary—not only was a woman fighting, which itself was almost unheard of, but she was also leading men into battle. Arriving outside the walls of Orléans in April of 1429, Joan must have indeed seemed like she was sent by God. Tiny and dark-haired, she rode a white charger and was dressed in a suit of white enamel armor, and she held aloft her *pennon*, a narrow banner of blue and white emblazoned with two angels and the word *Jesus*. Entering Orléans, Joan faced a huge crowd of deliriously happy civilians who, as one chronicler wrote, "felt themselves already comforted and as if no longer besieged, by the divine virtue which they were told was in this simple maid."

The Maid, as Joan of Arc was more generally known to the French people, immediately galvanized the defense of Orléans by going on the offensive. Leading charge after charge against the English—who shouted that she was a whore and a witch, and promised to burn her at the stake—she inspired the French army to new heights. Always in the thick of the fighting, alternately weeping and shouting praises to God, she was wounded in the neck by a crossbow bolt—a wound she had predicted the night before, telling her confessor that "tomorrow the blood will flow out of my body above my breast." But she was finally able to dislodge the English.

It was a great victory for the French, and Joan followed it up with further victories, capturing several towns in English territory, leading Charles to Reims, where he was crowned King Charles VII, and even leading a failed attack against Paris, then held by the English. Although she was captured by the English and finally put to death at the stake in May of 1431, Joan of Arc had transformed a nation.

A NEW ERA

After the dauphin became Charles VII, the tide turned for the French and they won a string of victories, ultimately defeating the English at the Battle of Castillon in 1453, a battle that most historians place as the end of the Hundred Years' War, although the English hung on to the port city of Calais for another hundred years.

The war had begun in medieval times—with battles over inherited land rights and chivalric codes of honor—and ended with the beginnings of modern nation-states. England, although bankrupt and bled dry, had a powerful sense of patriotism and a valuable patriotic myth in the actions of Henry V and his "band of brothers" at Agincourt.

France's nationhood revolved around a newly centralized government and a sense among the French people that they had come together to keep out foreign invaders. Uncounted hundreds of thousands had died in 116 years of never-ending war, but from the blood and ashes the modern era in Europe had begun to emerge. France and England were now about to coalesce into the countries that would do battle for 150 years over Europe and the soon-to-be-discovered New World.

CHAPTER 4

THE OTTOMAN WARS

"THE GREAT DRUM OF CONQUEST"

1354–1529

This series of conflicts, propelled by an ambitious people
with fierce and ruthless leadership, lasted 175 years
and shaped the rise of the Ottoman Empire as it
sought to conquer Europe.

On March 2, 1354, the Greek inhabitants of the town of Gallipoli (now called Gelibolu) awoke to the sound of rumbling. Then the earth began to shake and the town's wood and stone houses began to tumble, burying thousands in rubble. The early morning earthquake destroyed hundreds of villages in the area and leveled almost every building in Gallipoli. The dust rose up, obscuring the bright early sun as the sound of screams and moans filled the air.

The Greeks who survived were in a state of shock. In 1347, less than ten years before, the Black Death had touched down in Gallipoli on its way to devastate Europe, killing an untold number of townspeople. And now this. In great haste, climbing into any type of vessel that would float, the people of Gallipoli fled their town, sailing down the ancient strait known as the Hellespont (we now call it the Dardanelles) and into the Aegean Sea. Silence settled on the abandoned city of Gallipoli, except for the noise of crows calling and the ravening growls of prowling wolves. But across the water, on the Asiatic side of the Hellespont, in Anatolia, eyes were watching. The eyes belonged to an upstart warrior people called the Ottomans.

The Ottomans had only been around for fifty years or so—a pittance compared to the longevity of the Greeks and the Byzantium Empire. But by the mid-fourteenth century, the empire of Byzantium was long past its glory days. And these Ottomans, fresh and strong Turkish tribes buoyed by a newfound faith in Allah, had swept across Anatolia from their provincial capital near the Sea of Marmora. They conquered other tribes and consolidated them under their rule, until they reached the Asian shore of the Hellespont, where they could stare across the water at Gallipoli, a stepping-stone into Europe.

That March morning, seeing the smoke rising on the horizon, the Ottomans, under their leader, Sultan Orhan I, knew what to do. He sent his son Suleyman across the Hellespont with 3,000 troops and as many Turkish families as he could quickly find, and settled in the ruins of the city of Gallipoli, gaining the first Ottoman foothold in Europe.

The Greeks who had left recovered their senses, realized that they had opened the door to the Ottoman threat, and attempted to bribe Suleyman to get him to leave the city, but it was too late. A natural disaster was about to lead to 175 years of war—the longest war in European history—and a vast new empire to replace that of Rome and the Byzantines.

"THE RING OF A VAST DOMINION"

The Ottomans lived at the right time and in the right place, a prerequisite for any young people engaged in an empire-building war. The Byzantine Empire had fallen apart in the early thirteenth century, leaving a vacuum of power that was only partially filled by local warlords, whom the Ottomans either swept aside or co-opted. They were fierce fighters in the ancient mode of the Mongols, men who rode hardy ponies and called themselves *ghazis*—"warriors of the faith," that faith being Islam.

The Ottomans were also lucky in that their first three sultans—Osman, from whom the Ottomans derived their name, Orhan, and Murad I—were powerful warriors for whom no obstacle was too great. The long Ottoman Wars would have been greatly shortened had it not been for the determination and leadership displayed by these men.

The Ottomans also had a creation myth of sorts, which led them to believe that they were a chosen people—something that helped them endure the hardship of a long war. The story went that Osman, their first great leader, had when just a young tribal chief spent the night in the house of a devoutly religious Muslim. The Muslim had left the Koran on Osman's bedside table, and Osman stayed up all night reading it. When he fell asleep just before dawn, an angel appeared to him and said: "Since thou has read my eternal word with such respect, thy children and the children of thy children shall be honored from generation to generation."

In another dream he had while staying at the Muslim's house, Osman dreamed that a beautiful tree had sprung from his loins, one that grew so enormous that it covered the entire world. Then the leaves of the tree became sword blades, pointing to the city of Constantinople, the capital of the Byzantine Empire, which appeared in Osman's dream like "the precious stone of the ring of a vast dominion." As Osman was about to put the ring on his finger, he awoke, but the meaning of the dream was clear: he and his people were meant to conquer the world and make Constantinople their capital.

Cultural and religious myths—whether they belong to the Romans, the Greeks, or the Ottomans—are often a part of extended battles for empire, because they give a people a raison d'être that allows them to endure hardship and keep on fighting.

THE FIELD OF THE BLACKBIRDS

It was Osman who led the tribe from its obscure province in northwest Anatolia, but his son Orhan brought it into Europe. After taking over Gallipoli, Orhan led his armies into Thrace (in the westernmost part of modern Turkey), where he captured the ancient city of Adrianople, which he renamed Edirne, and which became the first capital of the Ottoman Empire. After Orhan died in 1362, his son Murad became sultan and continued Ottoman expansion into the Balkans. It was in the southern Balkans, on June 28, 1389, that Murad fought an epic battle against a Christian army of Serbs and Bosnians, with their allies the Hungarians and Albanians.

The battle took place in a mountain plain called for centuries the Field of the Blackbirds, or Kosovo Polje, a strategic point where Bosnia, Serbia, Albania, and Herzegovina all came together. The Serbian army outnumbered the Turks, but it lacked unity, mainly because the Serb leader, Prince Lazar Hrebeljanovic, had accused his own son-in-law, Milosh Obravich, of colluding with the Turks. In fact, it wasn't Milosh who had sold his soul to the Ottomans, but a Serbian traitor named Vuk Brankovic who conspired with Murad and arranged for his 12,000 soldiers to retreat just as the battle was beginning. Even so, the subsequent clash was long and bloody and remained so until Prince Lazar was captured and then beheaded on the battlefield. Even more dramatically, Milosh Obravich managed to

1. Mehmet II established his camp outside the land wall on April 7, 1453. The city was cut and the walls received a constant battering.

play dead, then rise up and strike Sultan Murad with his sword as Murad was touring the battlefield, killing him before being killed himself by the sultan's enraged bodyguards.

What transpired at Kosovo provided myth enough for both the Serbs and the Ottomans. Never mind that there are varying, often contradictory stories as to how Milosh managed to kill Murad—or that some historians believe that Milosh never existed at all, and that Murad was killed by a nameless Serb in combat. The courage of Milosh, the martyrdom of Lazar, and the perfidy of Vuk Brankovic created a legend that had the Serbs fighting for their nationhood, and losing it, at a very young age, the cream

The siege and fall of Constantinople in 1453 are shown here. The Ottomans were driven by a creation of myth of sorts, in which they believed that they were a chosen people meant to conquer the world and make Constantinople their capital.

4. On the night of May 28, the Turks broke in over the wall and through a small postern gate.

3. Mehmet sent Turkish ships overland round Pera on rollers and into the Golden Horn. Constantinople was now fully blocked.

2. A small Italian fleet broke through and was let into the Golden Horn, giving temporary relief.

5. Constantine XI was killed. For three days the city was sacked and looted

of their nobility left to rot on this desolate plain (see The Balkan Wars, chapter 12). Even down to the Bosnian Wars of the 1990s, the Serbs have sought to regain what they suspected they lost on the Field of the Blackbirds. Although factions of the Serbs made a temporary peace with the Ottomans, their loss would keep them fighting ferociously against their Muslim enemies.

The loss of Murad was a great blow to the Ottomans. Immediately after his death, Murad's oldest son was anointed Sultan Bayezid I; Bayezid's first act as sultan was to order the strangulation of his younger brother Yakub, in case there should be any threat to his throne—the first royal fratricide in the Ottoman dynasty, but not the last by any means.

TIMUR THE LAME

Although Murad had been a great fighter, he was also an able statesman. Bayezid, too, was a warrior of the first order, but he was not a diplomat and was often impetuous in his actions and rash in his judgments—something that would ultimately end up lengthening the Ottoman Wars. Still, at first Bayezid was successful. Taking a beautiful Serbian princess as his bride, he made peace with the Serbs and turned his attention to the jewel found in the ring his great-grandfather Osman had seen in his dream—Constantinople.

This ancient capital of the Byzantine Empire was located at the tip of the Golden Horn, the peninsula that juts out into the Bosporus, the straits that join the Black Sea to the Sea of Marmora. The fortress city, founded by the Roman emperor Constantine I in the fourth century on the site of the ancient Greek city of Byzantium, was strategically located at the point where Europe meets Asia and had been, for nine centuries, what one historian has called "the capital of [Eastern] Christian civilization," the center of the Byzantine Empire.

Byzantine influence had declined after a fractious army of Crusaders sacked it during the Fourth Crusade in 1203. Yet, it was still a powerful symbol of Christianity and a strategic point, and Bayezid was determined to be the Ottoman ruler who would capture it. In 1394, he laid siege to Constantinople, building a fortress upstream on the Asian side of the Bosporus to harass maritime traffic. But Bayezid, unlike Murad, had not been careful about guarding his flanks and moving slowly in his war of dominion.

While he was occupied in besieging Constantinople, the Christian countries of western Europe, where much alarm had been raised by the Ottoman victory in the Battle of Kosovo, gathered together a huge force of knights—some sources have it at as many as 100,000—and marched down the Danube to attack the Ottomans. Bayezid was forced to relinquish his siege and his army met the Christians at the town of Nicopolis (now Nikopol, Bulgaria) on September 15, 1396.

Sultan Mehmed the Conqueror sits on his throne at the time of the fall of Constantinople in this nineteenth-century Greek School painting. Captured Greeks are shown in the foreground, between two Turkish soldiers. A visionary leader, his goal was to build an empire that would lead the Ottomans into Western Europe.

Bayezid's troops lured the Christians into a trap, surrounded them, and annihilated them. In his exultant savagery, Bayezid had 10,000 Christian knights beheaded that day, until his own men were so sickened by the slaughter they begged their ruler to desist. Thinking that nothing now stood in the way of his great assault on Constantinople, Bayezid returned to besiege that city, but now found himself under attack from a strange and unexpected source.

From the east, from Samarkand, in modern-day Uzbekistan, there came a Mongol warlord whose name has come down in history as Tamburlaine, but whose real name was probably Timur Leng, or Timur the Lame. Timur represented the last of the waves of marauding Mongols who would terrorize the world, and he had decided that the Ottoman Empire, with Bayezid's attention elsewhere, would be ripe for the plucking, even though it, too, was Muslim. Timur's armies struck terror in the hearts of even the most hardened Ottoman warrior—they left huge pyramids of skulls behind them outside of conquered cities, and were less bent on colonization than sheer plunder and terror.

Bayezid once again left his siege to fight another threat, and his army met Timur's at Angora (now Ankara) in July 1402. But even the superb Ottoman fighters were no match for Timur's hardened steppe warriors, and the Ottoman army was devastated and obliged to retreat. Although he fought bravely until the end, Bayezid was captured and imprisoned by Timur. Transported everywhere in a cage, he was forced to watch his beautiful Serbian bride wait on Timur's table, completely naked. Within a year, Bayezid had died in captivity. Although Constantinople and the West lay open to Timur, he decided to return East and attempt to conquer China. He left in his wake a relieved Christian city of Constantinople, and civil war tearing the Ottomans apart.

MEHMED THE CONQUEROR

A prerequisite for any nation seeking to win an empire through long war is the ability to take setbacks, even major setbacks like the Ottoman loss at Angora, and keep on going. The Romans survived Cannae, the French Agincourt, and the Ottomans survived the loss of Bayezid and their attendant humiliation. But it would take fifty years for them to finally achieve their goals and conquer Constantinople. That they were able to do so was a credit to their leadership, in particular to Sultan Mehmed I, who to this day is known as Mehmed the Conquerer, a powerful, ruthless, charismatic leader who was as much a visionary as a fighter.

Mehmed was the son of Sultan Murad II, who had taken over control of the Ottoman Empire after civil war had torn it apart following the death of Bayezid. Murad II was a statesman and an intellectual first, a warrior second, and he had been willing to live in peace with the Christian world—at least until provoked, at which point he dealt mighty blows to armies of Christian Hungarians and Bulgarians that had dared to test his mettle.

But his son Mehmed, who became sultan at the tender age of nineteen in 1451, was to become the perfect Ottoman leader for conquest. Although he spoke Turkish, Greek, Hebrew, Arabic, Latin, and Persian, and cultivated numerous Christian acquaintances, he continued the cruel Ottoman tradition of fratricide by having an infant stepbrother drowned in a bathtub to thwart any possible threat to his power. Mehmed also read biographies of Alexander the Great in the original Greek and was determined to conquer the known world as Alexander had. He knew his classical world. As the historian Stephen O'Shea has written, Mehmed "saw himself not only as the sultan of the Turks, but as the Emperor of the Romans."

As a first step in this direction, Mehmed began his campaign to finally conquer Constantinople. He was serious and methodical about it. His first step, in the spring of 1452, was to build a fort across from the one that Bayezid had constructed, this time on the European side of the Bosporus. The Rumeli Hisari (the European Castle), as it is called, still stands upstream from the former Constantinople, a monument to the hundreds of stonemasons who constructed it. When it was completed in the astonishing time of four months, the Ottomans were able to strangle sea traffic attempting to reach Constantinople from the Black Sea.

MEHMED EMBRACED A RELATIVELY NEW TECHNOLOGY— ALWAYS A SIGN THAT A LONG WAR IS IN FOR EVEN LONGER DURATION. THIS WAS ARTILLERY.

Part of the reason for this was that Mehmed embraced a relatively new technology— always a sign that a long war is in for even longer duration. This was artillery. When he heard that a clever Hungarian cannoneer named Urban had been turned away when he offered his services to the Christians in Constantinople, he hired Urban, who designed a huge cannon to be placed in the Ottoman forts. Then Mehmed issued a warning to ships, telling them not to dare try to force passage to Constantinople. A Venetian ship challenged the Ottoman gunners and they blew it out of the water. When the surviving crewmen washed ashore, they beheaded them, all except the captain, whom Mehmed impaled.

This new technology, and Mehmed's evident determination, sent a chill down the spines of the Christians in Constantinople as 1453 began. The last Byzantine emperor, Constantine

XI Dragases, was a capable ruler, and he rallied his people as best he could, but the residents of the city were filled with panic when they heard that Mehmed had gathered a huge force and was literally paving new roads on which to march this vast host to Constantinople.

The army numbered about 100,000 men, but its fierce striking center consisted of 12,000 Janissaries. The Janissaries, from the phrase *yeni cheri*, meaning "new troops," were soldiers who had been abducted as boys from the ranks of Christian Serbs, raised as Muslims, and rigorously trained to be utterly devoted to the sultan. They were, at the time, the best soldiers in the world. Even greater surprises were in store when the Christians realized that the Turks, not known as a seafaring people, had actually built a navy under the direction of Mehmed that numbered 125 vessels, five times the fleet belonging to the Christians.

By April 2, 1453, Easter Monday, Mehmed had arrived outside the walls of Constantinople with his great army, while his navy ranged up the Bosporus. Constantine XI wrote to Mehmed: "It is clear that you desire war more than peace . . . so let it be according to your desire." And so the battle was joined.

"GO ON, MY FALCONS!"

In this epic siege, the sultan began by trying to batter down the walls of the city with Urban's huge cannonballs, but they were unable to breach them. Even at sea, the sultan failed, as his navy could not find its way around a huge boom laid across the entrance to the city near the strait of the Golden Horn. Enraged, the sultan flogged his admiral and then fired him, but then had another, brilliant idea: he could transport his ships overland and plunk them into the water behind the boom. He had his indefatigable engineers (always an unsung entity in war) build a new road and then lay down on it a track of greased timbers, upon which the ships were placed and rolled to their new position. Once there, they were dropped down into the water, much to the surprise and consternation of the Christians, who had Ottoman forces in front and behind them.

The siege went on for another seven weeks, with the Christians resisting mightily, although their food supplies dwindled rapidly. The sultan, growing impatient, offered the emperor one of two choices: his city could pay an enormous annual tribute to the Turks to survive as an independent entity, or Mehmed would allow all of the Christians to leave the city without being harmed. Constantine XI refused both options and Mehmed prepared his troops for a final assault on the walls of the city, to take place on May 29.

The next morning, to the cacophonous sounds of shrill whistles, kettledrums, horns, and ringing church bells, the attack began. Wave after wave of Ottoman soldiers threw ladders up to climb the city walls, while Mehmed's artillery sent huge balls smashing against perceived weak points. The Christians fought bravely, but the Ottomans breached Constantinople's defenses in several places after a hard day of fighting. Even so, the defenders resisted the Turks until Mehmed sent in his Janissaries, riding almost to the wall with them and shouting: "Go on, my falcons, march on my lions!" These white-coated soldiers attacked furiously, swarming over the walls, pillaging and killing.

Constantine XI tore off his royal robes, shouting: "The city is taken and I am still alive!" Waving his sword, he then plunged into the battle against the Turks and was never seen again. After allowing his men the traditional day's looting, Mehmed stopped the chaos and rode through the former Christian capital with his bodyguard, exulting. The city was now, and would stay, a Turkish possession. Ordering Edirne abandoned, Mehmed made Constantinople, which would be called Istanbul, his new capital. (The name Istanbul comes from the Greek phrase *eis ten polin*, which means "to the city"— most locals would point and pronounce these words when any Turks asked directions to Constantinople.)

"A FOREST OF CORPSES"

"The fall of Constantinople struck western Christendom with a sense of doom," the historian Lord Kinross wrote. Although most of the Christian countries and principalities of Europe had been too preoccupied with their own concerns to help save the city, the fact that the Ottomans now held the historic capital symbolized the relentless onslaught of Islam encroaching into Europe.

In actuality, Mehmed, though he could be notably ruthless, understood the importance and value of allowing conquered peoples to worship in their own faiths, and thus allowed the Greeks who remained in the city to retain their own Orthodox churches, priests, and patriarchs. And he set about rebuilding and repopulating Constantinople into a glorious city that was not only an Islamic capital but also a tribute to the eastern empire of the ancient Romans, whose heir he considered himself to be.

This is not to deny that his goal was worldwide dominion, a war of empire that would finally lead the Ottomans into Western Europe. In 1454 and 1455, his flanks now anchored by his capture of Constantinople, Mehmed led his forces into the Balkans, occupying much of Serbia as a base for continued expansion north. In 1456, he sent 150,000 men against the Christian country of Hungary, besieging its capital of Belgrade. But Mehmed was overconfident after his victory against Constantinople, and had not reckoned on the fierce resistance of the Hungarians of the city. They drove off even the Janissaries, surrounding and slaughtering them, trapping those who escaped into a moat around Belgrade and burning them to death. This so enraged Mehmed that he joined the fighting himself, but he was wounded with an arrow in the thigh and forced to withdraw.

It was a heartening victory for Christendom, but the Turks were not to be stopped. In 1458, Mehmed turned his attention to Greece and conquered those islands, which would remain a part of the Ottoman Empire until the early nineteenth century. In 1461, Mehmed returned to the Balkans, taking on the famous Vlad Dracul, known to history as Dracula, ruler of Wallachia. Dracul responded to news of the advancing Ottoman army by invading Ottoman territory and massacring 20,000 Ottoman soldiers and civilians, whom he impaled on stakes—thus Mehmed, at the head of his army, encountered the grisly sight of "a forest of corpses" along his line of march. But Vlad was vanquished, too, and Mehmed also attacked and conquered Bosnia. By 1477, he had also taken Albania, no easy task, as most Albanian fortresses were located in inaccessible, rocky places.

But by this time, Mehmed had siege tactics down to an art form. Rather than transporting cannon to such remote places, he cast them on the spot, used them to batter down walls, and then broke them up when he was through. Although the Albanians fought fiercely, Mehmed soon consolidated his forces there and was able to send parties of Ottoman raiders into northern Italy. These Ottoman warriors sacked towns and villages, crying "Mehmed! Mehmed! Roma! Roma!"

"THE GREAT EAGLE IS DEAD!"

Mehmed was now poised to make his assault on the heart of Christianity. He had been fighting the Venetians—the primary naval power in the Mediterr-

This map shows the range of the Ottoman Empire from 1451 to 1481 in gray. The Ottomans' success was due in part to the fall of the Byzantine Empire in the thirteenth century, leaving a vacuum of power only partially filled by local warlords, whom the Ottomans easily conquered.

The Ottoman Empire 1451-1481

B 25 C Long. East 30 of Greenw. D 35 E 40 F

UNGARY
MOLDAVIA
KHANATE OF CRIME
Azov 1471
1478
SEA OF AZOV
Crimea 1475
Crimea Tartars Taman
Bakchiserai Kaffa 1475

WALLACHIA
Severin
Tergovist
Braila
Dobruja
BLACK SEA
Aluta R.
Bukharest 1462
Giurgevo
Danube R.
Silistria
Nicopolis (Nikopol)
1393 Sistova
Sofia (Sredetz) Tirnovo (Trnova)
1382 Bulgaria Varna
Philippopolis (Plovdiv)
Maritza R. Chirmen
Adrianople (Edirne) 1361
Byzantine Empire
Constantinople 1453
Amasra (Amastris) 1461
Sinope
Samsun
EMPIRE OF TREBIZON
Trebizond 1462

OTTOMAN
Seres
Saloniki (Thessalonica) 1430
Thasos 1462
Gallipoli 1354
Bodonto
Scutari
Ismid (Nicomedia)
Isnik (Nicaea)
Kizil Irmak R.
Amasia
Karahissar
Terjan

1456 Lemnos
Brusa 1326
Sakaria (Sangarius R.)
Angora 1360
Sivas
Diarbekr

Lesbos 1462
To Genoa
Chios
Manissa (Magnesia)
Alashehr (Philadelphia)
Akshehir (Philomelium)
Akserai (Archelais)
Kaisarieh (Caesarea)
DOMINION OF THE CIRCASSIAN MAMELUKES

Negropont
Athens
Naupia
DUCHY OF NAXOS
Smyrna 1424
Ephesus
Mendere R. (Maeander)
Milassa (Miletus)
KARAMAN
Konia
1466
Karaman
Tarsus
Adana
Antioch
Euphrates R.

Tonemasia
Knights of S. John
Rhodes
Adalia (Attalia)
Selefke
Candia
Crete
KINGDOM OF CYPRUS
Nicosia
Famagusta
Tripoli

The Ottoman Empire 1451-1481

Empire
the
ond
tenegro

in 1451

Albania under George Castriota (Scanderbeg)
States under Latin rule
Venetian possessions
Genoese possessions
Dominion of the Circassian Mamelukes
Dominions of the Ottoman Turks

1443-1468

in 1451

Dominions of the Ottoman Turks acquired between 1451 and 1481

D.-Duchy; Desp.-Despotat, Rep.-Republic
The dates are those of acquisition by the Turks × Battle

Scale 1:15 000 000   100   0   100   200 Miles

25 C 30 D 35 E

anean and Aegean—for years, and several Turkish naval victories forced them to the negotiating table. In return for allowing them to keep certain bases and to trade unmolested with Ottoman cities, Mehmed's navy received a guarantee that Venice would not hinder any attack on Italy. In 1480, Mehmed made his first amphibious assault against Otranto, at the heel of the Italian boot, catching the town by surprise and massacring its inhabitants. However, as the Ottomans attempted to sweep north, they were repulsed by a force from Naples and compelled to withdraw.

Mehmed had faced worse defeats than this and come sweeping back with even greater success, but now he seemed to lose interest, or to spread his interests too thin. His forces attacked Rhodes, the island fortress of the Knights of St. John, the very last of the Christian crusaders, but were bloodily defeated. In the spring of 1481, Mehmed led his army on a campaign into the Middle East. As usual, he kept his destination secret—he may have decided to attack Egypt—but he never made it. Although only forty-nine years old, he had overindulged in liquor and food for years and suffered from numerous maladies, including arthritis, gout, and colitis. He had an attack of the latter while en route. His doctor attempted to give him a remedy, but it was ineffective—there were rumors that it was actually poison administered, in the true Ottoman tradition, by Mehmed's son Bayezid—and Mehmed the Conqueror died on May 4, 1481.

Europeans rejoiced at Mehmed's death, yet paid grudging respect to the great Ottoman leader—the Venetians received the news of Mehmed's passing from a messenger who cried: "The great eagle is dead!" For the next forty years, under two different sultans, Bayezid II and Selim I—Selim the Grim, as he was known, who to protect his throne murdered not only two brothers but also five orphan nephews—the Turkish war for empire advanced slowly but steadily. The Ottomans possessed land from the Aegean to the Nile to the shores of the Indian Ocean, although they had not been able to again push their way into Italy.

Suleiman I, who would become known as Suleiman the Magnificent, came to the Ottoman throne in 1520, at the age of twenty-six. Suleiman was brilliant, worldly, and quite aware of global politics. At the time, another brilliant young ruler, the Holy Roman Emperor, King Charles V of Spain, wanted to unite Europe under Habsburg rule—Habsburg being the Austrian royal house that controlled the Holy Roman Empire—but King Francis I of France resisted him. Suleiman secretly gave Francis hundreds of thousands of gold francs, seeing that a united Habsburg Europe would be a serious problem for the Turks. In the meantime, he set about conquering as much of the West as he could.

SETTLING OLD SCORES

One of the thorns in the Ottoman side was Belgrade, which had resisted the Ottoman attack under Mehmed in the previous century. With the persistence that characterized the Ottomans during their long war with Christendom, Suleiman crossed into Hungary to attack Belgrade again. He surrounded it and bombarded it with the superior Ottoman artillery and then tunneled mines under the bastion's walls and blew them up, which caused the garrison to surrender promptly. The newly victorious sultan now turned his attention to the island fortress of Rhodes, which also had warded off attack from Mehmed.

Rhodes was still held by the Knights of St. John under the leadership of their charismatic grand master, Villiers de I'Isle-Adam, who commanded 700 knights from France, Germany, England, Provence, and Italy, as well as 500 archers from Crete. At the end of July 1522, the Turks, personally led by Suleiman, landed a force of some 100,000 men, arranging them in a crescent shape around the castle walls. They immediately began bombarding the Christian knights, but Villiers de I'Isle-Adam had prepared for this and began an effective counter-bombardment. Cannon balls crisscrossed the air for a month, causing terrible damage to both sides, but without any break in the stalemate.

In September, Suleiman sent his sappers burrowing tunnels toward the walls of the fortress, but Villiers de I'Isle-Adam was prepared for this, too, and had hired an Italian mine expert who built counter tunnels through which his knights rushed to attacked the Ottoman diggers. When the Ottomans would set off a charge, they often found that its force had been dissipated by spiral vents the Christians had secretly dug.

At the end of September, the Turks unleashed a major attack against the city, but after ferocious fighting, the Christians drove it back, and the two sides settled once again into a stalemate that lasted into winter. The Turks had lost thousands of men, but the Christians were beginning to starve inside their citadel. Finally, at Christmas, the garrison agreed to surrender to generous terms given by Suleiman, which included ships to take survivors off the island. On January 1, 1523, Villiers de I'Isle-Adam led his battered but proud knights off the island, and it became an Ottoman possession, dispensing with the last threat to Suleiman's empire in the Aegean and eastern Mediterranean.

"THE RAIN FALLS IN TORRENTS"

Any long war depends not just on inspired rulers like Suleiman the Magnificent, but also on great war generals—on the Leonidases, the Hannibals, the Charles I's. Suleiman found his leader in his commander-in-chief Ibrahim Pasha, a thirty-one-year-old Greek, formerly a Christian, whom Turkish pirates had captured as a child and sold into slavery. He eventually came into the possession of Suleiman, who was impressed by his intelligence and determination. Ibrahim was so close to the sultan that he slept in the ruler's bedroom, and it was with Ibrahim that the sultan planned his next invasion: the ultimate conquest of Hungary as far as the Austrian border.

In the spring of 1526, Suleiman and Ibrahim set off for Hungary at the head of an army of 100,000 men. Campaigning through the summer, the Ottomans drove the Hungarians back across the strategic Drava River; the Christians finally gathered their army for a stand on the plain of Mohacs, 30 miles (48.3 km) north of the Drava. It was a foolish move. The plain gave room for the superb Hungarian cavalry to maneuver, but also was fertile ground for the far more numerous Ottoman horsemen.

The Hungarians were also impetuous, and opened the battle, on August 30, with a massive charge directly at the Ottoman lines. At first, the attack seemed to succeed as the Ottoman lines collapsed, but Suleiman had deliberately left his first line of offense weak, to lure in the Hungarians. The Hungarians charged up a hill and found the true Ottoman defense, the Janissaries, grouped around Suleiman's standards. As the Christian knights fought fiercely to break through to the sultan, the Ottoman artillery, which had been previously sited in the area, let loose, killing thousands of knights and breaking down their formation, allowing Turkish troops to encircle and slaughter them.

The king of Hungary died that day, as did most of the Maygar nobility and some 20,000 knights and soldiers. A vengeful Suleiman ordered that no prisoners be taken. Speaking of himself in the third person, Suleiman noted in his war diary for August 31: "The Sultan, seated on a golden throne, receives the homage of the viziers and the beys; massacre of 2,000 prisoners; the rain falls in torrents." Later Hungarian historians were to refer to the battlefield as "the tomb of the Hungarian nation."

Having successfully devastated Hungary and ended all resistance to Ottoman rule, Suleiman and Ibrahim then withdrew to Constantinople—now Istanbul—to plan for their ultimate goal: the capture of Vienna and surrender of Austria.

THE BELLS OF VIENNA

Three years later, at the beginning of campaign season in April of 1529, Suleiman the Magnificent and Ibrahim Pasha set off from Istanbul with an army of about 150,000 men, bent on finally destroying the forces of Christendom on their home ground. Driving up through the valley of the Danube, the sultan's armies reached Vienna in late September, having been delayed by torrential rains. The rains had not, however, doused the flames that the citizens of Vienna, behind their high walls, could see in the distance on the horizon—flames from burning towns and villages.

Despite this terrible sign of the sultan's wrath, the Viennese, under the command of Archduke Ferdinand, brother of Charles V, were determined to fight the encroachment of the Turks. They had done wonders to transform the defenses of their old medieval city, destroying all buildings within artillery range and clearing the ground to prevent fires. Around the city they built a new wall 20 feet (6 m) high, along with a deep moat; they also palisaded the banks of the Danube as it poured past the town.

Vienna had evacuated most of its old people, women, and children by the time Suleiman got to the city and opened fire with his cannon. Fortunately for the Viennese, the Turks had not been able to drag their heavy siege weapons through the muck and mire created by the unusually heavy rainfall that summer, and so only had cannons of lesser caliber that was unable to create a breach in the city's walls. Suleiman tried to resort to bluff, sending a message into the city that he would be having breakfast there within three days; after this period had passed, the Viennese released an Ottoman prisoner with a note for the sultan, telling him that his breakfast was growing cold and that he would now have to eat Viennese lead, provided by the guns barking from their walls.

SULEIMAN SENT A MESSAGE INTO THE CITY THAT HE WOULD BE HAVING BREAKFAST THERE WITHIN THREE DAYS; AFTER THIS PERIOD HAD PASSED, THE VIENNESE RELEASED AN OTTOMAN PRISONER WITH A NOTE, TELLING HIM THAT HIS BREAKFAST WAS GETTING COLD·

The Turks were not to be deterred by wordplay, of course. Their musketeers killed any soldier who poked his head over Vienna's battlements, while Ottoman archers shot showers of arrows blindly into the sky, so that they would fall among Vienna's streets and alleys, making it almost impossible for citizens to venture outside, even at night. The Turks tunneled into the walls to blow up mines, while the Viennese exploded countermines. Occasional breaches in the city walls from explosions would cause Turkish charges, which the Austrians would repulse with counterattacks.

At first, Suleiman encouraged his men by giving them gold ducats for Christian heads, but as time went by, bringing the Turks closer to winter, he had to beat his soldiers to the attack with whips and sticks. Finally, on October 14, Suleiman decided to launch one last, all-out assault on the city, sending thousands of troops into a breach in the wall that had been created by a carefully timed mine explosion. After hours of ferocious and bloody fighting, the Turks were driven back. Finally giving up, Suleiman killed all his prisoners (except those he

would sell into slavery) and turned back toward Istanbul, harried by Austrian cavalry. The bells of Vienna pealed in triumph—for, at last, the Turks had been stopped.

"THE GREAT DRUM OF CONQUEST"

Although the Ottoman Empire was far from an end, its long war to conquer Europe had finally reached its high-water mark. The war between Christendom and the Ottomans would certainly go on, but the defeat of Suleiman before Vienna in 1529 was, according to Lord Kinross, "one of the turning points in history. Sultan Suleiman finally failed . . . to penetrate into the heart of Europe."

In part, as Kinross points out, this was because of the bravery and skill of European knights, but it was also because Suleiman's lines of communication and supplies were simply stretched too far—it is almost 800 miles (1288 km) from Istanbul to Vienna. Supply lines figure into any long war for empire—the Persians were far from home base fighting the Greeks, and Hannibal ultimately did not win Italy because he could not keep his army fed. The Ottoman Empire would continue to grow, fight the Christians, and expand its cultural borders, but it had finally found a point beyond which it could not go.

During his last campaign, in 1566, the aging Suleiman the Magnificent had marched into what is now Croatia to attack an upstart prince there. Suleiman was to die, probably of a heart attack, before the successful investment of the prince's fort had begun. Hours before his death, he had turned to an advisor and said: "The great drum of conquest is not yet to be heard."

By this he meant the drum that would sound the attack of his troops, but his utterance can also stand for the beginning of the end of the long war of the Turks. At the mid-eighteenth century, the Ottoman Empire was still vast by any stretch of the imagination, extending from Morocco in the east to the Caspian Sea in the west, from the edges of Austria in the north to Yemen in the south, but its breakup was already beginning. Part of this was military defeats—losses to the Russians, Napoleon and the French, the Egyptians, and Greek rebels seeking independence chipped away at territory—but a good deal of it was internal, as sultan after sultan lived only for pleasure while a huge and corrupt bureaucracy exploited the citizenry.

When the Young Turks swept into power in 1913, they were merely administering the coup de grace to an empire that had, for a long time, been what Tsar Nicholas I of Russia famously called "the sick man of Europe." The days of Osman I, of Mehmed the Conqueror, and of Suleiman the Magnificent had now receded into dream and legend.

Suleiman the Magnificent is shown at the August 1526 Battle of Mohacs, in which his Ottomans slaughtered the Hungarian army. The king of Hungary died that day, as did some 24,000 knights and soldiers. A vengeful Suleiman ordered that no prisoners be taken. Hungarian historians later referred to the battlefield as "the tomb of the Hungarian nation." This sixteenth-century Ottoman School image is held at the Topkapi Palace Museum, Istanbul, Turkey.

Topkapi Palace Museum, Istanbul, Turkey / The Bridgeman Art Library International

"AS GOD IS MY WITNESS"
RELIGIOUS WARS

Religious fervor and zealotry
are at the heart of many long wars.

CHAPTER 5

THE JEWISH-ROMAN WARS

"NOT SO MUCH AS ONE SOUL"

66–135

Sparked by religious intolerance and lengthened
by intractable zealotry, the Jewish-Roman Wars caused
the Diaspora of the Jewish people, which would lead
to the beginning of the state of Israel
in the twentieth century.

The ancient fortress mountain of Masada rises 1,300 feet (396 m) above the Dead Sea, a stark reminder of the effect of religious zealotry on warfare. For it was here, in the year 73, that a group of almost 1,000 Jewish rebels—to be more precise, members of the fanatical wing of rebels known to the Romans as Sicarii, or "knife-wielders"—held off a determined assault by the Roman army and then, when all was lost, committed mass suicide. When the Roman commander General Flavius Silva finally led his army into the Sicarii stronghold, he found the bodies of 960 rebels—men, women, and children. Only two women and five children, hiding in a cistern, were alive to tell the Romans what happened.

Josephus, the Jewish rebel leader turned Roman historian who chronicled the First Jewish-Roman War, wrote of Masada: "These people died with this intention: that they would leave not so much as one soul among them alive to be subject to the Romans." *Not so much as one soul.* This phrase defines the three Jewish rebellions against Roman rule in Judea that occurred between 66 and 135. It is from these religious wars that we get the word *zealotry.* Religious fervor would be a major factor in lengthening wars in the millennia after the birth of Christ and is a major factor in the current conflicts that plague the world today.

PAYING TAXES TO ROME

The Jews first inhabited the city that would become known as Jerusalem and the area known as Judea—a fertile strip of land along the Mediterranean, at the junction of numerous land and sea trading routes—in the tenth century BCE, when the Israeli tribes under King David conquered the area. The Israelis were in turn conquered by the Assyrians and then by the Babylonians, who in 586 BCE took thousands of Jews into captivity in Babylonia. But after Persian king Cyrus freed them, they returned to Jerusalem, rebuilt their Temple, the heart of the Jewish religion, and lived there for hundreds of years. The Syrian Seleucid dynasty seized Jerusalem in 198 BCE, but thirty years later, all of Judea was freed by a successful revolt of the Maccabees, a Jewish liberation movement.

Thereafter, the Jews enjoyed a century of independence until the Romans under their great consul Pompey took advantage of a civil war between various Jewish religious factions to seize Judea and annex it to the Roman province of Syria in 63 BCE. Although the Romans at first allowed the Jews to have their own leaders—the famous Herod the Great was one of these—there were numerous violent clashes between Roman authorities and extremist Jews, known as Zealots, who wanted the Romans to leave Judea. (It was into this world, fraught with violent political and religious tensions, that Jesus Christ was born; some scholars believe that his message was one of Jewish zealotry and that Christ himself may have been a Zealot.)

In 6 CE, the strife in Judea had grown to such an extent that the Romans decided to place the country under more direct control by appointing procurators—civilian magistrates or governors who reported directly to the Roman emperor—which caused a great deal of dissension among the Jewish people. For one thing, taxes (which, at 19 percent of estimated income, were already quite high) now needed to be paid in money, rather than goods, which placed an almost intolerable burden on the people of a mainly agricultural society. And the taxes had to be paid in Roman coinage. Roman coins had pictures of their goddess Roma or their divine emperor, which broke the Jewish religious strictures against graven images and paying tribute to other gods. To make matters worse, the procurators who collected these impossible sums (Pontius Pilate was one) were in the main corrupt men who despised Jews.

The Jewish leadership became divided as the population became polarized. The high-ranking, conservative religious leaders known as the Sadducees wanted people to pay their taxes, cooperate with the Romans, and avoid bloodshed, while the more radical Jews of the sect known as the Zealots preached rebellion. Matters came to a head in the spring of 66 CE when a procurator named Gessius Florus enraged Jews by seizing money from the treasury of the Holy Temple in Jerusalem to make up for a shortfall in Judean tax payments. Rioting tore the city apart, and Florus sent in Roman legionaries along with Greek auxiliary troops to put it down. They did, but bloodily, killing 3,000 citizens of Jerusalem.

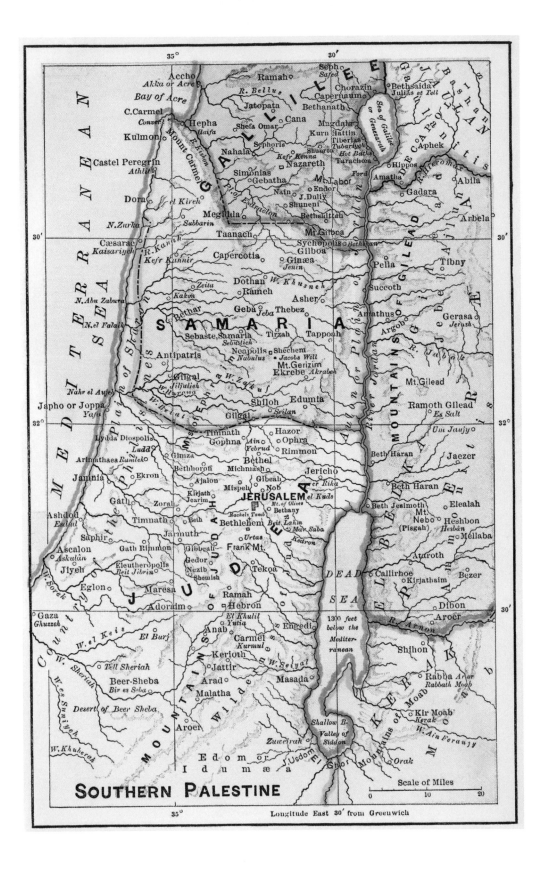

SOUTHERN PALESTINE

Scale of Miles

0   10   20

Longitude East 30' from Greenwich

ZEALOT RAGE

The stage was now set for the first of the Jewish uprisings in what would become the long and bloody conflict called the Jewish-Roman Wars. The Sadducees managed to convince Florus to remove all but one cohort of Greek troops from the city, which they thought might help cool tempers, but it was too late. The Sicarii, the most extreme of the Zealots, functioning much like a modern-day terrorist group, sent out assassins to stab to death prominent Sadducees on the streets. Even moderate Jews were targets, causing fear and panic to spread among the populace.

Then the Zealot leader Eleazar ben Hananiah, the captain of the Temple guard and the son of a former high priest, convinced those who followed him that they should not make any more of the animal sacrifices that they were required by Roman law to make to Emperor Nero. Finally, Eleazar's forces turned to open warfare, massacring the Greek troops left in the city after most of them had surrendered.

This type of killing was a sign of the terrible hatred that is a hallmark of never-ending warfare. The Jews had been impoverished by decades of severe taxation, had their citizenry murdered, and had their religion scorned. It was in particular the profanation of the Temple by the seizing of proceeds its citizens had meant for the upkeep of their religion that enraged most Jews. The situation worsened almost immediately, from a Roman point of view, because the Roman governor of the region, Cestius Gallus, who was stationed in Antioch, Syria, was inept at best. He led an army to assault the Zealots in Jerusalem, but just as it seemed the Romans would defeat the Jews, he withdrew them.

On their way back to Syria, in November 66, the Romans were ambushed by Hananiah's Zealot troops at the pass at Beth-Horon, a strategic point on a road leading out of Jerusalem where, a hundred years before, the Maccabees had defeated a Seleucid force. An awareness of history is an important thing in a small people fighting an empire. The Zealot troops rained arrows, spears, and rocks down upon the Roman soldiers. As the Romans ducked for cover, they were attacked from the front by a large Zealot force. Unable to maneuver or form up into ranks in the crowded and narrow pass, 6,000 Roman soldiers were killed or wounded.

Up until that point, it was the worst defeat suffered by troops of a rebellious province in Roman history, and an important one in terms of morale for the Zealots. More and more Jews began to flock to their banners, and the Zealots spread out from Jerusalem, taking small Roman outposts all over Judea and Galilee. They also set out to seize major ports along the Mediterranean, hoping to make it more difficult for the Romans to land troops.

A map of ancient Palestine shows Judea. Roman governors ruled the province, burdening Jewish inhabitants with heavy taxes, scorning their religion, and murdering citizens, all of which fueled the bloody uprisings to come. Note the fortress mountain of Masada on the Dead Sea, where nearly 1,000 Jews committed mass suicide rather than be ruled by the Romans.

© North Wind Picture Archives / Almay

"THE MULE DRIVER"

In Rome, Emperor Nero was infuriated when he heard that this small province would dare to rise against the might of the Roman Empire. Like most Romans, he had little or no understanding of the power of religion in the lives of the Jewish people. The Jewish religion was interwoven with every aspect of the Jewish culture, from birth to death. When the Romans trampled upon this, they trampled upon a centuries-old way of life.

Fortunately for the Romans, Nero made an unusually good choice for the job of destroying the Jews: the general Titus Flavius Vespasianus. Fifty-eight years old in 67, Vespasianus, known in English as Vespasian, had successfully commanded a legion during the invasion of Britain and been awarded with greater and greater honors, which included being made governor of Africa in 63. However, thereafter his personal fortunes took a downturn as he fell into debt and was then dismissed from the royal court for falling asleep during one of Nero's endless musical recitals. Nero appointed him because of his reputation as a tough, patient, and stubborn fighter—Vespasian's nickname among his men was "the Mule Driver"—and that is exactly what the Romans got.

A war fought against guerillas who are inspired by both religion and patriotism is one of the most difficult ones for an imperial country to wage, which is why Vespasian was the right commander at the right time. Landing 45,000 Roman legionaries in Judaea, he began attacking Jewish fortresses one by one, patiently surrounding them, searching for a weak point, finding it, and then exploiting it. Little quarter was given in these battles by either side, with the Zealots either committing suicide at the end or being put to the sword by Vespasian's men.

In the spring of 68, slowly approaching the outskirts of Jerusalem, Vespasian learned that Emperor Nero had committed suicide after the Roman Senate declared him a public enemy. In the chaotic year that followed—one that saw civil war in Italy and four different emperors upon the Roman throne—Vespasian delayed assaulting Jerusalem while he awaited orders from Rome. When, in 69, he himself was named emperor—his age, honesty, and stability being what the Romans sought—he left control of siege operations against Jerusalem in the hand of his son Titus and headed home.

THE FALL OF JERUSALEM

The siege that Titus—a future emperor of Rome himself—conducted against Jerusalem was a classic one. It was the spring of 70 and the city had been surrounded for more than a year. Although much of this delay was caused by the fact that Vespasian had been awaiting clarity over the situation in Rome, it had worked out strategically for the Roman army. During the lengthy period, the Jewish rebels within the city had begun fighting among themselves.

One faction consisted of Zealots who had been responsible for many of the Jewish victories in the countryside over the past year. Another was a strange group led by John of Gischala, a Galilean who had his men dress, according to the historian Josephus, like women, even "plaiting their hair," wearing eye shadow, and dousing themselves with perfume. This had the effect of momentarily confusing their enemies long enough for them to plunge a dagger into their chests. The third faction was a stark desert group led by Simon ben Giora, who sought a social revolution that was close in nature to the type that Karl Marx would later write about.

This was a bloody internecine conflict that took place in the streets and alleyways of Jerusalem, its chief weapon being assassination. It weakened the Jewish forces, but in the long run, nothing could have stopped the Roman juggernaut. In May of 70, with a shower of arrows and the thudding of huge battering rams, Titus sent his forces crashing against the city's walls. It was no easy task. Jerusalem had three walls—the first 20 feet (6 m) high and the two inner ones 30 feet (9 m) high and 15 feet (4.6 m) thick.

But the Roman army was expert at siege tactics. For them, siege was not a long investment, hoping to starve the enemy out or wear him down—that tactic, which we recognize today, began in the Middle Ages. Instead, the Roman siege was an aggressive, offensive action, a *repentina oppugnatio* ("violent assault"). In this case, the Roman frontline troops brought up movable wooden towers 75 feet (23 m) high, from which they showered down spears, stones, and arrows on the city's defenders. In the meantime, Roman battering rams shook Jerusalem's outer wall, day after day.

After fifteen days of fierce attack, the Romans broke through the first wall of defense and the Zealots retreated to their second wall. Four days after that, the Romans broke through that and the Jews were at last forced behind their final line of defense. As those on the ramparts fought bravely, parties of Zealots and Jewish civilians, seeing that destruction was near, began to escape through Jerusalem's extensive series of sewers. To stop this, Titus ordered a huge wall to be built around the city, a structure 4½ miles (7.2 km) around, replete with thirteen forts, which was completed in just three days' time, according to the writer Josephus, at the cost of denuding the once heavily forested hills surrounding the city.

Showing that he was fighting a war without mercy, Titus had those Jews who surrendered to Roman forces crucified in full view of the city's defenders. By early July, legionaries at last breached the last defenses of Jerusalem and drove its defenders into

three hilltop fortresses, including the Temple. Knocking the Temple doors down with battering rams, the Romans set fire to it, driving the last remaining Zealots out and slaughtering them.

The bloody fighting didn't end even then, for Titus hunted the Jews through Jerusalem's sewers and subterranean water tunnels until these doomed brick caverns ran red with blood. Titus kept 2,000 men, women, and children with which to celebrate his brother Domitian's birthday—by sending them into gladiatorial rings to be torn apart by wild animals.

As a parting gesture, Titus ordered the entire city of Jerusalem destroyed, leaving only a portion of the wall on the western side—which is today's Wailing Wall—standing to protect his garrison of legionaries.

"THE COURAGE OF THE JEWS"

Writing at the end of his history of the Jewish-Roman Wars, Josephus describes the Romans surveying the dead Zealots at Masada and goes on to say: "Nor could they do other than wonder at the courage of the Jews' resolution and the immoveable contempt for death which so great a number of them had shown when they went through with such an action as [the mass suicide]."

The first Jewish-Roman War officially closed in 73, when Masada fell, but in actuality the war never really ended at all. The "courage of the Jews" impressed the Romans so much that they made it their practice in the years post-Masada to hunt down entire lineages of Jews and attempt to exterminate them, understanding that their enemy never gave up. This, along with the general devastation of the war (perhaps one million Jews died in seven years; Roman losses are unknown, but certainly in the thousands), led thousands of other Jews to emigrate from the country to different parts of the Roman Empire.

One ingredient of long warfare is long memory, and the Jews in the years after the First Jewish-Roman War never forgot the horrors perpetrated on them, their country, and their religion. The Romans owned the known world at that time, so there were few places the Jews could go that would be outside the reach of those who had despoiled Jerusalem and its Temple. Still, many Jews joined existing Jewish communities in Egypt, Cyprus, and Cyrenaica, which is the northeastern part of modern-day Libya, making lives for themselves as tradesmen, farmers, and herders.

Around 115, the Roman emperor Trajan, an able administrator who sought to consolidate the borders of the Roman Empire, launched a war against Parthia (which encompassed modern-day Iran and Iraq and parts of modern-day Afghanistan) and Armenia. As he was busy waging what would turn out to be successful actions in these

PREVIOUS PAGE: Violence broke out following the Roman destruction of the Temple of Jerusalem, shown here in this nineteenth-century oil painting by Francesco Hayez. Jews considered the Roman taking of Temple monies sacrilegious, more evidence of Roman intolerance of their religious beliefs.

Kunsthistorisches Museum, Vienna, Austria / The Bridgeman Art Library areas, a major Jewish revolt began in Cyrene, the largest town in Cyrenaica. It was led by a man named Lukuas (sometimes called Andreas), who may have been a messianic figure, since the first thing that Lukuas ordered his followers to do was destroy the pagan temples of Apollo, Artemis, Hecate, Demeter, Isis, and Pluto, all Greek gods, and to attack those who worshipped them. "Seized by a terrible spirit of rebellion," as the Greek historian Eusebius wrote, they burned these temples to the ground.

Thousands of Greek citizens (all Roman subjects) were killed by the Jews, and many more fled to Alexandria, Egypt, where there was a population of perhaps 150,000 Jews, making it the largest Jewish center outside of Judea. Even though the Jews in Alexandria had nothing to do with Lukuas and his followers, they were persecuted, and many of them massacred, by the enraged Greeks who had lost property and family members in Cyrene. The following year, in 116, the Jews of Egypt had their revenge, destroying Roman and Greek temples in Alexandria and, with especial symbolism, despoiling the tomb of Pompey, who had captured Jerusalem two centuries before.

"THEY WOULD COOK THEIR FLESH"

The origins of and much of what occurred during the Kitos War, as the Second Jewish-Roman War came to be known, remains shrouded; it did not have an historian like Josephus to record the story. But it is obvious that the Jews, feeling themselves to be an oppressed minority, rose up with a vengeance. Interestingly, the Kitos War began not in Judea, but in the provinces where diasporic Jews had gone subsequent to being ousted from Jerusalem.

The Kitos War—*Kitos* is a corruption of the name Lusius Quietus, the Roman commander who eventually put down the revolt—was an especially bloody one. The Roman historian Dio Cassius wrote of the first rebels under Lukuas, or Andreas:

> Meanwhile the Jews in the region of Cyrene had put one Andreas at their head and were destroying both Romans and Greeks. They would cook their flesh, make belts for themselves of the entrails, anoint themselves with their blood, and wear their skins as clothing. Many they sawed in two, from the head downwards. Others they would give to wild beasts and force still others to fight as gladiators. In all consequently, 220,000 perished. . . .

Dio Cassius, writing within fifty years after these events, may have been prejudiced against the Jews, but other sources say that Libya was practically depopulated after the Kitos War, lending some credence to Dio Cassius's casualty figures (he also stated that 240,000 died in Cyprus, where the revolt would spread). The atrocities that Dio Cassius attributes to the Jews were the same ones that the Romans had perpetrated against the Zealots they had defeated in the First Jewish-Roman War. Obviously, the war against the Romans had never really ended. Kept alive by simmering hatred, it burst into flame again.

In 116, Lukuas led his army into Alexandria to join the rebellious Jews there, and put the city to the torch after the Roman governor and his troops fled for their lives. In the ensuring months, the Jews terrified Egypt, despoiling the countryside and attacking the city of Thebes. The Jewish revolt now broke out in Cyprus, under another charismatic leader named Artemion, and spread to regions the Romans had newly conquered in Parthia.

Emperor Trajan had to do something. In 117, he sent two Roman legions to the area under the command of Lusius Quietus (Quietus, originally a Berber from Morocco, was one of the few blacks to succeed in the Roman military world of that era). Quietus's men made fairly easy work of Lukuas and Artemion's armies—which, according to some sources, were less armies than armed mobs—but then went further. Because Trajan was afraid that the Jews would rise up again and that their revolt would spread farther into the empire, he ordered Quietus to wipe out as many Jews in Egypt, Parthia, Cyrenaica, and Cyprus as he could. The killing was so effective in Cyprus that not one Jew remained and Jews were then forbidden to set foot on the island.

In major cities like Alexandria and Cyrene, Lusius confiscated Jewish property to pay for the reconstruction of the destroyed temples and also attempted to force Jewish children to be raised as secular Greeks. Once again, as with the First Jewish-Roman War, all this persecution merely made the Jews more resentful and prolonged the war. And their religion began to take an even deeper messianic turn. As the war ended in 117, some Jews were predicting that the end of the world was imminent.

THE NEW REVOLT

Judea after the First Jewish-Roman War had never been a quiet place. There were almost continuous instances of Jewish hostility to Romans—the mood of the country remained so rebellious that many Roman legionaries, having finished their twenty-year stint, were not discharged. There had been insurrections in Judea during the Kitos War—in fact, Lusius Quietus had been sent to put them down and had then stayed on as procurator, as reward for his services.

The second rising against the Romans was led by a man many Jews considered the Messiah, or Son of David—Simon bar Kosiba, or Bar Kokhba, depicted in this 1927 miniature by Arthur Szyk. The uprising was temporarily successful, enough to prolong the war, but ultimately ending with Roman victory and the death of Bar Kokhba.

Emperor Trajan died at the end of 117, to be replaced by Hadrian, who mistrusted Quietus's popularity among the Romans and had him executed. Shortly after this, Hadrian told the Jews of Jerusalem that he would rebuild the city (which had not yet recovered from being razed by Titus) and allow them to rebuild their own Temple as a Jewish Temple. However, in 130, Hadrian visited Judea and announced that he had changed his mind. His plan now was to have the entire city rebuilt into a Roman city with a huge temple celebrating the Roman god Jupiter. Historians can only speculate as to why he changed his mind—possibly because the Jews had reacted so emotionally to his first offer to allow them to keep their Temple that he feared they might use it as a rallying point against him. In any event, according to the historian Haim Hillel Ben-Sasson, in his *A History of the Jewish People*, Hadrian now decided "to convert Jerusalem into a pagan city, without regard for its past or its place in Jewish thought and aspirations."

And he did one more thing. Hadrian hated any religion or religious practice that he considered exotic and unusual, and one of these practices was circumcision, which he equated with castration. He therefore banned circumcision under penalty of death. This ban was not aimed just at the Jews, but because circumcision was a primary religious rite of the Jews, it struck them where they lived. (There is another, more moderate historic interpretation of Hadrian's ban, which reads it as a ban only on circumcision of boys who have not yet reached the age of consent.) And so they began again to secretly prepare for war against the Romans. Dio Cassius says that Jewish armorers would damage swords and spears given to them to repair, so that the Romans would reject them—and then the Jews would turn them back into functioning weapons in hidden armories.

The Jews bided their time and finally chose to revolt in the beginning of 132, possibly because the ongoing Roman construction work in Jerusalem had caused the tomb of Solomon to collapse, a sacrilege within a sacrilege. All over Judea, armed Jewish guerillas now rose up, attacking Romans in small outposts.

SIMON, PRINCE OF ISRAEL

Little is known about the beginnings of the revolt, but from fragments of letters and documents found in caves in the Judean desert by modern archeologists, we now know that the charismatic leader of the Jews was a man known as Simon bar Kosiba, or Simon, Prince of Israel, which indicates that he was a messianic figure. He was also known as Bar Kokhba, or "Son of the Star," which is how this Third Jewish-Roman War became known as the Bar Kokhba War.

Simon bar Kosiba was a real figure whose presence can be tracked by the letters he wrote, containing orders and land grants he made as his forces took over more and more of Judea and Galilee from the Romans. They track from the very first days of the rebellion, in April of 132, to the last days, in November of 135, indicating that bar Kosiba was in charge from the very beginning.

Many of his followers thought he was the messiah, the Son of David—there were rumors that he could shoot flames out of his hands to smite his enemies—while others did not. These included Jewish Christians who also joined in the fighting against the Romans and whom bar Kosiba supposedly ousted from his ranks if they refused to renounce Jesus.

The Bar Kokhba Revolt was the largest and bloodiest of the Jewish-Roman Wars, at once a continuation and a culmination of the first two conflicts, in which religion, nationalism, and extreme rage—Dio Cassius speaks of Roman troops being afraid to approach the Jewish rebels because of their "desperate anger"—all came to a head. Everything that had caused the conflict to go on as long as it did now lay at the heart of the terrible fighting between Jews and Romans.

THE BAR KOKHBA REVOLT WAS THE LARGEST AND BLOODIEST OF THE JEWISH-ROMAN WARS, AT ONCE A CONTINUATION AND A CULMINATION OF THE FIRST TWO CONFLICTS, IN WHICH RELIGION, NATIONALISM, AND EXTREME RAGE ALL CAME TO A HEAD.

At first, the Jews were successful, possibly beyond even their own dreams. Fighting against the Roman Tenth and Sixth Legions, the rebels were able to seize control of all of Judea, and much of the rest of the countryside. They may possibly have taken Jerusalem, although this is uncertain. For two and a half years, Simon bar Kosiba and his men ruled over a sovereign nation. They issued coins that showed the Ark of the Covenant and the Star of David and carried phrases such as "the freedom of Israel" and "the redemption of Israel." They gave land that had been taken by the Romans back to Jewish farmers.

Roman governor Tinius Rufus tried harsh measures. According to the Greek historian Eusebius, "He moved out against the Jews, treating their madness without mercy. He destroyed in heaps thousands of men, women, and children, and under the law of war enslaved their lands." Even so, Simon bar Kosiba and his men were able to control most of the country.

"WHO COULD HAVE OVERCOME HIM?"

The Romans then sent in Publius Marcellus, the governor of Syria, who brought with him Syrian legions as well as legions from Egypt and Arabia. The Jewish rebels beat these back, severely damaging the Roman Twelfth Legion (although not completely destroying it, as some sources have it). After that, in 133, the Jewish forces appear to have fought their way to the sea and may even have participated in a naval battle against the Romans, although this is uncertain.

Finally, in late 133 or early 134, Hadrian sent in Julius Severus, the governor of Britain, with his own legions and legions brought from the Danube. The Roman forces, with a dozen legions fighting, now far outnumbered those of Titus some sixty years before. They were able to push the rebels out of Galilee and fierce fighting now ensued in Judea. The Jewish rebels probably used guerilla hit-and-run tactics against the larger enemy force. According to Dio Cassius:

> The rebels did not dare try to risk open confrontation against the Romans, but occupied the advantageous positions in the country and strengthened them with mines and walls, so that they would have places of refuge when hard pressed and could communicate with one another unobserved underground; and they pierced these subterranean passages from above at intervals to let in air and light.

Slowly, the Jews were pushed back through Judea in a series of bloody actions. The Romans themselves moved cautiously, as Dio Cassius once again wrote:

> Severus did not venture to attack his opponents in the open at any one point, in view of their numbers and their fanaticism, but—by intercepting small groups, thanks to the number of his soldiers and under-officers, and by depriving them of food and shutting them up—he was able, rather slowly, to be sure, but with comparative little danger, to crush, exhaust and exterminate them. Very few Jews in fact survived. Fifty of their most important outposts and nine hundred and eighty-five better known villages were razed to the ground.

At last the Jews, Simon bar Kosiba among them, were pushed back to their fortress village of Betar, near a range of hills about three hours southwest of Jerusalem. There Kosiba and his command made their last stand in the spring and summer of 135. The Jews never surrendered, fighting until the last man. According to tradition, the Romans found the body of Simon bar Kosiba, cut off his head, and brought it to Emperor Hadrian, who reportedly said: "If his God had not slain him, who could have overcome him?"

"THE NOSTRILS OF THEIR HORSES"

In terms of barbarity, the war was the worst one of the three conflicts fought between the Jews and the Romans. The Romans supposedly wrapped children in the Torah and set them afire. According to Dio Cassius, 580,000 Jews died. However, Dio went on, so many Romans also perished that the emperor, in his letter to the Senate, "refrained from using the customary introductory phrase: 'I trust you and your children are well; I and my troops are well.'"

The Romans got their revenge. They rooted out Jewish fighters in caves across the Judean desert (although there is archeological evidence that Jews remained in these caves for years). They refused to allow the Jews of Betar to bury the dead of the revolutionary fighters for seventeen years, leaving their bones strewn over the countryside. As retaliation, according to the Talmud, the Romans massacred so many Jews, rebels or not, that blood rose to the level of "the nostrils of their horses." So many Jews were sold as slaves in marketplaces in Hebron and Gaza that they were worth less than a horse's ration of grain.

Emperor Hadrian now refused to allow Jews to set foot in Jerusalem—a detachment of the Tenth Legion was stationed near Jerusalem until the fourth century, expressly to oust any Jews attempting to enter the city (those caught were imprisoned and sometimes tortured to death). In fact, Hadrian renamed Jerusalem Aelia Capitolina, dedicating it to Jupiter. Hadrian placed his equestrian statue in the Holy Temple.

The long wars of the Jews against the Romans were now truly over. There would not be another Jewish army until the twentieth century and Judea would stop being the center of Jewish religion and thought. Once again, as with the Carthaginians in the Punic Wars, a country that fought a long, destructive war against the Romans was destroyed. Well, the country was destroyed, but not the people. The Jewish religion and culture continued and thrived throughout all the centuries of the Diaspora, until the Jews finally returned to Israel in the mid-twentieth century—occasioning yet another long and bloody war (see chapter 7).

CHAPTER 6

THE TROUBLES IN NORTHERN IRELAND

BY BALLOT AND BULLET

1966–1998

Although Ireland had been a flash point of rebellion against the British, the so-called Troubles in Northern Ireland, beginning roughly in 1966, was a bloody war of terror that saw the Irish Republican Army fighting against both the British and the Protestant paramilitary forces.

Compared to larger-scale wars, the 3,600 lives lost during the thirty years of the Troubles in Northern Ireland seem, at first glance, to make the war a relatively benign affair. That is, until you read about the way many of those were killed.

Some, innocent civilians, were assassinated in their homes simply because they were related to combatants. Others, members of the Protestant Ulster Defense Association (UDA) or the Catholic Provisional Irish Republican Army (PIRA), were tortured when taken prisoner by their enemies. One man, a Catholic, was hanged from the roof of a garage by ropes and slowly stabbed 147 times. Another was dropped repeatedly on his head on a concrete floor. Both sides favored executing enemies by "hooding" them and then shooting them in the back of the head.

When a nonlethal lesson was delivered, "kneecapping"—shooting a bound victim behind both knees with a handgun—was preferred. From 1973 to 1979, during some of the worst violence in Northern Ireland, the police counted 756 victims of this practice—531 Catholic and 225 Protestant. One in five of those shot in this fashion were crippled for life, but even so, most preferred it to the other favored method of punishment, which was tarring and feathering. The tar used was actually thick diesel oil, which, if inhaled for too long, could permanently damage one's lungs. Quite often a person was badly beaten before being tarred, and when hospital workers attempted to remove the tar from fractured bones, agony ensued.

The Troubles were, at their essence, religious wars, although layers of other grievances added to the problem, such as economic inequality. Wars of faith are some of the most violent in world history. They are also some of the longest, for cycles of violence—an eye for an eye, a tooth for a tooth—repeat themselves endlessly.

"THE ENGLISH GAVE US THE FAMINE"

Northern Ireland, as one historian has written, "was born in violence." The roots of the conflict go back a millennium. The English King Henry II invaded the country in 1169. The Irish did not take kindly to the foreign occupiers, and the English were continuously putting down rebellions. Henry VIII made a final attempt to completely conquer the country during the sixteenth century, and after years of brutal warfare under the reign of his successors Elizabeth I and James I, the country was brought under English control.

The roots of the Troubles began during the early seventeenth century, when the English government gave Protestant settlers large land grants in many areas of Ireland, particularly the northern part of the country, and then passed a series of harsh laws that discriminated against Catholics, confiscating land that belonged to the Irish and disenfranchising those who remained Catholics.

Irish rebels, mainly Catholic, fought the English in the great rebellion of 1641 and in the Jacobite War of 1689–92. During another rebellion in 1798, the firebrand lawyer Wolf Tone made league with the French and very nearly overthrew the English in Ireland, until an unlucky storm in the English Channel destroyed a French army on its way to invade Ireland. Without the help of the French, an estimated 40,000 Irish died, many of them tortured to death by the English, although—in a tradition that would continue—the Irish rebels were no slouches in committing atrocities against the English or any of their own countrymen they perceived as traitors. In one notorious incident in 1798, 100 to 200 loyalist prisoners were set upon by rebels, herded into a barn, and burned to death.

Irish unrest against English occupation continued in the nineteenth century, as they fought against the penal laws, which barred Roman Catholics from election to the House of Commons and forbade the Irish from passing land on to a single heir, forcing them to split up farms among many people, thus shrinking the size of their plots, often down to fewer than the three acres needed to sustain a family. These laws went into effect while absentee English landlords controlled huge plots of land.

During the Potato Famine of 1845–1849, such practices contributed to the death of one million Irish and the emigration (to the United States, Canada, and Australia) of one and a half million more. An Irish saying of the time went: "God gave us the potato blight, but the English gave us the famine," meaning that with their tiny parcels of land, Irish peasants had even less chance of surviving the depredations of the killer fungus that blackened potatoes in the ground.

THE CREATION OF NORTHERN IRELAND

In the twentieth century, Irish dreams coalesced around the idea of home rule or home government, in which the Irish would be able to tend to their own affairs, even if Ireland remained a member state of the British Commonwealth. Supporters put forth numerous home rule measures in the British Parliament, but the Protestant Irish who predominated in the northeastern part of the country ferociously opposed them. They called home rule "Rome Rule," meaning that they would be under the control of the Catholic majority in the country.

During the armed Easter Uprising of 1916, Irish poets and intellectuals tried to force the British government to implement home rule. The British quickly put down the rebellion but made the mistake of executing sixteen of the rebels, which brought the sympathy of the Irish firmly on the side of the Rising, as it was known. In an attempt to pacify the country, the British government in 1920 passed the Government of Ireland Act, which divided Ireland into two separate political entities, each with certain powers of self-government.

The Protestants of Northern Ireland—Ulster Protestants as they were known, because Northern Ireland is in the province of Ulster—praised the act, but Catholics in the rest of the country rejected it because it partitioned Ireland and because two of the counties that would be included in Northern Ireland (Fermanagh and Tyrone) actually had Catholic majorities. A bloody civil war broke out, in which the newly formed Irish Republican Army (IRA) battled British and Protestant forces. Finally, in 1921, a treaty was signed creating the Irish Free State, consisting of twenty-three southern counties and three counties in Ulster. The other six counties of Ulster became Northern Ireland, which remained part of the United Kingdom. In 1949, the Irish Free State became an independent republic. But the troubles of Northern Ireland were only beginning.

"ONE MAN, ONE VOTE"

Armed hostilities between Catholics and Protestants subsided after 1921, for the most part, but simmering hostilities remained in Northern Ireland for the next forty years.

In 1920, the British government passed the Government of Ireland Act, which divided Ireland into two separate political entities, the Catholics being a minority in the newly created Northern Ireland. A bloody civil war ensued. Here, British troops arrest two Sinn Féin members following a raid on the Ministry of Labor offices in Dublin in 1920.

The six counties of Northern Ireland had a two-thirds Protestant, or Unionist, majority, which was exacerbated by the gerrymandering of local election districts to favor Protestants, even in predominantly Catholic, or Nationalist, areas.

Another problem for Catholics seeking self-determination in the North was that people who owned properties or businesses in different districts could vote both individually and as businesses, garnering up to six votes. Most business and property owners were Protestants, so this practice, which had long been abolished in England, severely limited Catholic electoral participation. Catholics lobbied for "one man, one vote," but they were unsuccessful.

Inequity plagued Catholics in other forms. They were discriminated against when it came to public housing and jobs—according to one study, Catholic men were two and a half times more likely to be unemployed than Protestants. Poor Catholics in cities such as Londonderry (known as Derry) and Belfast lived in what the historian Tim Pat Coogan has called "appalling slum conditions." Day-to-day living conditions were abysmal. Because most available public housing went to Protestants, many Catholics lived in converted army barracks.

But the 1960s brought changes. The conservative prime minister of Northern Ireland, Viscount Brookeborough, stepped down in 1963 after twenty years and a former Anglo-Irish army officer named Terence O'Neill took his place. O'Neill sought to alleviate the

Magilligan Strand

Giants Causeway

DONEGAL

Derry City

DERRY

Donegal

U L S T E R

ANTRIM

TYRONE

Northern Ireland

Belfast

Sligo

FERMANAGH

ARMAGH

DOWN

SLIGO

MONAGHAN

Mountains
of Mourne

Westport

LEITRIM

CAVAN

Cooley
Hills

MAYO

ROSCOMMON

LOUTH

C O N N A C H T

LONGFORD

Kells

Newgrange

Galway

WESTMEATH

MEATH

GALWAY

Hill of Tara

OFFALY

DUBLIN

KILDARE

Dublin

The Burren

L E I N S T E R

Glendalough

CLARE

LAOIS

WICKLOW

Limerick

CARLOW

LIMERICK

TIPPERARY

KILKENNY

M U N S T E R

WEXFORD

KERRY

CORK

WATERFORD

Blarney

Cork

plight of the Catholics to some extent. He went so far as to meet with the prime minister of the Republic of Ireland—the first time in forty years the two officials had met—and also reached out to the Nationalist groups in cities such as Belfast and Derry.

However, Unionist extremists, whose views found a mouthpiece in the Reverend Ian Paisley, a fundamental evangelical preacher who had entered politics, considered even such relatively tame gestures to be anathema. Paisley organized numerous protest marches, at one point in 1963 even staging a demonstration when the flag in front of the Belfast city hall was lowered to half-mast after the death of Pope John XXIII (whom Paisley called "the Roman anti-Christ").

In 1966, the first sectarian violence broke out. April of that year was the fiftieth anniversary of both the Battle of the Somme and the 1916 Easter Uprising. The Battle of the Somme, in which more than 50,000 British and Protestant Irish soldiers became casualties, was a flash point for Protestant violence because many Irish Catholics, opposed to the British government, had not served in World War I.

A group calling itself the Ulster Volunteer Force (UVF), originating in the mainly Protestant area around Shankill Road in a working-class section of Belfast, began targeting and attacking Catholics. The first three victims of the war were not in any way connected with the IRA. One was a seventy-seven-year-old Protestant widow who was burned to death when the UVF attacker threw a gasoline bomb at a Catholic pub. The second casualty was a Catholic man who had apparently shouted "up the rebels" while staggering home from a night's drinking. The UVF shot him to death. The third victim was a teenage Catholic bartender who walked out of his pub one night and was shot down. Catholics almost immediately began rioting and Terence O'Neill responded by banning the UVF, but the Troubles had already begun.

"THE ONE THING I CANNOT FORESEE"

Great causes can lead to long wars, as can the emulation of folk heroes, and the embattled Catholic minority in Northern Ireland had both cause and folk heroes aplenty. Irish Catholic agitation against Protestant rule went back hundreds of years, and the young Irish fighters rising now from the streets of Belfast and Derry had legendary heroes in Wolf Tone, Patrick Pearse, and Michael Collins, as well as generations of songs and poems about fighting the oppressors—be they British or Protestant Irish.

Because it was the 1960s, another factor came into account: civil rights. The Northern Ireland Civil Rights Association (NICRA) was founded in 1967. Although it did not call for an end to the partition of Ireland, NICRA did present the government

The map shows the border between Northern Ireland and the Republic of Ireland. When the British government divided Ireland in 1920, Protestants of Northern Ireland praised the act, but Catholics in the rest of the country rejected it because it partitioned Ireland and because two of the counties that would be included in Northern Ireland (Fermanagh and Tyrone) actually had Catholic majorities.

of Northern Ireland with a list of seven demands, which included "one man, one vote"; an end to discrimination in public housing allocation and civil service jobs; and the redrawing of electoral districts to fairly represent their voter population. Such NICRA members as John Hume and Bernadette Devlin, influenced by Martin Luther King Jr. and the American civil rights movement, led huge Catholic civil rights marches.

Boisterous armies of Unionist marchers organized by Ian Paisley often opposed these marches. The most pivotal march of the period occurred on October 5, 1968, in Londonderry. The Unionist government at first banned the march, which only served to inflame marchers and swell the size of the crowd. Then the Royal Ulster Constabulary (RUC) reacted violently by hosing the peaceful marchers (who were singing "We Shall Overcome") with water cannons and then wading in to beat them with clubs—with the entire scene captured for Ireland, and the world, by news cameras.

Even though Terence O'Neill attempted to make concessions to the Catholic protestors, they were too little and too late, and he knew it. Writing in a private letter to a friend at Christmas in 1968, he said: "What a year! I feel 1969 will be worse. The one thing I cannot foresee in 1969 is peace. . . ."

He was right. Another Catholic march in early January 1969 in a rural area of County Londonderry saw protestors attacked by Unionist thugs swinging clubs. The RUC simply stood by.

THE BATTLE OF BOGSIDE

Terence O'Neill resigned in April 1969, at the beginning of what is traditionally known in Northern Ireland as "marching season." The Irish hold huge parades or marches in the spring and summer to commemorate events of the past, which may at first sound innocuous, but is not. Most of the parades are organized by Protestant fraternal orders closed to Catholics—groups such as the Apprentice Boys, the Loyal Orange Order, and the Black Preceptory.

One of the great occasions commemorated by such Unionists is the 1609 Battle of the Boyne, the famous clash in which Protestant King William defeated Catholic King James, thus cementing England's hold over Ireland. The march that began on July 12, 1969, took hundreds of thousands of Orangemen (so named because of their support of King William of Orange) through Catholic towns, ghettos, and neighborhoods in the six counties. Enraged Catholic mobs met these marchers in Belfast and Derry. The violence came to a head in August as Catholics in the Derry enclave of Bogside decided to battle it out with Unionists and the RUC in what one historian has called "a full-scale uprising."

Local teenagers set up barricades to keep Orange marchers from entering their neighborhoods and battled with police trying to tear them down, throwing gasoline

Gasoline bombs explode, scattering riot police, during the Battle of Bogside in Derry in August 1969. The violence so was intense that the Northern Ireland prime minister asked for—and received—British troops to quell the hostilities.

bombs, bricks, and anything else they could get their hands on. When the police were able to tear apart a barricade, hundreds of Orangemen would come charging in, destroying Catholic property and attacking any Catholics they encountered.

What became known as the Battle of Bogside lasted for days and spread to other cities. Rioters in Belfast neighborhoods such as Shankill and Falls Road clashed viciously, with pistol and rifle shots ringing out. In both towns, the police used tear gas against Catholic neighborhoods.

The scenes were surreal and violent. The darkened streets (streetlights were the first thing destroyed by mobs on either side) were filled with shouts, screams, shots, and explosions. As a report filed by a British inquiry into the riots later said: "In the Crumlin road [district of Belfast] . . . were to be found and stumbled over all the clutter of urban rioting—barricades, debris, flames, and liquid petrol. Normal traffic movement had stopped: the noise of hostile, jeering crowds, the crackle and explosions of burning buildings, and the shattering of glass had enveloped the area."

Eight people died in a two-week period, four of them killed by the RUC, including an eight-year-old boy killed in his bedroom by a stray machine gun bullet fired by an armored car. Seven hundred and fifty people on both sides were injured. Finally unable to handle the rioting, the new prime minister of Northern Ireland, James Chichester-Clark, asked for and received British troops. A new era in the war had begun.

THE PROVISIONAL IRA

The IRA, or Irish Republican Army, had been in existence since the early 1920s, but was now undergoing an identity crisis. Part of its stated goal was to protect the Catholic neighborhoods of Northern Ireland from Protestant aggression, but it had failed to do so, mainly because the leadership of the IRA had not expected the level of violent assault directed against Belfast and Derry, and in any event had few weapons. But with failure to help the poor Irish of these Catholic ghettos, the IRA lost face. A popular Catholic graffito of the time was: "IRA = I Ran Away."

Around 1970, a new, far more violent wing of the IRA now arose, calling itself the Provisional IRA ("provisional" after the provisional government that had been briefly set up by Easter rebels during the Uprising of 1916). This group, popularly known as the Provos, would turn itself into what one historian has called "an aggressive killing machine" whose stated goal was "combined defense and retaliation."

On the Protestant side, groups had now organized themselves into what became known as the Ulster Defense Association, the goal of which was the same as that of the

Provos—to protect Protestants and retaliate against Catholics. An eye for an eye, a tooth for a tooth, and so the pattern for the long war became entrenched.

The third warring faction now became the British army, whose job was mainly patrolling Catholic neighborhoods in areas such as Derry and Belfast. Although they were supposedly there to keep the peace, they quickly alienated the local Catholic populations in places like Bogside in Derry and the Falls Road area of Belfast. At one point in July of 1970, following a clash between Catholic and Protestant rioters, British soldiers ousted 20,000 Falls Road residents to search for hidden arms. Although they found 100 weapons and 20,000 rounds of ammunition, the British seriously angered the population by damaging homes as they ransacked them. They also shot and killed three Catholic men and accidentally crushed another to death beneath an armored vehicle.

None of these men were PIRA members; in fact, a good portion of the Falls Road population did not support the Provos and had expected the British troops to protect them from violence. But overnight, as one local politician put it, "the population turned from neutral or even sympathetic for the military to outright hatred of everything related to the security forces."

It was a watershed moment, the kind that creates long wars—a relatively unbiased group of people so abused that they turn into relentless enemies. The Provos now became heroes to many in the poor neighborhoods like Falls Road. One of these heroes was Billy McKee, an IRA commander at the time. In June of 1970, Protestant marchers again attempted to march through Belfast, and McKee met them at St. Matthew's Church, a Catholic church in East Belfast left unprotected by the British army. With eleven Provos, McKee fought off the Orangemen in what he later described as the PIRA's "first main battle," a fierce melee in and around the grounds of the church. McKee, shot five times, barely survived, and one Catholic and two Protestants were killed (although it later turned out that the one Catholic killed was a civilian accidentally shot by the PIRA during the gun battle).

BLOODY SUNDAY

Violence grew steadily throughout 1970 and 1971, with the Provos beginning to plant bombs in an attempt to murder security forces. One such explosion killed instead five innocent civilians in County Tyrone. In another incident, three Scottish soldiers who had been drinking in a Belfast pub were taken, drunk, to a road outside the city and shot to death by Provos. All were in their teens; two were brothers. The citizens of Scotland and England were outraged at the cold-blooded nature of the killings and called for more British troops to find the killers.

In March 1971, Prime Minister Chichester-Clark resigned and was replaced by Brian Faulkner, who in an attempt to gain control of Northern Ireland instituted internment for suspects—detaining them indefinitely without trial. As with most of the measures the Northern Ireland authorities were taking at the time, this only made the situation worse. Most Provos had gone on the run to escape being captured; often the men pulled in on the dragnets were innocent. As the British mounted operations to attempt to capture the IRA, Belfast civilians, now completely on the side of the Provos, banged the sidewalks with trash can lids to give warning. One observer gave a picture of the chaos:

> There was the ominous rattling of hundreds of bin-lids as communities sent out a call to arms and for defenders to man the ramparts. Buses were being hijacked on all sides, cars were dragged from burned out showrooms . . . anything was being used to make barriers. Milk vans were being commandeered and the bottles used to make petrol bombs, pavements were being ripped up for missiles and to build barricades. Smoke, fire, noise and impending disaster was everywhere.

According to statistics gathered by David McKittrick and David McVea in their book *Making Sense of the Troubles*, of the 150 civilians who died in Northern Ireland during the second half of 1971, almost half were Catholic, and twenty-nine of these were killed by soldiers. The army claimed that many of these twenty-nine had been armed, but for the most part this turned out not to be the case.

Suspicion and hatred of the British security services reached an all-time high on January 30, 1972, a day that would be forever remembered in Northern Ireland as Bloody Sunday. On that day, a group of Catholic marchers gathered in Bogside to protest internment. At first peaceful, the march turned violent as the marchers began to hurl stones at the watching police.

But then the British army showed up in the form of the British Parachute Regiment, in armored personnel carriers commonly referred to as PIGS. The hardened paratroopers carried SLR rifles that fired high-velocity bullets, instead of the rubber bullets usually fired by the police at rioters. They opened fire on the crowd and killed thirteen people (a fourteenth died later) in twenty minutes. The army claimed that IRA members in the crowd carried guns and nail bombs, but no evidence of this was discovered, and a 2000 inquiry into the events of Bloody Sunday conducted by the British government found that the behavior of the paratroopers "bordered on reckless."

A mural in the Shankill Road area, a mainly Protestant, working class section of Belfast, declares the Loyalist position. Both Protestant Loyalist and Catholic Republican positions were fairly intractable, resulting in repeating cycles of violence.

© Steffan Hill / Alamy

"THE LOWEST LEVEL OF HUMAN DEPRAVITY"

The Bloody Sunday attack set off an even more vicious cycle of violence. A priest who observed the attack and gave the last rites to the dying said: "A lot of younger people in Derry who may have been more pacifist became quite militant as a result of it." Gerry Adams, who was to become head of Sinn Féin, the political branch of the IRA, wrote later: "Money, guns, and recruits flooded into the IRA." The activist Bernadette Devlin, who at the age of twenty-one had become the youngest woman ever elected to Parliament, physically attacked the British Home Secretary on the floor of the House of Commons, slapping him and pulling his hair, after he claimed that the British paratroopers had fired only when they were fired upon.

Such responses were mild compared to what happened next. In May, the IRA planned a retaliatory bomb attack on the 16th Parachute Regiment's headquarters in Aldershot, England. However, they hastily placed the bomb outside of a kitchen instead of a barracks. When it blew up, it killed five women, a gardener, and a Catholic priest. The IRA then kidnapped and shot a nineteen-year-old Derry man named William Best, who had been serving in the British army. Next, the Provos set off a bomb near a Belfast restaurant in a crowded shopping district. One hundred and thirty people were injured, including two sisters shopping for a wedding dress—both women lost their legs. On March 20, the Provos set off another bomb in Belfast, this time a car bomb, which killed six and injured 100.

It was a sorry tale typical of long wars. Had the British not reacted so violently on Bloody Sunday, had the IRA not responded so indiscriminately, it is possible the Troubles in Northern Ireland could have been shortened, but now there was no end in sight, and the British government took even more repressive measures. Because of the growing level of violence, Prime Minister Edward Heath removed control of all security from the government of Northern Ireland and appointed a secretary of state for Northern Ireland affairs. In response, the entire Northern Ireland Parliament resigned in protest, and Heath responded by introducing "Direct Rule," with Northern Ireland being governed directly from London.

It did little good. The IRA continued its campaign of violence, making 1972 the bloodiest year of the Troubles, with almost 500 dead. Although most of the deaths were due to the Provos, the UDA claimed numerous attacks. In July, a group of drunken Protestant loyalists broke into the home of a Catholic family, killed a mentally handicapped man, and raped his mother; when the case was brought to court, a lawyer told the judges: "We have reached the lowest level of human depravity."

On July 21, on a day that came to be called Bloody Friday, the IRA set off twenty-two bombs in Belfast in the space of an hour, killing nine people and injuring 130. Five or six of the bombs were car bombs, which were rapidly becoming a favored weapon of the Provos—the car itself acts as deadly shrapnel when the bomb shreds it. Some warnings were called in by the IRA, but there were also several hoax warnings, which further confused the issue. The loss of life and the terror created were almost unbearable. A police officer responding to one of the bomb scenes said: "You could hear people screaming and crying and moaning. The first thing that caught my eye was a torso of a human being lying in the middle of the street."

These indiscriminate killings on the part of the Provisional IRA were intended to create panic and inspire a ferocious response on the part of the British, and they did, with British troops moving into ghetto neighborhoods and virtually holding poor Catholics hostage. But public opinion in most of Ireland was firmly against such attacks. Many of those killed were Catholics; almost none were soldiers. The Bloody Friday attack was considered so reprehensible that, thirty years later, the PIRA actually issued an apology to the victims.

ATTEMPTS AT COMPROMISE

In March 1973, the British government publicized plans for a new Northern Ireland assembly that would "seek a much wider consensus than has hitherto existed . . . the objective of real participation should be achieved by giving minority interests a share in the exercise of executive power."

In other words, any new Northern Ireland Parliament would have to have proportional representation of Catholics and power would need to be shared. Further, Heath and his ministers suggested creating a "council of Ireland," which would give a partial say in the affairs of Northern Ireland to the Republic of Ireland—one of the greatest fears of the Protestants, who did not want to be a minority in a largely Catholic state.

Elections held in June 1973 showed that a majority of Protestants and Catholics in Northern Ireland wanted power-sharing agreements; that is, they were moderates who hoped to cooperatively govern the country. But most Protestant radicals were against giving any power in Northern Ireland to Catholics and lobbied fiercely against any concessions. The Ulster Workers' Council, a coalition of Protestant trade unions, called a worker's strike that crippled Ireland in May 1974. Three days later, bombs went off in Dublin, killing twenty-five people, and in the border town of Monaghan, killing seven more. It was the worst single atrocity of the Troubles. The bombs were set off by the outlawed Ulster Volunteer Force (UVF), although the organization did not admit responsibility for the act until 1994. There are those who believe that British intelligence may have had a hand in helping to plan the explosions. This has never been proven.

It was another pattern found to lengthen sectarian war—moderates who represent the majority attempting to compromise, only to have the efforts sabotaged by radical minorities. The British government, now headed by Harold Wilson, reinstated direct rule of Ireland and the sickening violence went on throughout the next few years; 1975 and 1976 were particularly bad. Statistics gathered by David McKittrick and David McVea show that almost 600 lives were lost during these years; most of the dead were killed by the Provos. The litany of gruesome death was particular to Northern Ireland and to religious warfare. More Provo bombers set off explosives in London, taking the war home to the British people.

Several attacks in late 1975 killed fifteen people. In January 1976, Provo gunmen in County Armagh in Northern Ireland took eleven Protestant textile workers from a minibus, lined them up, and shot them. Ten died and one survived with eighteen bullet wounds in what was called the Kingsmill Massacre. The Ulster Volunteer Force responded by murdering other Catholics. One particular member of the UVF, Lenny Murphy, was most likely a sociopath. Leading a gang called the Shankill Butchers during the period of 1975 to 1977, he was responsible for the especially savage murders of seven Catholics who were abducted in the night hours and murdered with butcher knives. Many were tortured for hours before being killed. Murphy, described by one law enforcement official as a "ruthless, dedicated terrorist with a sadistic streak," was later murdered by the IRA.

Perhaps a prime example of the senseless deaths and tragedy that occurred around this time happened in Belfast on August 10, 1976. The British army shot an IRA gunman speeding away at the wheel of his car, which careened onto the sidewalk, striking a Catholic woman named Anne Maguire, who was walking with three of her children, ranging in age from eight years to six weeks. All the children were killed. Maguire herself was in a coma for several weeks. She apparently never fully believed her children were dead, often talking to them and claiming that she could see them.

She and her husband and remaining daughter moved to New Zealand to get away from the violence of Belfast. There, Maguire had another daughter, but she could never recover from the trauma. After leaving her family a note that read, "Forgive me—I love you," she cut her throat and wrists with an electric carving knife.

"I'LL WEAR NO CONVICT'S UNIFORM"

Anne Maguire's tragedy inspired the Peace People's Movement, led by Maguire's sister and Betty Williams, a Belfast woman who had witnessed the crash, which held huge rallies and garnered international attention that included the Nobel Peace Prize of 1976. But this and other peace movements and initiatives did not last and the war ground on inexorably, despite the majority of people in Northern Ireland and the Republic of Ireland wanting it to stop. Ironically, while most people reviled the violence fostered by the IRA, it was the actions of a few IRA prisoners that would ultimately help lead in the direction of peace.

Since 1972, the British had given their paramilitary IRA prisoners some of the rights of prisoners of war, such as the right to wear their own clothing, to be policed by their own "officers," and to be segregated from the main prison population. They were known as Special Category prisoners. However, in 1976, the British government decided that it did not want to dignify people it considered terrorists by such a designation, and so it announced that the IRA prisoners would be placed in the general prison population and classified as ordinary criminals.

Most of these prisoners were held in the infamous Maze prison near Belfast—also known as Long Kesh—which, by 1975, held about 1,100 Special Category inmates. Maze was a sprawling compound surrounded by barbed wire whose inmates lived in World War II—era Nissen huts, which added to the aura of the Provo prisoners as POWs. But the British government forced the Provos to move to newly built cell blocks (known as H-Blocks because of their shapes) and to wear prison uniforms and perform prison work.

The Protestant prisoners held in the Maze reluctantly acceded to this, but not the Catholics, who fiercely protected their identity. A song written by IRA member Francis Brolly went:

> I'll wear no convict's uniform,
> Nor meekly serve my time,
> That England might
> Brand Ireland's fight
> Eight hundred years of crime.

In 1976, Provo prisoners went on a "blanket strike," refusing to wear prison clothing and donning only blankets. At the same time, they refused to wash, smearing themselves and their cells with excrement and garbage. This led to force washing with fire hoses on the part of the guards and prison administration, as well as beatings of prisoners. It was quite dangerous to be a prison guard in the Maze at the time—from 1976 to 1980, the IRA murdered nineteen Maze guards outside of the prison.

However, the protest by the "blanket men," as they were called, did not receive widespread attention. The IRA sought another tactic. In October 1980, seven Maze prisoners went on a hunger strike, demanding the right to be restored as Special Category prisoners. At the time, the British government was reeling from several same-day IRA attacks that took the lives of eighteen British paratroopers as well as the prominent Briton Lord Mountbatten, who was blown up along with his yacht. Prime Minister Margaret Thatcher announced that "the government will never concede political status to the hunger strikers or to any other person convicted of criminal offenses."

Thus the stalemate was set. The first hunger strike of 1980 was called off in December, with most of the participants near death, when the IRA mistakenly thought that the British government had made concessions. The second hunger strike began in March 1981, led by an IRA member named Bobby Sands. Born in 1954, Sands was a Belfast native who had been sentenced to fourteen years in prison for possession of a gun while on an IRA operation. Sands could not have been more perfect as the leader of a strike that was meant, to a certain extent, to humanize the IRA in front of the world and portray the organization as a victim of British cruelty, David McKittrick and David McVea write. Sands had not been convicted of any IRA atrocities, but merely of carrying a gun. He was also handsome, with flowing hair. "The fact that [Sands] looked more like a rock drummer than a ruthless terrorist was important in the propaganda battle that raged all around the world," the authors write.

During Sands's hunger strike, which lasted sixty-six days, the IRA had a stroke of luck. The Catholic Member of Parliament from Fermanagh in Northern Ireland died of a sudden heart attack, and an election was held to fill his vacant seat. IRA propagandists put Sands up for the election, and he won. The British government now had an MP who was a terrorist on a hunger strike. This embarrassed the British, but also made many within the IRA realize that there might be broad support for the organization if political means were sought to resolve issues.

Bobby Sands died of starvation on May 5, 1981, but not before becoming a worldwide folk hero. The British government did not make any concessions to the IRA as a result of the hunger strikers (nine more of whom would die before the strike ended in August), but the IRA had gained worldwide prestige and understood that it had more political support than it thought possible. It would not give up violence. But, as an IRA official asked at the time: "[What if] with a ballot box in one hand and the Armalite [an automatic rife] in the other, we take power in Ireland?"

PEACE

The bloody violence of the war in Northern Ireland would continue, but Sinn Féin, the IRA's political wing, would contest, and win, more and more elections. In 1983, Sinn Féin leader Gerry Adams became the Member of Parliament from West Belfast. However, the Provos continued their campaign of violence. Shockingly, in 1984, as Thatcher attended a conference in Brighton, England, she was nearly killed by an IRA bomb planted in the hotel room next to hers. (Five others were killed, and thirty-four wounded.)

Despite this, she continued to try to work on a compromise agreement for Northern Ireland, and a year later, she helped engineer the Anglo-Irish Agreement, which confirmed that Northern Ireland would remain independent from the Republic of Ireland—a victory for the Protestants—but that Northern Ireland would not be allowed to rule itself independent of Great Britain unless it agreed to power-sharing, something the Catholics deeply desired. This did not please radicals on either side, but was accepted by moderates on both sides. The violence in Northern Ireland continued, but more and more disputes were being settled in elections, and those who committed the violence, be they IRA or UDA, became marginalized.

Finally, an agreement was reached in 1998, with the mediation help of the U.S. government, which became known as the Belfast Agreement, or the Good Friday Agreement. Radical groups on both sides were to disarm, paramilitary prisoners were released early by the British government, and power sharing was agreed upon. Northern Ireland would continue to remain independent, with the Republic of Ireland dropping any constitutional claim to its six counties. The Good Friday Agreement was endorsed by Northern Ireland voters in a referendum, Great Britain dropped direct rule, and the agreement went into effect in 1999.

Has it been effective? Northern Ireland still has a long way to go toward peace, and as of 2010, there has been an upswing in violence, possibly because economic hard times have set in after a period of Irish prosperity. The formation of such groups as the "Real IRA," a violent splinter group responsible for settling old scores from the war via murder, is problematic. In an attack in March 2009, the Real IRA killed two British soldiers. However, the Good Friday Agreement still holds and Northern Ireland is, for the time being, at peace.

CHAPTER 7

THE ARAB-ISRAELI WARS

WHEN WAR IS A FACT OF LIFE

1948-ONGOING

After the destruction of the Ottoman Empire in World War I, many Jews dreamed of the establishment of a Jewish state in the Middle East. The increase in Jewish immigration to Palestine caused clashes between Jewish and Arab populations that in 1948 broke out into open warfare, which has continued virtually uninterrupted ever since.

The modern state of Israel is comprised of a narrow strip of land between the Mediterranean Sea and the Jordan River, covering 8,522 square miles (22,072 square km). This makes it one of the tiniest nations on earth—nineteen Israels could fit inside the American state of California. Yet despite its size, Israel has been fought over more fiercely, and for a longer period of time, than almost any country in the world.

It is the locus of a still-unresolved religious war that has drawn in surrounding countries as well as almost every major world power. In an era of nuclear weapons, the Arab-Israeli conflict can be said to threaten the very existence of the world. All for a patch of earth dubbed, from biblical times, "the land of milk and honey."

Like many long religious wars, the Arab-Israeli conflict is a war of survival. Each side considers the threat signature of the other so high that surrendering is unthinkable. Peaces have been negotiated with regularity since the first clash in 1948, but each segment of the war leaves unresolved conflicts that extend the war, making these peaces null and void. Both sides have engaged in fiercely violent acts. And yet, both sides contain men and women who are profoundly religious and have a powerful belief in an all-encompassing deity. The Arab-Israeli conflict has gone on for so long, in so many different incarnations, that is it hard to imagine the world without it.

PARTITION

The Jewish people originated in Palestine, in the fertile strip of land they called Israel (meaning "He has striven with God"), which they ruled from about 1000 BCE onward. Although they were conquered by the Assyrians and later the Babylonians, who dragged them off into captivity, they returned to Israel in the sixth century BCE, and rebuilt their Temple in their holy city of Jerusalem. They were well established when the Romans conquered the Holy Land in the first century after the birth of Christ. Following the bitter Jewish-Roman Wars (see chapter 5), most of the surviving Jewish people dispersed around the world, many carrying with them a fervent dream of returning to their lost land.

After the fall of the Roman Empire, Palestine was ruled by numerous occupiers— Byzantines, Arabs, Seljuk Turks, Crusaders, and Mamluk and Ottoman Turks. All of these, except the Byzantines and the Crusaders, were Muslims. Palestine became for centuries a Muslim land and a relatively quiet part of the world.

By the 1880s, 25,000 Jews lived there, a distinct minority surrounded by hundreds of thousands of Arabs. By this time, the fervent dream of the Jews had turned into a religious-political movement, Zionism—Zion was a name for one of the fabled hills of Jerusalem—which called for Jews to return to their traditional homeland. By the beginning of World War I, there were 100,000 Jews living in Palestine, making up 15 percent of the total population. (Palestine at this time was not a separate state, but an area between Jerusalem and Beirut, part of the Ottoman Empire.) This community was called the *Yishuv*, meaning settlement, and Arabs viewed with suspicion its swelling numbers and growing prosperity.

With the defeat of the Turks in World War I, Palestine—consisting of what would become Israel, the West Bank, the Gaza Strip, and Jordan—became a British protectorate. Great Britain had promised self-determination to both the Arabs and the Jews and in 1922 divided Palestine into two territories. The land east of the Jordan River would become Transjordan (today's Jordan), while the land to the west remained Palestine.

Almost immediately, armed clashes between Jewish and Arab forces began as each vied for more territory. The Arabs of Palestine were especially concerned about the growing number of Jewish immigrants and by the Jews of the Yishuv buying up more and more Palestinian land. World War II arrived and with it the Holocaust, which brought world attention and sympathy to the homeless plight of the Jews. After the war, more and more political pressure was put on the British government to allow a Jewish homeland in Palestine. Great Britain resisted, but the United Nations (UN) interceded and in November 1947 passed Resolution 181, which called for the partition of Palestine into both a Jewish and a Palestinian homeland.

BLOODY CIVIL WAR

The Jews and Arabs had very different views of the Partition. The Jews, led by their charismatic first prime minister, David Ben-Gurion, had originally wanted all of the land that made up the ancient state of Israel—that is, the land from the Mediterranean to the Jordan River, and even some areas that were in 1947 a part of Transjordan. Instead, they got only half of this area, with Palestinian Arabs getting the other half. However, their dream of having a Jewish state was finally realized, even if the full Zionist dream of a state encompassing all of ancient Israel was not. Ben-Gurion decided that, for the time being, this was acceptable to Israel, but as Thomas Friedman points out in his book *From Beirut to Jerusalem*, Ben-Gurion and many of Israel's founders did not give up the Zionist dream of uniting *all* of Israel. This would seriously lengthen the Arab-Israeli conflicts of the half-century to come.

The Palestinian Arabs, on the other hand, felt that the UN had been influenced by Jews who held powerful political positions in countries around the world. From their point of view, half of their own homeland was being torn away from them. In 1947, there were 650,000 Jews surrounded by twice as many Palestinian Arabs and also 40 million sympathetic Arabs in the surrounding countries of Syria, Egypt, Transjordan, Iraq, and Lebanon. War was inevitable and both sides knew it. Even before Great Britain withdrew its mandate and Israel proclaimed itself a sovereign state on May 14, 1948, civil war flared between a makeshift Jewish army known as the Haganah (meaning "defense"), along with its more radical terrorist arms, the LHI, better known as the Stern gang, and the IZL, better known as the Irgun, and a group called the Arab Liberation Army (ALA).

Like most civil wars, this one was violent and bloody, with numerous civilians caught in the crossfire. Arab snipers took up positions in Tel Aviv buildings and randomly shot Jewish civilians. The LHI in response randomly picked five Arabs, kidnapped them, and executed them. Much of the fighting centered on the city of Jerusalem, sacred to both Arabs and Jews. The Jews held the so-called New City of Jerusalem, while the Arabs surrounded much of the Old City. Fighting also focused on supply roads into Jerusalem and other Jewish strongpoints. Large, organized bands of Arabs under the lead of influential commanders, but not necessarily the more centralized authority of the ALA, headquartered themselves in villages and attacked Jewish truck convoys with mortars and machine guns.

A map showing the West Bank and the Gaza Strip, which have been hotly contested areas in the Israeli-Arab struggle since the middle of the twentieth century.

Library of Congress

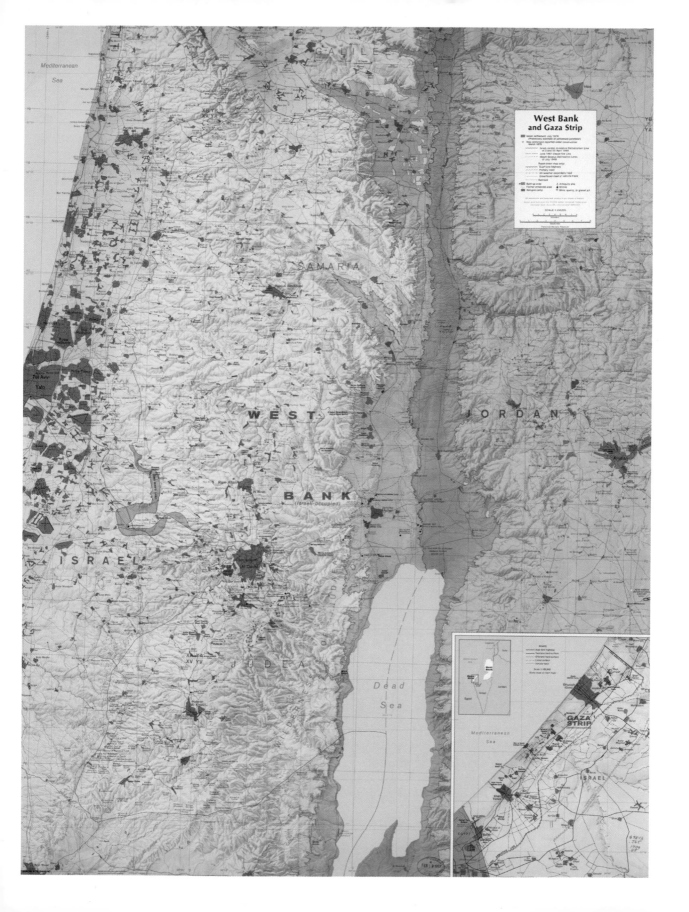

West Bank and Gaza Strip

Mediterranean Sea

GALILEE

SAMARIA

JORDAN

W E S T

B A N K
(Israeli-occupied)

I S R A E L

Tel Aviv

Yafo

Netanya

J U D E A

Dead Sea

GAZA STRIP

ISRAEL

EGYPT

Mediterranean Sea

Although these fighters were brave, there was as yet little Arab nationalism in Palestine—almost no sense of the Arabs fighting together as a single united force, as the Jews did—and a disturbing trend began: thousands upon thousands of Arabs began to flee their homes to escape the fighting. Jewish civilians, with nowhere to go, stayed put.

A MAJOR VICTORY—AND THE SEEDS OF LONG WAR

The Jews took heavy losses and labored under serious shortages of arms and other supplies, and for a while, as the world watched, they reeled under the Arab attacks. But then in April 1948 David Ben-Gurion planned a major attack, code-named Operation Nachshon, which opened up an essential road corridor to besieged Jerusalem and also killed one of the most charismatic Arab leaders of the time, Abd al-Qadir al-Husseini. The Israelis had little time to rest on their laurels, however. When the British mandate ended and Israel proclaimed itself a state, there was a pan-Arab invasion consisting of armies from Egypt, Syria, Transjordan, Iraq, and Lebanon. The ALA, heavily funded by these countries, also took a major part.

The civil war had been difficult, but this was now a war where professional armies surrounded Israel. Most of the watching world expected the Jews to be crushed. Both sides started out with relatively small armies, which then grew rapidly in size. The Hagana forces numbered 30,000 in May 1948, although within six months these would rise to 108,000. The Jewish commando groups—the Arabs thought of them as terrorists—numbered perhaps 4,000 in total. The Jews had only small arms—rifles, machine guns, and mortars—and no tanks or heavy artillery. However, in May 1948, most of the Jewish fighters were reserves, with only 2,000 being fulltime members of the Hagana.

The invading Arab armies numbered about 20,000 in total—5,500 Egyptians, 6,000–9,000 Arab Legionnaires, 6,000 from Syria, 4,500 from Iraq, and a handful of Lebanese, Palestinian irregulars, and foreign volunteers. Arab forces would total 80,000 by October. However, these forces were amply supported by a much larger and more organized supply and command infrastructure than that possessed by the Israelis.

At first, the pan-Arab forces won the expected victories. Transjordan troops took control of the Old City of Jerusalem, while Egyptians overran Jewish settlements in the Negev Desert in the south. But by July, the now-consolidated Jewish army (called the IDF, or Israeli Defense Force) took central Galilee and pushed the Arabs back. After a four-week cease-fire called by the UN, fighting broke out again and this time the Israelis pushed the Arab countries back on all fronts, taking control of all of the Negev Desert (with the exception of the Gaza Strip).

In 1962, charismatic Israeli Prime Minister David Ben-Gurion, second from left, is surrounded by his general staff (from left to right): David Elazar, Ezer Weizmann, Yitzchak Rabin, and Abraham Adan. Ben-Gurion and many of Israel's founders did not give up the Zionist dream of uniting all of Israel—something that would lengthen the Arab-Israeli conflicts.

Between February and May 1949, Israel signed separate truces with all her enemies except Iraq, which refused to sign a treaty. It was an amazing and unforeseen victory for Israel. Its forces had taken 400 Arab towns and villages, and had increased its original land allotment under the UN Partition by 30 percent. But in victory lay the seeds of future episodes of the long war. Six hundred thousand Palestinian refugees had fled or been expelled to other Arab countries, where many of them lived in slum conditions and held simmering resentments against the Israelis. Too, there were many Israelis who fostered the hope that such a victory, with its attendant gain in territory, would be only the first of many that would put the ancient territory of Israel back in Jewish hands.

A NEW WAR IN THE MAKING

Armistices had been signed, but there was no sense that the tensions between the Israelis and their Arab neighbors were over. Although the Arab countries had stopped fighting, they still did not recognize Israel as a state. As far as they were concerned, the peace was merely a truce, to buy time to prepare for the next round of hostilities. Almost immediately following the armistices, irregular Arab forces known as *fedayeen* (meaning "freedom fighters" or "self-sacrificers") began to raid Israeli kibbutzim and commit sabotage against water and electrical facilities. There were no immediate major attempts to attack Israel, however, because the surrounding Arab countries were so traumatized by their defeat.

Dissatisfaction with the performance of Arab leaders was high. Radical Muslims assassinated the Egyptian prime minister even before the war ended. In July 1951, King Abdullah of Jordan, who was about to sign a secret peace accord with Israel, was assassinated by a young Palestinian terrorist. (Wounded in the attack was Abdullah's grandson, Prince Hussein, who would become king of Jordan a year later.) The Syrian government was rocked by several military coups.

And in Egypt, a group of army officers lead by Lieutenant-Colonel Gamal Abdel Nasser took control July 22–23, 1952. Nasser, born in 1918, preached a philosophy of pan-Arab nationalism, of Arab countries joining forces with Egypt against the Western powers, and by extension Israel, which was supported by these powers. Nasser became a serious concern for the Israeli government after he signed a huge arms deal in late 1955 with the Soviet bloc state of Czechoslovakia, receiving a massive amount of tanks, fighters, bombers, destroyers, submarines, and patrol boats. This made Egypt the best-armed country in the Middle East, with a four-to-one superiority over Israel in all areas of heavy weaponry, ships, planes, and vehicles.

Nasser declared economic war against Israel by blocking Israeli vessels from traveling through the narrow Straits of Tiran, which led to the Red Sea and access to African and Far Eastern markets. Worse, Egypt blocked access to the strategic Suez Canal to Israel and Israeli-bound shipping, and Nasser then nationalized control of the Suez Canal Zone, ousting the French and British, who had been stationed there for eighty years by treaty. Fedayeen raids increased, killing hundreds of Israeli citizens; then, in October 1955, Egypt signed a joint military pact with Syria (and later Jordan).

David Ben-Gurion and Israel could see that war was coming and knew that Israel's chief hope lay in a preemptive strike against Egypt and Nasser. He worked out a secret deal with Great Britain and France in which Israel would feign a surprise attack against the Suez Canal, which would give the French and British an excuse to send in troops to "protect" the Canal Zone. In the meantime, Israel would launch an attack in the Sinai Peninsula, with the immediate goal of freeing the Straits of Tiran for Israeli shipping.

"A WORK OF ART"

The British military historian Basil Liddell Hart later called the Israeli attack "a work of art." It was a model for future Israeli attacks, one that would make the Israeli military feared throughout the Middle East. The Israeli attack began on October 29, 1956. Israeli paratroopers landed only 24 miles (38.6 km) east of the Suez Canal, acting as if they would attack there, while prop-driven World War II–era Israeli planes swept in 12 feet (3.7 m) off the ground and used their propellers to cut telephone lines, thus severing vital Egyptian communications.

The Israelis—led by such future heroes as Rafael "Raful" Eitan, Mordechai Gur, and Ariel Sharon—at first launched their attack into the Sinai in a deliberately scattered and piecemeal way, puzzling Egyptian commanders, who could not decide whether this was an invasion or a sortie in force intent on punishing fedayeen raids. By the time major operations began two days later, the Egyptians were reeling.

Despite heavy resistance, Israeli forces drove to within 10 miles (16 km) of the Suez Canal by November 2, while British and French commandos seized the canal itself. By November 5, the war in the Sinai Desert was over. The Israelis had captured the Gaza Strip and the entire Sinai Peninsula; however, the intervention of both the United Nations and the United States forced Israel to relinquish the Gaza Strip and the Sinai, and Great Britain and France to withdraw from the Suez Canal, after assurances that the Egyptians would allow free passage of shipping. Israeli ships were still not allowed through the canal, although with UN help, they now passed through the Straits of Tiran.

As a result of the Sinai Campaign of 1956, Nasser's prestige in the Arab world increased—paradoxically, it would seem. Although his troops had been soundly beaten on the battlefield, the UN had intervened before he could be completely defeated, and thus Nasser could claim that he had never had to surrender Egyptian forces. The world had condemned the French, British, and Israeli attack (the Suez was, after all, in Egyptian territory), and the British and French governments both suffered upheaval because of the invasion.

The Israelis benefited as well: Israeli military planners, knowing that the long war was nowhere near over, figured they had bought by their fiercely successful attack at least another decade in which to develop their defenses. As historian Michael Oren writes, the war only led to more war: "If a new status quo had been created, it was one of inherent instability, a situation so combustible that the slightest spark could ignite it."

BUILDUP TO WAR

The June 1967 War—the so-called Six-Day War—would become the most pivotal and far-reaching conflict in the Arab-Israeli Wars. The decade after the Sinai War saw Israel rapidly developing itself as a nation, increasing in population, and instituting a major irrigation project that diverted water from the Jordan River into the Negev Desert, turning much of the parched land there arable. But conflict was only as close as the young state's borders.

In 1964, a thirty-three-year-old Palestinian radical named Yasser Arafat co-founded the Palestinian Liberation Movement, vowing to drive Israel from the lands that had once belonged to the Palestinians. (Arafat would become head of the Palestinian Liberation Organization [PLO] in 1969.) With funding from Nasser and Egypt, Arafat's organization, along with several smaller ones, made numerous fedayeen raids across Israel's borders, attacking water transfer stations, electrical facilities, and the like. In northern Israel, Syria shelled Israeli kibbutzim repeatedly from the Golan Heights.

Israel retaliated by striking back at Syria with punitive raids that grew larger and larger, especially after Syria began its own Jordan River irrigation project that, carried to completion, would have dried up the source of Israel's water. Jordan also sent in fedayeen to attack Israel, which responded with more retaliatory raids. The vicious cycle of attack and revenge attack—a staple of long religious wars—was repeating itself.

In this modern religious conflict, however, the stakes were a great deal higher because of the involvement of the world's major powers. The Soviet Union continued

Bodies of Palestinians killed in 1982 in the refugee camp of Sabra lay in the middle of a road in West Beirut. The deaths occurred after Israel allowed the Lebanon Christian militia to enter the camps and ferret out PLO members. Instead of handing them over to the Israelis, the militia murdered hundreds of refugees. A commission of inquiry found that Israel bore "indirect" responsibility for the massacres.

to arm Syria and Egypt, while France and West Germany gave aid to Israel. The United States, a friendly presence for Israel, was not yet the huge bastion of aid for that country, in part because of the United States' continued preoccupation with and involvement in the Vietnam War.

In April 1967, all of the simmering tensions came to a head when Israeli fighters shot down six Syrian jets during a battle near the Israeli-Syrian border after a Syrian raid into Israeli territory. The Soviets warned Syria that Israel's armed forces were engaged in a full-scale buildup near the Syrian border. This in fact was not true, and historians to this day do not know whether the Soviets simply had their intelligence wrong—something that is hard to believe, given their capacity for gathering information—or whether they deliberately gave disinformation to the Syrians, hoping to see a war with Israel.

Syria had recently signed a mutual defense pact with Egypt, and now both of these countries, alarmed, began a rapid military buildup along their borders. To make matters worse for Israel, Nasser successfully demanded the withdrawal of the UN troops that had been guarding the Gaza Strip and Sinai Desert. Nasser then resumed blockading Israeli shipping in the Straits of Tiran, one of the main impetuses for the Sinai invasion of 1956.

STRIKING EARLY

Seeing this, Israeli leaders—Prime Minister Levi Eshkol, his chief of staff Yitzhak Rabin, and Defense Minister Moshe Dayan—decided they had no other choice but to launch a preemptive military strike. On the morning of June 5, 1967, some 250 Israeli jets—all but twelve of the country's military airplanes—swept in over Egypt, flying as low as 20 feet (6 m) off the ground to avoid radar detection.

The Egyptian pilots had thought any Israeli air strike would be launched at dawn, an hour before; they had already flown defense sorties, seen nothing, and landed. Their planes were parked on the ground at eleven different airfields and the pilots themselves were eating breakfast when the Israeli planes hit, first dropping special bombs to break up runways, and then strafing the parked jets.

Surprise was complete, and in just forty minutes the Egyptians lost half of their air force—more than 200 planes—to only eight jets lost by the Israelis. A second wave the same morning attacked fourteen bases and destroyed another 107 planes for a total of 304 out of 419 aircraft. The Israelis lost nine planes and suffered damage to another six. This stunning attack was to set the tone for the fast-moving drama that became the Six-Day War, images of which were flashed around the world via television and photojournalism.

The war quickly escalated, in part due to misinformation given to Nasser by his underlings. Afraid to tell him the truth about the loss of the crème of his air force, they told him that the Israeli attack had failed, that Israeli losses had been "staggering," and that Egyptian jets were even now pounding Israeli airfields. Egypt spread this news to its allies Syria and Jordan, both of which joined the fight, certain of victory. Each got a rude awakening when Israeli jets attacked their air bases and military installations.

THE WAR WAS ALMOST UNBELIEVABLY SUCCESSFUL FOR THE ISRAELIS. IT HAD LOST 800 FIGHTERS. BY COMPARISON, THE EGYPTIANS ALONE HAD LOST 10,000 TO 15,000 MEN.

The battle now turned to the ground, where Israeli armed forces—including tens of thousands of civilian reservists called to take arms—fought against Syria, Egypt, Jordan, and Iraq in five more days of desperate struggle. However, without the support of the jets Israel destroyed on the first morning of the war, the Arabs were lost and their armies were routed on all three fronts—the West Bank of Jordan, the Sinai Desert in Egypt, and the Golan Heights, on the Syria-Israel border. By the time of a UN cease-fire called on the evening of June 11, the Israeli Defense Force (IDF) had captured the Sinai Peninsula, all the way to the east bank of the Suez Canal, the West Bank of the Jordan (including East Jerusalem), and the Golan Heights in Syria, where for so long Syrian guns had been able to reach far into Israeli territory.

The war was almost unbelievably successful for the Israelis. It had lost 800 fighters. By comparison, the Egyptians alone had lost 10,000 to 15,000 men. Eighty-five percent of Egypt's military might—planes, tanks, artillery—was destroyed; the Jordanians suffered nearly as badly. Even more important, the Israelis had taken 42,000 square miles (108,780 square km) of new territory and united its capital, Jerusalem. And this time, the Israelis were determined to hang on to this new territory.

A NEW ROUND OF VIOLENCE

After the Six-Day War, Israel experienced an unprecedented period of prosperity and international prestige. The United States now became a firm backer of the country and began to supply it with military hardware and assistance. But here—as in other long wars—from the seeds of victory grew discord. Along with the territories the Israelis had captured—territories that finally did realize the ancient Zionist dream of a Jewish state in all of ancient Israel—came one million Arabs who were living within these areas.

The Israeli leadership now faced serious questions as to how to treat these Arabs and what, exactly, would be the makeup of the future Israeli state. In the meantime, the PLO, based in refugee camps inside Jordan, sent more and more infiltrators into the West Bank, initiating a wave of terrorist actions against the Israelis. During 1970 and 1971, King Hussein of Jordan expelled the PLO from his country after fierce fighting, but it traveled to Lebanon and then to Syria, continuing terrorist attacks on Israel and Israeli targets. These reached their apex at the Munich Olympics in 1972, where PLO guerillas killed eleven Israeli athletes and coaches in an attack that horrified the entire world.

In the meantime, Egypt, still stunned to have lost so badly in the Six-Day War, kept up a three-year-long clash with the Israelis in the Sinai Desert—the so-called "War of Attrition" fought with artillery duels, jet planes, and lightning raids across the arid wastes of the Sinai. It was an attempt to slowly bleed Israel, and it continued until Nasser died in 1970.

He was replaced by President Anwar El Sadat, who now planned yet another—a fourth—war against Israel. This time the Arabs caught the Israelis by surprise. The Yom Kippur War began on October 8, 1973, when Egypt and Syria launched a two-prong attack. With the somewhat complacent Israelis unprepared (as well as observing the major religious holiday of Yom Kippur), Egyptian forces overwhelmed the Israelis in the Sinai, pushing them back 15 miles (24 km), while Syrian forces had the same success in the Golan Heights.

However, the Israelis—helped to a great extent by U.S. intelligence planes like the SR-71 Blackbird, which pinpointed the location of Arab troops—rallied. In a three-week-long war, they drove to within 65 miles (104.6 km) of the Egyptian capital of Cairo and 35 miles (56.3 km) of the Syrian capital of Damascus. Only the threat of direct military intervention by the Soviets caused them to stop. A cease-fire treaty brokered by both the Soviets and the Americans ended the war, and, once again, the Arab nations had failed to defeat Israel.

OPERATION PEACE FOR GALILEE

In a sense, however, the Yom Kippur War had some positive outcomes. Even though they lost, the Egyptians were able to recover some of the fighting honor they had left on the field of battle in the disastrous Six-Day War. And after four bloody wars, there were Arab nations now willing to agree that Israel would need to be dealt with peaceably. At the Camp David Accords in September 1978, Anwar Sadat signed a peace treaty with Prime Minister Menachem Begin of Israel, which recognized Israel and returned the Sinai Peninsula to Egypt.

However, the cycle of violence was just starting up again in a new way with the end of this last "conventional" war between the Arabs and the Israelis. Terrorist organizations such as the PLO and others that had sprung up did not want to see any recognition of Israel as a state, so they stepped up their campaigns against her. Anwar Sadat was assassinated in 1981 by one Egyptian group that hoped to throw the peace process into disarray. The PLO continued to attack from Lebanon, attacks that caused the Israeli citizens in Galilee, the region closest to the Lebanese border, to live in fear. The Israelis responded with jet strikes and commando raids, but this did not stop the PLO from building camps in southern Lebanon and training thousands of fighters there.

Finally, after radical Palestinians had attempted to assassinate the Israeli ambassador to Great Britain on June 3, 1982, the Israelis had had enough. All sides had known for awhile that Israel would go into Lebanon, and the Reagan administration was repeatedly informed during the first half of 1982 that it would happen. One historian speculated that the attack was ordered by radical Palestinians "specifically in order to provoke an Israeli attack on the PLO in Lebanon." It was at this point that, in a sense, Jewish fortunes changed for the worst. Attacking on June 6, in a massive invasion named Operation Peace for Galilee, Israeli forces drove all the way to Beirut, battling the PLO as well as elements of the Syrian armed forces that were supporting the PLO. By the end of the summer, the Israelis had surrounded and trapped the PLO; finally, with the assistance of U.S. mediators, the Palestinians negotiated a truce to leave Lebanon for Syria.

However, a bloody atrocity occurred of the type that is all too commonplace in long religious wars. After Bachir Gemayel, the Christian president of Lebanon, was assassinated by the Syrians on September 14, 1982, for agreeing to make peace with the Israelis, the Israeli army occupied West Beirut. On September 16, it allowed the Lebanon Christian militia, also known as the Phalangists, which had been waging a civil war against the Muslims, to enter the Sabra and Shatila refugee camps. The population of these camps consisted mainly of Muslim Palestinians and Lebanese civilians who had fled from the fighting in southern Lebanon. While the Israeli army closed off the exits to the camps, the Phalangists, enraged at the assassination of Gemayel, went through them, ostensibly to find remaining PLO fighters and hand them over to the Israelis.

Instead, the Phalangists murdered hundreds of refugees (possibly several thousand, the number is still in dispute) in cold blood. The UN declared the slaughter an act of genocide. A commission of inquiry within Israel—instituted after major protests not

Smoke rises up over Jerusalem on February 22, 1948, following the explosion of car bombs by Arab irregulars that killed 52 Jewish civilians and left 123 injured, an example of the increasing violence as the deadline for the partition of Palestine approached in May 1948.

© Trinity Mirror/Mirrorpix/Alamy

just from Palestinians but also from Israeli civilians—found that the Israeli army bore "indirect" responsibility for the massacre, after evidence was presented that Israeli officers knew what was going on, but failed to stop it. Defense Minister Ariel Sharon was forced to step down from office as a result, although he would later be elected prime minister.

"SHAKING OFF"

Israeli would eventually withdraw her forces to a so-called "buffer zone" in southern Lebanon, but was forced to maintain a presence in Lebanon for twenty years. The occupation of Lebanon—though it achieved the goal of pushing the PLO away from Israel's borders—changed the way many in the world (and within Israel) looked at the country. Instead of the fiery young state fighting for its life, it began to seem a heavily armed occupying power that was party to a bloody massacre of an already oppressed people.

This shifting of perceptions led to a continuation of hostilities, especially after the intifada in 1987. *Intifada* is an Arab word that means "shaking off," and the intifada was an uprising in the Palestinian territories of Gaza, the West Bank, and East Jerusalem against Israeli rule. What was different about the intifada was that it was not engineered by the PLO leadership; in fact, the uprising took Arafat and his generals (headquartered now in Tunis) by surprise. The intifada began in December in the Jabalia refugee camp in the Gaza Strip, after four Palestinian refugees were killed in a traffic accident near an Israeli checkpoint, an incident that was rumored to be Israeli revenge for the killing of an Israeli several days before. Palestinian youths burned tires and attacked IDF forces and Israeli police.

As with the war in Northern Ireland, scenes of street rioting in Gaza, with young men throwing rocks and bottles at Israeli tanks and armored vehicles, filled the media and brought new attention to a Palestinian cause that many people had ceased to pay any heed to. Because the uprising was spontaneous and, at first, not organized around terrorist attacks, it made the world understand the plight of a people who had been crowded into refugee camps for years and lived in dire poverty without medical care and proper schooling.

By the early 1990s, the intifada had turned far more violent, with suicide bombers working for the newest radical Palestinian organization, the Islamic Resistance Movement, known by its Arab acronym Hamas, regularly entering Israeli territory from Gaza or the West Bank and blowing themselves, and dozens of Israeli citizens, up. Palestinians—many of whom held menial jobs working for Israeli businesses or private Israeli citizens—began to knife Israelis on the street in random acts of terror. More and more Israelis began calling for Israel to be sealed off from Palestinian territory or even to cede these areas, captured in the 1967 war, completely.

In 1992, newly elected Israeli prime minister Yitzchak Rabin seized upon these sentiments to help negotiate a peace with PLO leader Yasser Arafat, a peace that was ratified by the Oslo Accords. Israel pledged to withdraw its forces from parts of the West Bank and the Gaza Strip, while it affirmed the Palestinian right to self-government. In return, Arafat and the PLO recognized Israel as a state and committed themselves to policing the areas the Israeli army would withdraw from.

The Oslo Accords pleased extremists on neither side. In February 1994, a fanatical Jewish settler walked into a holy Muslim shrine and gunned down thirty worshippers. Later that year, a Hamas radical blew up himself and twenty-two Israelis on a city bus in Tel Aviv. In 1995, Yitzhak Rabin himself became a casualty, assassinated by a Jewish extremist opposed to peace with the Arabs.

The Oslo Accords were a first ray of hope in the long Arab-Israeli War, but the real peace is a long way off. Since the death of Yasser Arafat at the age of seventy-five in 2004 and subsequent waning of power of the PLO, Hamas has been Israel's chief terrorist opponent within the Palestinian territories of the Gaza Strip and the West Bank, while Hezbollah—meaning "the Party of God," an Islamic militant group—has fought the IDF from Lebanon.

Israel's hawkish prime minister Ariel Sharon completely withdrew Israeli settlements from Gaza in 2005, surprising most observers, but since then Israel and Hamas have waged pitched battles following terrorist rocket attacks on Israeli territory. Israel continues a blockade of Gaza that strangles the area economically. There are those on both sides who continue to seek ways for these two peoples to find mutual ground, but for the time being, peace remains elusive, and war—or the threat of war—the status quo.

"AS A FISH SWIMS IN THE SEA"
GUERILLA WARS

Great Mao's dictum that a guerilla
should move among the landscape
and population "as a fish swims
in the sea," avoiding major conflict,
can make war interminable.

CHAPTER 8

THE SEMINOLE WARS

"A TRIBE WHICH HAS LONG VIOLATED OUR RIGHTS"

1817–1858

The Seminole Wars took the form of three bloody conflicts that pitted the U.S. against Florida's elusive Seminoles, ending with their near extinction and a blueprint for the American Indian wars to come.

The United States army soldiers garrisoned at Fort Scott, Georgia, just across the Apalachicola River from the Seminole village known to the whites as Fowltown, were understandably nervous. On November 21, 1817, their commander, Major General Edmund Gaines, had sent them to drive the Seminoles from Fowltown and burn their homes because their chief, Neamathla, had refused the Americans the right to cut timber on Seminole land. The attack of the soldiers had been successful in that Fowltown was destroyed, but the now-homeless band of Seminoles, led by Neamathla, were lurking somewhere in the thick forest to the south, near the border with Florida.

And Fort Scott was running out of supplies. There was hope, though. A shipment of arms, food, and clothing was scheduled to come up the Apalachicola from the Gulf of Mexico at the end of November, and so General Gaines sent a lieutenant, R. W. Scott, and a detachment of troopers to meet it. Arriving near the gulf, Scott found the shipment and the contingent of men accompanying it. Unfortunately, many of these men were sick with fever; seven had brought along wives and children. Making the best of it, Scott headed back upriver in two boats, bringing along women, and possibly the children (records conflict on the latter).

Concerned about the Seminoles, he sent a message on ahead to his commander, which read: "Mr. Hamby [a civilian trader who worked as an interpreter] informs me that Native Americans are assembling at the junction of the river, where they intend to make a stand against those vessels coming up the river; should this be the case, I am not able to make a stand against them. My command does not exceed forty men, and one half are sick."

Poling the unwieldy flat-bottomed boats upriver, the men tried to stay in the center of the stream, but the currents pushed them toward shore. On November 30, as the boats—now about 15 miles (24 km) south of Fort Scott—drifted once again toward the thickly forested banks, they were raked by musket fire. Numerous soldiers were killed as the Seminoles leaped from the woods and grabbed hold of the boats, grounding them in the shallow water near shore. What followed was an orgy of shooting, stabbing, knifing, and, finally, scalping, as the river ran thick with gore and shrieks pierced the mangrove swamps.

When it was over, forty whites were dead. Six soldiers escaped by swimming desperately through the water to the opposite shore, and one civilian, Elizabeth Stewart, was taken hostage. (Stewart was found alive by a rescue party seven months later, with no idea why her life had been spared.)

Thus, in the space of a little more than a week, the longest Indian war in U.S. history began. It was what would later become known as a guerilla war—fought in swampland and deep forest, with hit-and-run raids and ruthlessness on both sides. The war went on as long as it did, according to historians John Missall and Mary Lou Missall, because of "the sheer determination of the participants . . . The government was as determined to remove the Seminoles as the Seminoles were to resist that removal."

In the end, the U.S. government prevailed. And the near-extermination of the Seminoles became a blueprint for future American Indian wars.

"WILD ONES"

As far as Native American tribes went, the Seminoles were of a relatively recent origin. They were the remnants of tribes of the Creek Confederacy—a loose grouping of bands such as the Alabamas, Apalachicolas, Hitchitis, Oconis, and Chiahas, called Creeks by white traders who had to paddle up creeks to find them in their remote locations in what is now Georgia, Alabama, and Mississippi. These tribes themselves were the remnants of the once-grand southeast confederations that had been destroyed by European steel and, especially, European illnesses, in the centuries following Columbus landing in the New World.

The tribes that became known as the Seminoles was actually made up of several small bands of Native Americans—predominantly from the Creeks and related tribes—that began to drift into Florida at the beginning of the eighteenth century, gradually pushed south by British settlers. Florida at the time was a Spanish possession, even if the Spanish government, weakened by strife with the British, had abandoned most of the northern part of the state. There the tribes that would become the Seminoles settled, capturing and raising cattle the Spanish had left behind, hunting, farming, and raiding north into the British colonies, particularly Georgia, where settlers returned the favor by mounting numerous small attacks against the Seminoles. The Spanish called them *cimarrones*, meaning "wild ones" or "runaways," which eventually became corrupted into the word *Seminoles*.

And yet the Seminoles were not so wild. They were a matriarchal society that lived in log houses, some raised on stilts above the marshy ground. They practiced communal farming and raised horses. They were fierce warriors, but those white men who approached them unencumbered by prejudice found them generous hosts.

However, after the American Revolution, as more and more whites began to spread into the southeastern United States, the Seminoles became a hated tribe. This was in part due to the fact that runaway slaves took refuge across the border with the Seminoles, who refused to give them back to the white slave hunters who came looking for them. Many of the blacks were in fact also enslaved by the Seminoles, but with no shackles. They had the chance to marry and raise families, and their only real obligation was that of paying a yearly stipend to their owners. Being a slave to a Seminole was, in the words of John and Mary Lou Missall, "perhaps the best life that an British slave could hope for." Indeed, many former slaves became some of the best warriors the Seminoles had.

At the beginning of the nineteenth century, the Spanish hold on Florida was growing ever more tenuous. As the French Revolutionary Wars tore through Europe, Spain simply could not afford an overseas possession tied to the heart of an aggressively growing young country—a nation which, in 1804, bought most of the land west of the Mississippi from France, further isolating Spain in the Florida peninsula. Americans looked hungrily at the poorly protected land there. They considered the land mainly uninhabited—unless you counted the Seminoles, which most Americans in the southeast, General Andrew Jackson among them, most certainly did not.

"AN ENORMOUS LAND GRAB"

Andrew Jackson is one of those larger-than-life figures possessed of almost superhuman determination and a powerful ability to hate—much like Hannibal Barca—who can make long wars extend decades longer. Born in 1767 in South Carolina, Jackson did not so much experience as escape his childhood. He was raised on a hardscrabble farm and, as a boy of thirteen during the Revolutionary War, received a saber slash across the

PERRINE'S
NEW
MILITARY MAP
ILLUSTRATING THE
SEAT OF WAR.

Entered according to Act of Congress, in the year 1862, by
C. O. PERRINE,
in the Clerk's Office of the District Court of the State of Indiana.

SOUTHERN PART
OF
FLORIDA

Map Division
5 ~ JAN 1964
Library of Congress

forehead for refusing to shine a British officer's boots. He then survived smallpox and the deaths of both parents and two of his brothers.

Moving to Tennessee after the war, Jackson became a lawyer, landowner, and merchant, a congressman, and finally a U.S. senator, in 1797. During the War of 1812 against the British, Jackson was appointed a major general and began a ferocious campaign against the Creek, especially the militant Red Sticks warriors of Chief Red Eagle, who had taken advantage of the hostilities to attack the whites.

Finally cornering them in March 1814 at the Battle of Horseshoe Bend, in what is now Alabama, Jackson slaughtered hundreds of Red Sticks. Even though many of the Creek tribes had not sided with the Red Sticks, Jackson forced them all to sign a treaty giving the U.S. government 23 million acres (93,078 square km)—about three-fifths of the present state of

Charles O. Perrine's 1862 map "Illustrating the Seat of War" shows the key areas throughout Florida fought over by the U.S. Army and the elusive Seminoles. The Seminole Wars dragged on so long because of the tribe's intimate knowledge of the area and ability to disappear into its swamplands and elude the enemy.

Alabama and one-fifth of Georgia. It was, as one historian has written, "an enormous land grab [that] ensured the ultimate destruction of the entire Creek Nation."

And Jackson was only just getting started with the tribes of southeastern America. After vanquishing the British at the Battle of New Orleans in early January 1815, in the process ending the War of 1812 and becoming a national hero, he turned his eyes on the Cherokee and Choctaw, forcing them to cede 2 million acres (8,094 square km) of land in Georgia, Alabama, and Tennessee and making them remove their people to land in Arkansas and Oklahoma.

After that, the Seminoles loomed large in Jackson's range of vision. They refused to cede the whites land in southern Georgia that Jackson claimed had been given him by the Creeks. The Seminole habit of protecting runaway slaves and the fact that invading Florida would give him a pretext to confront the Spanish drove Andrew Jackson to war against the Seminoles. The massacre of Lieutenant Scott's detachment on the Apalachicola was all the incitement he needed.

"INSULTED OUR NATIONAL CHARACTER"

On December 28, 1817, about a month after the Scott party massacre, General Jackson received a letter from President James Monroe that read: "This day's mail will convey to you an order to repair to the command of the troops now acting against the Seminoles, a tribe which has long violated our rights & insulted our national character." Monroe then made the interesting statement: "This is not a time for you to think of [stopping]. Great interests are at issue. . . ."

Naturally, Jackson had to believe that "great interests" meant more than the conquest of the Seminoles—meant, in fact, the wresting of Florida itself from the Spanish. Still, he wanted to be clear what Monroe meant. He wrote back, saying: "Let it be signified to me through any channel . . . that the possession of the Floridas would be desirable to the United States, and in sixty days it will be accomplished."

Monroe never replied and later claimed that he was ill when he received Jackson's letter and did not even read it—not a likely claim. In retrospect, it seems clear that Monroe wanted Jackson to use the Seminoles as an excuse to bloody the Spanish in Florida (if not outright conquer them) but wanted to ensure deniability at the same time. In a sense, during this First Seminole War, the Seminoles were merely a pawn in a much larger game of empire.

In January 1818, Andrew Jackson set out for Fort Scott from Tennessee with 1,000 volunteers, arriving there in March after a grueling forty-six-day march over bad roads. At the fort were 500 regular army troops belonging to General Gaines's command as

President Andrew Jackson, shown in this c. 1896 chromolithograph, referred to the war with the Seminoles as "this Punic War" because of the length of the conflict. Both wars featured guerrilla tactics that served to drag out the fighting.

well as about 800 Georgia militia. Combined with about 1,400 Creek warriors who had sided with Jackson against the Seminoles, this was by far the most formidable force in the area. After provisioning his army, Jackson marched down the Apalachicola and entered Florida's Panhandle region about March 13, heading for the Seminole villages around Lake Miccosukee. The Seminoles faded away before Jackson, watching from hiding as he burned their town of Tallahassee on March 31.

On April 1, he attacked the town of Miccosukee, the largest Seminole habitation in the area, and nearly captured hundreds of Seminole men, women, and children. However, Jackson's men mistook friendly Creeks for Seminoles and, in the ensuing firefight, the real Seminoles escaped.

At this point, Jackson turned south and headed for the Spanish fort of St. Marks, about 10 miles (16 km) from the Gulf Coast. Jackson demanded that the Spanish commandant surrender the fort, claiming that he had aided and abetted the Seminoles. Greatly outnumbered, the Spanish commander surrendered to Jackson. Within the fort, Jackson found a British trader named Alexander Arbuthnot and two important Red Stick Creek and Seminole chiefs. He hung the chiefs immediately and would, on April 29, execute both Arbuthnot and another British trader named Robert Ambrister, allegedly for "inciting" the Seminoles against the Americans. The evidence for this was scanty at best.

Jackson now turned his attentions to the Seminole villages along the Suwannee River in east Florida. However, as he approached each one, the Seminoles inside fled into the woods and swamps, a classic guerilla avoidance of a larger and better-armed force. The only serious fight Jackson's troops had during the campaign was on April 12, on a village of Red Stick Native Americans that had fled to Florida after the Creek Wars. Jackson's troops killed forty Red Sticks and took 100 women and children captive.

As Jackson marched on, he was harassed on his flanks by a small force of black Seminoles—escaped slaves who had become warriors in the tribe. Once again, whenever the whites attacked, these fighters simply melted away into the northern Florida wilderness. Finally, having burned every Seminole town he could find, Jackson marched to the Spanish city of Pensacola, captured it on May 24, and notified President Monroe that the Seminole War was over. He had captured "the hot beds," he wrote, "essential to the peace and security of our frontier."

"AN EXERCISE IN FUTILITY"

Jackson's short foray into Florida accomplished a number of things—his execution of two of their citizens enraged the British government, while his show of force and capture of two Spanish forts convinced the Spanish government that Florida was going to be impossible to hang on to (and, in fact, it ceded Florida to the United States by treaty the following year). But one thing he did not in the least accomplish was the defeat of the Seminoles.

Jackson's actions in Florida were classic harbingers of long war. He destroyed the Seminoles' villages, made them destitute and homeless, but aside from the two chiefs he executed, he did not destroy the Seminole leadership at all, and he barely touched the rank and file of the tribes. In fact, he never once met the Seminoles in open battle, because they were careful to avoid the fate of the Red Sticks. The First Seminole War was, as the historian Joe Knetsch has written, "an exercise in futility."

The Americans did not even know how many Seminoles lived in Florida—a best guess at the time, although an overestimate, was 22,000, along with 5,000 black slaves—nor had they even explored the vast tracks of land in northern and eastern Florida where most whites had not been since the Spanish had retreated from that part of the country.

The Seminoles, for their part, took heart. Jackson and his army had not defeated them, and they now continued their cross-border raids into Georgia even as the Americans officially took over Florida from the Spanish in 1821, with Andrew Jackson named the state's first military governor. Although the cross-border raids were a nuisance, they did not yet add up to open war. The U.S. government instead mounted a policy of attempting to populate Florida with settlers—a tough sell for many Americans, because the climate, though temperate in the winter, was brutally hot in the summer, a time called "the sickly season" by many would-be homesteaders because of the prevalence of malaria and yellow fever. The government was also hampered by the fact that much of the territory it had inherited from Spain was unexplored, except along the coastlines.

The presence of the Seminoles further inhibited U.S. efforts to populate Florida, and for a time, the government attempted to parlay with them. In 1823, the government negotiated the Treaty of Moultrie Creek, giving the Seminoles a large tract of land in the center of Florida as a reservation, along with an annuity of $5,000 a year for twenty years, farm implements and livestock, a school, and even the services of a blacksmith, also for twenty years, by which time it was assumed the Seminoles would become farmers who posed no threat to the whites. The Seminoles also agreed—a major concession—to give back any runaway slaves who tried to join their tribes, as well as the slaves already with the tribes.

For the next three years, most of the Seminoles stayed on the reservation, but—as would happen repeatedly with Indian reservations the U.S. government set up in the West—there were serious problems. Not used to intensive farming as their sole way of survival, they were starving. The Seminoles still had not returned blacks who were longtime members of their people, and it seemed unlikely that they would. And

numerous bands of Indians who had not been signatory parties to the Treaty of Moultrie Creek continued to rove through Florida, attacking isolated white settlers.

However, until about 1830, relative peace reigned in Florida, which was slowly being filled with white settlers and land speculators. But in 1828, Andrew Jackson, the Seminoles' nemesis, was elected president of the United States and continued his longtime plan for dealing with the southeastern Indians by removing them west of the Mississippi River, to Arkansas and Oklahoma. In 1830, Congress passed the Indian Removal Act; in the next few years, Creeks, Cherokees, and other tribes signed "treaties" agreeing to what was essentially forcible emigration west.

"THE DISPLAY OF TOO LITTLE FORCE"

Faced with an extraordinary amount of pressure, many Seminole chiefs signed the Treaty of Payne's Landing in May of 1832. The treaty, which was ratified by the U.S. Senate in 1834, called for the Seminoles to move west by 1835. But a delegation of Seminole chiefs that went west for a visit to the Creek reservation in Arkansas came back extremely disillusioned—not only was the climate cold and arid, but also the Creeks insisted that their chiefs and their laws should govern the Seminoles. In the meantime, black Seminoles refused removal, claiming (and rightly so) that they would be taken back into slavery under the whites. Because many of them held powerful positions within the Seminole Nation, their voices convinced others to resist removal.

Late in 1834, government agents noticed that the Seminoles had taken most of their annual stipend and were buying guns and powder with it. Soldiers carrying mail between forts were attacked and killed. Even more significantly, a Seminole chief named Charlie Emathla, who had agreed to take his small band west, was murdered in 1835 on an isolated trail by a fellow Seminole who believed Emathla had betrayed his people. His killer was the fiery young Osceola, whom the whites would soon hear a great deal more from.

Despite these warning signs, the U.S. army had only 550 men in north and central Florida, augmented by perhaps 500 civilian militia, many of whom did not even possess muskets. Most of these soldiers were concentrated in isolated forts. From one of these, a commander wrote his superior: "We have fallen into the error committed at the Commencement of every Indian War: The display of too little force—the attempt to do too much with inadequate means."

The attempt to do too much with inadequate means. These are words that can apply to almost every long war between a larger developed nation and a supposedly smaller, less advanced one, from the Jewish-Roman Wars all the way to the French and American

Seminole leader Osceola posed for this oil portrait by artist George Catlin in 1838. Catlin painted him while he was imprisoned at Fort Moultrie, South Carolina. Osceloa died almost immediately after the sitting of a throat infection, and, in Catlin's opinion, a "broken spirit."

wars in Vietnam and beyond. It is an essential ingredient for long wars: underestimating one's less well-armed and well-organized enemy, thinking that Native Americans are far easier to crush than British regulars, that Afghani irregulars are no match for the queen's best regiments, that bombs can destroy Viet Cong hiding in jungles.

The Americans would pay for this miscalculation in the Second Seminole War—the longest single war they ever fought against the Native Americans—which started in the final weeks of 1835. On December 18, Osceola and a band of fifty or sixty warriors attacked a Florida militia supply wagon near Pensacola, killing eight and wounding six. Shortly afterward, a large force of Seminoles led by another charismatic leader, King Philip, attacked and destroyed a sugar plantation near St. Augustine.

Finally, in late December, a detachment of 110 troopers led by Major Francis Langhorne Dade was sent from Fort Brooke on Tampa Bay north to the more isolated Fort King in the center of the territory, which was being threatened by Seminoles. On the morning of December 28, Dade and his men were ambushed by about 180 Seminole warriors led by their chief Micanopy, firing from behind pine trees and palmettos. The whites took position behind a rude breastworks they had thrown up and fought back, but by mid-afternoon, Dade's force had been completely wiped out, except for two wounded soldiers who somehow managed to make it back to Fort Brooke.

The Dade Massacre, as the whites called it (to the Native Americans it was a victorious battle), was as well known in its day as Custer's Last Stand later became and set the tone for the bloody years of war that were to follow.

"AND THE BUZZARD LIVE UPON HIS FLESH"

As tensions mounted leading up to the Second Seminole War, the U.S. government decided to ban the sale of gunpowder to Seminoles—previously, only blacks had been refused the ability to buy gunpowder. Hearing of this, Osceola proclaimed: "The white man shall not make me black. I will make the white man red with blood; and then blacken him in the sun and rain . . . and the buzzard live upon his flesh."

Just as Andrew Jackson had become the pivotal warrior of the First Seminole War, Osceola was to become that warrior in the Second Seminole War—the man whose power, cunning, and courage kept the war going far longer than it might have otherwise. Many whites thought Osceola was the head of the Seminole Nation, but he was not. Instead, as the Missalls have written, "he became the 'war spirit' of the Seminoles, the one man who best defined their struggle." Osceola was born in 1804 and may have been part white—his mother had married a white trader named Billy Powell and Osceola was often referred to as Powell. The name Osceola is derived from the Creek name Asi-Yoholo; in fact, his mother was a Red Stick Creek and Osceola was one of the Creeks driven out of Georgia after Jackson's defeat of the Red Sticks at Horseshoe Bend.

In a sense, this mixed ancestry made him the perfect Seminole—of many origins, toughened by hardship, and determined not to leave yet another homeland he had found. He rose to become chief of a small band of Seminoles, about 100 or so, but his power extended far beyond them, because he was so articulate and because he was daring. Just before the Second Seminole War began, Osceola had been imprisoned overnight by a U.S. Indian agent named Wiley Thompson, with whom he had quarreled. Osceola vowed revenge and got it. Even as the Dade Massacre was occurring, he and a small band of warriors were waiting in the forest outside of Fort King. When Thompson and a friend stepped outside of the fort for an evening walk, Osceola and his men shot the agent fourteen times and killed his friend as well.

As 1835 ended, the news continued to be bad for the U.S. government. Seminoles led numerous coordinated attacks against white settlements on the east coast of Florida south of St. Augustine, essentially causing settlers to abandon the eastern coastline. General Duncan Clinch led a beefed-up force of some 750 Tennessee volunteers and regular army into Florida to find the Seminoles, but his fate signified the difficulties of fighting a guerilla force in its own country. The whites had very little idea of the nature of the land in Florida and had to depend on guides who were themselves Seminoles— who may or may not have been turncoats.

On his way to attack Indian settlements to the southwest of the Withlacoochee River, Clinch found himself, on New Year's Eve day, unable to cross the river because he could not find the ford. He decided to ferry his men across in a leaky canoe, the only water transport he had, six men at a time. Half of the men got across when they were ambushed by Seminoles hiding in a nearby hammock (one of the dense stands of hardwood trees that dotted the Florida marshland). A withering fire cut down the soldiers. With half their force still on the opposite bank, the regular army troops could not stay where they were and survive, and so they mounted a bayonet attack that forced the Seminoles back. But, stunned and bloodied, Clinch retreated, leaving the Seminole villages intact.

A SEASON OF DEFEAT

More setbacks followed for the whites, with Osceola leading numerous ambushes that devastated soldiers and settlers alike. Washington was forced to mobilize as quickly as possible. A respected officer, General Winfield Scott, was placed in charge of the war effort in Florida. Scott ordered General Edmund Gaines to march from New Orleans with 1,100 men to attack the Seminoles, but Gaines found himself at the exact same unfordable spot on the Withlacoochee Clinch had arrived at just two months previously.

This time, Gaines sent men out to discover the ford, but when he attempted to cross, a waiting ambush of Seminoles led by Osceola himself began to cut his men down. It was a sizable force—perhaps 1,500—and after taking losses Gaines quickly built a small fortification and hunkered down for a siege. First, however, he sent a message to General Clinch in a nearby fort, telling him to come and attack the Seminoles from the rear.

This was a plan that might have worked, because the Seminoles were unused to tactical maneuvering, but Winfield Scott was a meticulous and even prissy soldier (his men called him "Old Fuss and Feathers") and tended to move slowly. By the time he gave Clinch the okay to come after Osceola, Gaines's men were starving, and the Native Americans, once again undefeated, had withdrawn. Winfield Scott then made his invasion of Florida with three columns of men totaling 5,000, and managed to cross the Withlacoochee without incident, but in what would become a pattern for the war, they simply could not find the Seminoles, who had melted away into the marshland and hammocks, ready to fight on their own terms.

The Seminoles used their superior knowledge of the landscape to extend the war against an enemy they could not possibly hope to best in open, set-piece combat. While Scott's men blundered through eastern Florida looking for him, Osceola and 250 warriors attacked Fort Defiance on June 9, being driven off only after a fierce fight in the broiling sun. The Seminoles even attacked the lighthouse at Key Biscayne, near present-day Miami, burning it down in hopes of luring ships to crash upon the shores.

As full summer's fierce heat hit them, the army began to retreat, abandoning garrisons such as Fort Alabama, Fort Defiance, and Fort King. The "sickly season" was upon them and men began to drop with fever like flies. By the time 1836 came to a close, Winfield Scott had abandoned his attempts to destroy the Seminoles and was replaced by General Thomas Jesup.

"OUR HOPES ARE ALL BLASTED"

Jesup tried—as many a commander in long guerilla wars after him would try—to beat the Seminoles by different tactics. He increased his forces to 7,000 men and sent smaller parties, instead of large columns, deep into the Florida wilderness, tirelessly pursuing the Seminoles. He was unscrupulous, playing on Southern fears of a slave uprising to garner a large volunteer militia force. (Jesup told the governor of Georgia: "This is a negro . . . not an Indian war.")

He kept his men constantly on the guard, so easy victories that the Seminoles had earlier won through surprise were harder to come by. Burning villages and driving off livestock wherever he found them, he finally convinced hundreds of Seminoles to agree to being removed to the west. In June, 700 Seminoles were being held in a detention camp near Fort Brooke, preparing for their journey west, but the poorly defended camp was attacked by Osceola, another Seminole leader named Sam Jones, and 200 followers, who freed those in detention and led them back into the wilderness.

Because there were perhaps only 1,500 Seminole fighters in Florida, these 700 restored nearly 50 percent of their fighting force. It was a daring raid that extended the war, a fact recognized by the whites at the time. One Southern newspaper headline read: "Our hopes are all blasted. We have war again."

Jesup wasn't giving up easily, however, and he could be ruthless. He kept up the pressure on the Seminoles on all fronts and began to find, somewhat to his surprise, that many black Seminoles were surrendering. Living constantly on the run, unable to enjoy familiar comforts and hunt and grow crops, many blacks had been brought to starvation level, particularly those who were less well assimilated into the tribes. Many Seminoles, hiding deep in the swamps, had the same issues and were willing to talk.

In October, Osceola, who was apparently ill, agreed to come to meet a white commander near St. Augustine under a white flag, to negotiate a possible truce agreement. Under Jesup's direct orders, Osceola was arrested, put in irons, and brought to the fortress in St. Augustine (he was later transferred to Charleston, South Carolina). Even the whites were horrified by Jesup's tactics—a white flag of truce was a respected convention of war—but Jesup robbed the Seminoles of their chief war leader. Osceola died of malaria three months later.

In a sense, however, Jesup's actions prolonged the war. It is possible Osceola would have died of illness anyway (it is hard to imagine a healthy Osceola wanting to parlay) and having been taken prisoner in a way that even whites considered unfair made him more of a martyr to Seminoles, some of whom had not even approved of his firebrand tactics. The war would go on, and it would get bloodier.

Seminole chief Billy Bowlegs, shown here in an 1895 photographic print by Arthur P. Lewis, and a few hundred Seminoles tried to live peacefully in the Big Cypress Swamp area in Florida. The federal government offered them hundreds of thousands of dollars to move, but the Seminoles refused, so powerfully attached were they to their land.

Library of Congress

"DISEASE UNKNOWN"

In the months and years that followed, the Americans tried everything to bring the Seminoles to heel and drag them westward. In the Battle of Lake Okeechobee, on Christmas Day 1837, Sam Jones and his Seminoles were defeated in what the whites claimed was a major setback—but only a dozen Seminoles had been killed before the rest disappeared into the swamps. Ferocious fighting continued, with the Seminoles continuing to prey on small army posts and isolated settlements. Governor Robert Reid of Florida, seeking to fan hatred of the Seminoles, described in a letter to the Florida legislative council the scene of one such settler massacre near the Apalachicola River:

> I found Mrs. H., lying prostrate on the ground . . . with her throat cut, a ball shot through her arm, one in her back, and a fatal shot in the head . . . Her youngest son . . . lay near her side, with his skull fractured by a pine stick which lay near him. He exhibited signs of life . . . and faint hopes are now entertained of his recovery. Had you witnessed the heart-rending sight of Mr. H. embracing his little son and calling him by his nickname, 'Buddy! Buddy! Buddy!' . . . and then running to the corpse of his wife, throwing his arms around her, crying out, 'My wife! My dear wife! Oh! my dear wife!' I know your feelings would have given way as mine did.

Starving and hungry, a large band of Seminoles approached General Jesup in 1838 with the idea that they would cease fighting if they could only just stay where they were, in the wilderness south of Lake Okeechobee, and Jesup, knowing what fierce fighters they were, agreed to take the request to his superiors in Washington. However, the U.S. government, refusing to countenance any such idea, ordered Jesup to continue his campaign.

Jesup, seeing little hope for the kind of victory Washington wanted, asked to be relieved of his command, and was replaced by General Zachary Taylor, future hero of the Mexican War and president of the United States. Taylor's plan was as good as Jesup's had been—to garrison Florida with dozens of tiny forts and constantly patrol Seminole territory, even to the extent of penetrating the Everglades and the Big Cypress Swamp, where the remnants of the Seminoles were deeply hidden.

It did little good. After two years of bloody yet inconclusive guerilla warfare, Zachary Taylor left in 1840 and still the war went on. It took its toll on both sides. Three hundred army officers had resigned since the beginning of the conflict in 1832. What we would call combat fatigue or post-traumatic stress was at an all-time high. After a march through the steaming Everglade swamps in search of Seminoles, one officer, a colonel, went into his tent and ran his sword through his eye and into his brain. His official cause of death? "Disease unknown." Another later wrote in a letter home: "Florida is certainly the poorest country that ever two people quarreled over. It is in fact a hideous region to live in . . . why not in the name of common sense let the Native Americans have it?"

Ultimately, however, the Seminoles suffered more than the whites did. Fewer in number and resources, on the run for years from adversaries who were now employing bloodhounds to hunt them down, most of them surrendered in 1842 and agreed to be transported west. Three thousand Seminole men, women, and children were transported, leaving several hundred deep in the swamps of southern Florida, led by men like Sam Jones (nearly ninety years old) and Billy Bowlegs, a hereditary chief. The war had cost the United States nearly 1,500 dead, although 1,100 of these had died of disease. It had cost the United States treasury $30 million.

And it still wasn't over.

BILLY BOWLEGS AND THE BITTER END

On the face of it, Billy Bowlegs was an odd name for a fearsome warrior, but that is only what the whites called him—not because he rode horses excessively but because the Seminole chief who preceded him was named Bolek. Born in 1810, Billy was known to the Seminoles as Holato Mico, or Halpuda Mikko, meaning "the Alligator Chief." Billy had fought bravely during the Second Seminole War and was one of the few powerful Seminole chiefs left from that period.

Following the end of the war in 1842, he and a few hundred followers attempted to live peacefully in the Big Cypress Swamp, but the federal government never ceased in its efforts to try to convince Billy to remove himself and his tribe west. In 1852 and again in 1854, Billy and other chiefs were taken to Washington, to show them the might of the federal government, and offered literally hundreds of thousands of dollars to move their tribes. Yet these Seminoles refused, so powerfully attached were they to their land. And it is a testament to the ferocity of the Seminole warrior that Washington felt so threatened by such a small group.

The army also tried more forceful persuasion, building forts on Seminole territory and constantly patrolling Seminole hunting paths. This was bound to lead to a confrontation, and it did. In December 1855, a small patrol of U.S. soldiers under Lieutenant George Hartsuff came upon what they thought was a deserted Seminole village and, seeing bananas growing, helped themselves to bunches of them. In another version of the story, however, they rampaged through the banana cultivations, destroying them. It is still not entirely clear what happened.

In any event, the village was not deserted—the Seminoles had simply fled as the patrol came through—and when they discovered the theft or destruction, they attacked the soldiers' camp, killing four men. The Third, and last, Seminole War had now begun. Some historians believe that Hartsuff's patrol was a deliberate provocation, hoping to incite just such an incident—to "see old Billy cut up," as one soldier wrote home later—but there is no real proof of this.

What is real is that an already long war was extended even further because a powerful nation was terrified of a few hundred Indians, many of whom lived impoverished lives in swampy and inaccessible areas. Compared to the Second Seminole War, the Third was small change. Once again, federal troops and bloodhounds poured into the area, and once again the Seminoles, led by Billy Bowlegs, eluded them and struck isolated outposts in southwestern Florida. The war lasted two and a half years and involved no major battles; instead, it was bloody ambush after bloody ambush, with whites and Seminoles being picked off one by one. Children on both sides were killed. Both sides began the dreadful practice of scalping their enemies alive. Finally, leading a hunted life became too much for most of the Seminoles, and Billy Bowlegs and his followers surrendered in May 1858. Thirty-eight warriors and eighty-five women and children boarded a steamer that took them to Oklahoma. Billy Bowlegs would die there of disease a year later.

AN ALREADY LONG WAR WAS EXTENDED EVEN FURTHER BECAUSE A POWERFUL NATION WAS TERRIFIED OF A FEW HUNDRED INDIANS, MANY OF WHOM LIVED IMPOVERISHED LIVES IN SWAMPY AND INACCESSIBLE AREAS.

After forty years of war, most of the Seminoles had been destroyed, but a band of 150 or so remained in Florida, stubbornly refusing to move, remaining in hiding deep in the swamps. They became famous in U.S. history. As time went on and the Native Americans of the Far West were subdued—in some cases almost erased from the face of the earth—the Seminoles and leaders such as Osceola took on a romantic aura for the very people who had done so much to destroy them. They were the Native Americans who never surrendered, and their names dot Florida towns, rivers, and auto dealerships.

But little was romantic about what happened to the Seminoles. In a long and grinding war of attrition against an intractable foe, they were vanquished.

U.S. troops travel by boat as Seminoles hide on the shore during the Seminole Wars in Florida in this circa 1845 painting by John F. Clymer. The conflict led to the near extinction of the Seminoles.

CHAPTER 9

THE ANGLO-AFGHAN WARS

"THE GREAT GAME"

1839–1919

This fifty-year-long war began in 1839 when the British attempted to remove an Afghan emir, fearing the Russian influence over him. The bloody war that broke out waged throughout the nineteenth century and saw Great Britain facing similar difficulties to what the Russians and Americans have faced in the twentieth and twenty-first centuries.

In 1808 Mountstuart Elphinstone, a twenty-nine-year-old Scottish political affairs officer who worked for the British Raj in India, was sent as an envoy into the mysterious country of Afghanistan—the "Kingdom of Caubul," as the British thought of it at the time—to contact its ruler, Shah Shuja-ol-muk.

He took with him 400 Anglo-Indian soldiers as well as 600 camels and twelve elephants carrying expensive presents for the shah. Huge crowds of curious people met him as he entered Peshawar, the shah's winter capital—most Afghans had never seen an Englishman before. However, the fine fowling pieces and bolts of cloth Elphinstone carried with him on his elephants could not begin to compare with what he found the Afghan king wearing: a crown with 9-inch (23 cm)-long spikes covered with diamonds and a suit of armor speckled with emeralds. From a bracelet around the shah's wrist dangled a brilliant gem, the 104-carat Koh-i-noor diamond, which supposedly carries a curse that the owner will possess the world but also suffer misfortunes.

The fact that the Koh-i-noor would by 1850 become a prize specimen in the British crown jewels, to be worn by Queen Victoria and later Queen Elizabeth (for the curse is rumored to strike only men, not women), should not in any way be construed to mean that Afghanistan would also become a jewel in the British crown. In seventy years of long and bloody warfare, the best the British could do was keep parts of the country pacified, while much of the rest of the land bided its time, waiting to rise again.

Like many foreigners who fought over the land later, the British found Afghanistan to be a country of contradictions. As one British officer was to write: "Sensuality of the grossest kind and murder, abominable cruelty, treachery or violent death are never long absent from the thoughts of a people than whom none in the world are more delightful companions or of simpler, gentler appearance."

"THE GREAT GAME"

Afghanistan has always been a land warred over by great powers. Lying between Persia (modern-day Iran) on the west and India on the east, with the old khanates of Central Asia to the north—Khiva, Bukhara, and Samarkand—it was an ancient invasion route to the rich plains of India. The rugged Hindu Kush mountains run across the center of the country, making such passages difficult, and Afghani tribespeople—fiercely clannish and murderous in their anger—have resisted any attempts to conquer them. Yet, as the British empire builders in India were all too aware at the beginning of the nineteenth century, every successful invasion of India from Alexander the Great onward had come through Afghanistan, from the northwest. And to the northwest lay the burgeoning new power of Russia.

It is true that invasions have found their way through the rugged landscape of Afghanistan, but few invaders have ever stayed. In their wars in Afghanistan in the nineteenth century, the British would find the conflicts hopelessly lengthened and ultimately unresolved due to a similar series of issues that faced the invading Russians in the 1980s and the U.S.-led coalition forces in the first decade of the twenty-first century. Imperial powers move slowly over difficult terrain, tribespeople use the landscape to disappear following hit-and-run tactics, and—as the British discovered—Islamic warriors on a jihad do not know the meaning of defeat.

The reasons for Elphinstone's 1808 mission to Afghanistan were relatively simple. Napoleon Bonaparte of France and Tsar Alexander I had signed an 1807 treaty (the Treaty of Tilsit), which made them allies against the British. And there could be no greater prize for a combined French-Russian attack against the British in the east than India, the colony that was destined to become "the jewel in the crown." Such an attack, launched in Persia, would have to come through Afghanistan. Therefore, Elphinstone was in the mysterious country to prevail upon Shah Shuja to sign a treaty of friendship with the British, in which he promised to oppose any foreign troops attempting to pass through Afghanistan. Unfortunately for the British, the shah was deposed in a coup shortly after signing such a treaty in June 1809 and Afghan disintegrated into civil war, unable to provide the British with a needed buffer against foreign aggression.

Even though a combined Russian-French invasion of India never materialized—for Great Britain was to defeat France and vanquish Napoleon at the Battle of Waterloo in 1815—the Russians marched steadily southward through the Caucasus, defeating Persia in numerous important battles so that, by the early 1830s it essentially controlled the Persian shah and ruling dynasty in Tehran. As one British politician put it, "The resources of Persia [are] at the disposal of the Court of St. Petersburg."

For their part, the Russians did not appreciate the British interfering with what Russian tsars thought of as their "Eastern Destiny" by making steady advances in the area east of Afghanistan, in what is now Pakistan—Punjab and Baluchistan. Inexorably, both countries were encroaching on each other's dreams of empire, and Afghanistan lay between them. Thus, in the 1830s, what became known as "the Great Game"—a name popularized by Rudyard Kipling in his 1901 novel *Kim*, but actually coined by a British intelligence officer—began. The Great Game involved geopolitical maneuvering on a grand scale, in which each country attempted to thwart the ambitions of the other through spying, subterfuge, and the threatening or bribing of allies. What neither Russia nor, especially, Great Britain counted on was the formidable fighting spirit and utter tenacity of the Afghanistan people.

"AUCKLAND'S FOLLY"

By the late 1830s, both Britain and Russia had powerful agents in Kabul, attempting to influence Dost Mohammad, the capable ruler who had taken control of the Afghanistan capital and much of the surrounding countryside. The Russian envoy was Captain Ivan Viktorovich Vitkevich, while the British spy was Captain Alexander Burnes. Both men, in the time-honored tradition of espionage, were supposedly there to open trade missions, but, in fact, each wanted Dost Mohammad's support.

Alexander Burnes was a dashing character, thirty-two years old, who had made his name and fortune as an explorer, traveling through Afghanistan in native dress. He was brave, intelligent, and sensitive to the chaotic Afghan political scene, the shifting alliances between tribes, and power struggles between leaders (although he had a weakness for Afghan women, which would ultimately prove fatal). Burnes recognized Dost Mohammad as a strong leader and advised the British to back him, but in the blunder that would lead to the First Afghan War, the British governor-general of India, Lord Auckland, placed harsh terms upon the Afghan leader, insisting that Dost Mohammad sever all ties with the Russians, oust Vitkevich from his capital, and also make peace on less than honorable terms with the Hindu Sikhs, who had been pushing into Afghanistan from the east.

This British map from the late nineteenth or early twentieth century shows both Afghanistan's strategic location and its mountainous terrain. The British sought to use Afghanistan as a buffer against foreign aggression. However, Imperial powers move slowly over difficult terrain, tribespeople use the landscape to disappear following hit-and-run tactics, and—as the British discovered—Islamic warriors on a jihad do not know the meaning of defeat.

Reproduced from *Afghanistan From Darius to Amanullah* (1929)

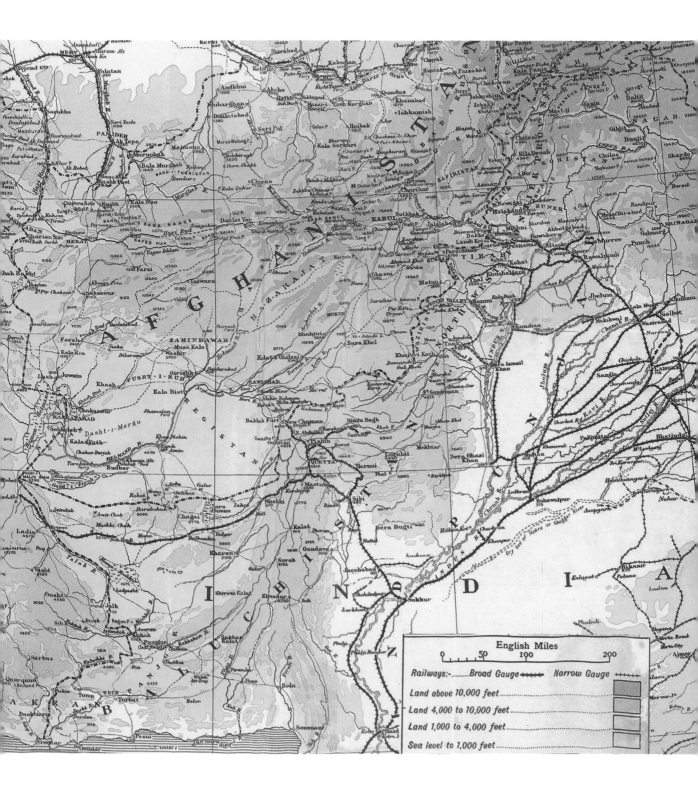

English Miles

0	50	100	200

Railways:- Broad Gauge ━━━━━ Narrow Gauge ━━━━━

Land above 10,000 feet

Land 4,000 to 10,000 feet

Land 1,000 to 4,000 feet

Sea level to 1,000 feet

When Dost Mohammad naturally refused to accept these terms, Auckland decided to bring back former Afghan leader Shah Shuja, who had been leading a life of exile in India, protected by the British, and had not ruled in Afghanistan for almost thirty years. Placing a puppet ruler on the throne of a sovereign country is a tactic used by imperial powers in long guerilla wars—see the Vietnam Wars, chapter 10—but it generally backfires and tends to extend the cycle of violence. The people over whom the puppet is placed naturally tend to resent this and rebel, while the puppet himself tends to be weak—after all, he is a puppet—and far too dependent on his puppeteer. The result is confusion and violence.

In October 1838, Lord Auckland issued his Simla Manifesto—Simla was the summer capital of the British Raj—laying forth the reasons why the British were sending troops into Afghanistan along with Shah Shuja. To keep India safe from foreign aggression, he said, Britain needed a strong leader in Kabul. Auckland also claimed that British troops would leave Afghanistan as soon as the shah was placed back on his throne. The British, Auckland said, were not invading Afghanistan, merely protecting what they saw as its legitimate leader from "foreign interference and factious opposition."

The Afghans greeted Auckland's claims with derision, but the British were at the height of their power and arrogance. The young Queen Victoria had just been crowned a few months before and it seemed the empire could do anything. However, within a few years, Auckland's decision on Afghanistan would be known as "Auckland's Folly." The old Afghan hand Mountstuart Elphinstone was one of the few Britons to protest at the time, issuing a warning: "I have no doubt you will take Candahar and Caubul and set up Shuja; but for maintaining him in a poor, cold, strong and remote country, among a turbulent people like the Afghans, I own it seems to me hopeless . . . I have never known a close alliance between a civilized and an uncivilized state that did not end in mutual hatred in three years."

Prescient words, but no one paid attention.

"THE KING'S EXECUTIONERS AMUSED THEMSELVES"

In December 1838, a mixed force of British, Bengali, and Sikh troops sent out from different locations in the Punjab and India entered Afghanistan by way of the southern Bolan Pass and hooked up with each other near Quetta, in southwestern Afghanistan, in April 1839. The Army of the Indus, as it was called, numbered some 20,000 fighting men and thousands of camp followers—wives and children, as well as cooks, personal servants, peddlers, and prostitutes.

At first the march was successful. The size of the invading army so frightened the defenders of the strategic city of Kandahar in late April that they fled to Russian protection in Persia. The Army of the Indus then moved north for Kabul without opposition, but even so, the British were already beginning to understand how hard things were going to be in Afghanistan. When Shah Shuja held ceremonial parades in the towns they passed, few people turned out to see him; it was apparent that no one was longing for his triumphal return after thirty years. So many camp followers died of starvation along the rugged line of march that "jackals fattened" on their remains. As an unexpected difficulty, there was little wood available in the rocky vastness of the country, so that when a Hindu died, there was no way to cremate the body, as religious dictates called for, causing numerous Sikh desertions.

In July, British forces attacked the Afghan fortress city of Ghazni, where the defenders, led by Akbar Khan, one of Dost Mohammad's sons, put up a spirited battle. British forces won the day and entered the city, forcing its surrender and capturing nearly 1,600 prisoners. These prisoners were treated well, except, one British officer noted, for a group of fifty men, all wearing black shirts, whom the shah ordered beheaded. The officer had stumbled on this horrid scene as he walked through the fortress. He watched as "the King's executioners amused themselves with hacking and maiming the poor wretches indiscriminately with the long swords and knives."

What the officer did not realize what that these black-shirted Afghan fighters were *ghazis*, Islamic fundamentalists fighting a holy war against the infidel—both Christian and Hindu—intruders. In a prefiguring of the wars that would wrack Afghanistan at the end of the twentieth century and the beginning of the twenty-first, Dost Mohammad had called for a jihad against the invaders. Led by fanatical clerics, or mullahs, who promised martyrdom if they died in battle, these ghazis would become more and more a factor in the British battle against the Afghans. The ghazis were, in the words of historian David Loyn, "men prepared to die for a cause bigger than Afghan nationalism, and the forerunners of al-Qaeda." Shah Shuja was taking no chances with such fighters—he had ordered all of them to be killed immediately

"LET HIM RULE US IF HE CAN"

After the British victory at Ghazni, Dost Mohammad fled with his forces to Bukhara, and the British carried Shah Shuja to Kabul in triumph, entering the city in August 1839. However, what should have been apparent earlier became clear to the British now—the shah had little local support and depended completely on the British military presence to shore him up. A powerful Afghan leader told the British: "You have brought [Shah Shuja] by your money and arms into Afghanistan. Leave him now with us Afghans and let him rule us if he can."

But, of course, the British did not dare leave the shah to his own devices. They became an occupying force, but, as is typical of long guerilla wars, one with power mainly centered in Kabul and a few other fortress towns. Outside, in the Afghanistan wilderness, ghazis and other tribal fighters ruled. Although Dost Mohammad was defeated in late 1840, and eventually surrendered to the British, going into exile in India, the insurgency against the British not only continued but also gathered strength. "This country is one mass of loose gunpowder," wrote Sir William Hay Macnaghten, head British political officer in Kabul.

Much of the fighting British troops had to put down took place in Helmand province in the southwestern part of the country, where fighting rages today between coalition forces and the Taliban. Ironically enough, Britain was so preoccupied with trying to contain Afghan tribal fighters that Russia was able to continue its inroads into Central Asia, strengthening its hold on Persia and beginning to move into Khiva to the north—exactly the opposite of the results that the British desired.

The Afghan guerilla fighters were formidable. Armed with *jezails*—long muskets that they fired with deadly accuracy—they practiced classic hit-and-run tactics, striking at British forces from hidden positions high in mountain passes, then vanishing, only to reappear and strike again. Numerous skirmishes and battles took their toll on British forces, making duty in Afghanistan a highly dangerous one. The Afghans took few prisoners and their women scoured battlefields for British wounded, armed with long knives. It did not do to be caught alive by these women. As Kipling wrote in his poem "The Young British Soldier":

> When you're wounded and left on Afghanistan's plains
> And the women come out to cut up what remains
> Jest roll to your rifle and blow out your brains
> An' go to your Gawd like a soldier.

But, back in Kabul, British officers and their ladies tried to act as if theirs was a normal posting in some colonial town—they avidly pursued horse racing and cricket. Yet Afghan intrigue and the usual bumbling of senior British officials in Afghanistan conspired to make their lives far more dangerous than they knew. In the summer of 1841, Sir William Hay Macnaghten cut in half the subsidies paid to local tribal chieftains—essentially bribes to keep them on the British side—because London had decided the war was becoming far too expensive. Thoroughly sick of Afghans and Afghanistan, Macnaghten was ready to head back to India to assume a new post in the

George Eden, the first Earl of Auckland, is shown in an 1815 engraving by George Stodart. In a major blunder, Eden's insistence that Afghanistan sever all ties with Russia led the British to install a puppet ruler—and resulted in Afghan resentment, internal uprisings, guerilla attacks, and prolonged conflict.

Getty Images

fall of 1841; Sir Alexander Burnes, who had been knighted by the queen and was now a lieutenant colonel, would take his place as head political officer in Kabul. Burnes had once had a good reputation among the Afghans, but now he was soundly reviled, as rumors, mainly true, spread through Kabul that he had dallied with numerous Afghan women, including the wife of a powerful tribal chieftain.

Right around this time, the warlike Ghilzai clan, which controlled the passes in eastern Afghanistan leading to Peshawar and safety in India, rebelled because their subsidy was cut; they attacked and ransacked a British supply caravan. If they continued to rampage, they would close off access to India. Macnaghten therefore sent Brigadier Robert Sale to give the Ghilzai a "trouncing," but Sale—a brave soldier known as "Fighting Bob" who left his wife, Lady Sale, behind in Kabul—was caught in late October in an ambush on a mountain pass. Sale eventually fought out of this ambush, although his column took sixty-seven casualties and he himself was wounded in the leg. He cornered the Ghilzai on October 22 and was ready to make a final charge that would destroy them, when George MacGregor, his political officer, made a deal with the Ghilzai leader, promising to give him his full British subsidy again if he and his men would protect the passes out of the country.

BETRAYAL

This turned out to be a major mistake, because the Ghilzai, merely buying time, had no intention of keeping such a deal—and it made the British appear weak, as if they were buying protection from their enemies. Within a week, the Ghilzai had regrouped and were attacking British columns again. On the evening of November 1, a different drama played itself out in Kabul. A powerful Afghan clan chief accused Alexander Burnes's men of abducting his favorite mistress, claiming Burnes had aided and abetted in the kidnap, as well as other indignities perpetrated against Afghan women. Early in the morning of November 2, an angry mob attacked Burnes outside his house and stabbed him to death along with his brother, who had fought to protect him.

The uprising in Kabul now became general and the British in the town made haste to retire to their cantonment, just north of Kabul. The army in Kabul was commanded by the aging and somewhat infirm General William Elphinstone (a cousin to Mountstuart), who was indecisive from the start—his favored response to the apocalyptically bad news going on around him was: "This is most distressing!" The cantonment was not a fort, but rather a large area about 1,200 by 600 yards (1,097 by 548.6 m), protected by ditches and low walls that could be scaled by anyone "with the facility of a cat," as one British officer wrote sarcastically. There were several small British forts in the area, which were the scene of savage fighting with Afghan tribal forces—numbering as many as 20,000—that were closing in around the Kabul cantonment. With General Sale forced to retire to Jalalabad, in what is now eastern Pakistan, to keep from being surrounded and destroyed by his enemies, Kabul was without protection.

In December, Sir William Hay Macnaghten made an agreement with Akbar Mohammad, Dost Mohammad's son and leader of the surrounding Afghan forces, which stated that the British would evacuate Kabul if the Afghans supplied the now-starving garrison with rations. The Afghans did not live up to their part of the bargain, but requested another parlay, this time on December 23, which Macnaghten was to attend personally.

THE ARMY IN KABUL WAS COMMANDED BY THE AGING AND SOMEWHAT INFIRM GENERAL WILLIAM ELPHINSTONE, WHO WAS INDECISIVE FROM THE START—HIS FAVORED RESPONSE TO THE APOCALYPTICALLY BAD NEWS GOING ON AROUND HIM WAS: "THIS IS MOST DISTRESSING!"

Despite being warned about possible Afghan treachery, Macnaghten showed up with several of his officers. The Afghans seized them all and Akbar Mohammad personally murdered Macnaghten on the spot. Macnaghten's body was then dismembered. His head was put on a pike, while his bloody hands were waved mockingly in front of his former officers, now prisoners. His torso was paraded through Kabul's Great Bazaar, within sight of the British watching through spyglasses from their cantonment.

THE RETREAT FROM KABUL

There followed an episode that would become famous in British history—the epic retreat of 700 British troops, 34 British women and children, 3,500 Indian and Sikh soldiers, and 12,000 camp followers from Kabul. Under supposed safe passage granted by Akbar Mohammad, the British left Kabul in falling snow and subfreezing weather early on the morning of January 6, 1842, their destination being Jalalabad. Within two days, after the Afghans had finished looting the cantonment, they had set upon the British, harassing them along their line of march, and demanding hostages and any valuable goods the British still had with them. The Afghan tribes used treachery as a weapon; with little choice but to trust them, General Elphinstone acceded to their demands, and then the killing began all over again.

After living in exile for thirty years in India, Shah Shuja-ol-muk was brought back to power by the British as a puppet ruler who would protect their interests in Afghanistan. The Shah had little local support and depended completely on the British military presence to shore him up; concurrently, the insurgency against the British gathered strength.

Reproduced from *Afghanistan From Darius to Amanullah* (1929)

When the column reached the Khoord Kabul Pass on January 8, they camped overnight, exhausted. They had left a trail of dead and dying behind in the freezing weather; the air in the mountains was so cold that "frost tortured every sensitive limb," as one survivor wrote. Now more a mob than an army, masses of camp followers and soldiers poured through the pass at first light, only to be attacked by Ghilzai tribesmen, who ambushed them. During the course of a day's fighting, 3,000 of the Indian soldiers lost their lives, as did thousands more camp followers. The corpses were so thick that Lady Sale, Fighting Bob Sale's wife, wounded in the wrist, had to carefully pick her way along the pass, lest she step on former comrades.

Akbar Mohammad then sent a message suggesting that the British allow him to take all the British women and children present, for safe passage. Although Elphinstone and the surviving British officers could not trust him, they felt they had no alternative, and so turned over Lady Sale and the other civilians. The march toward Jalalabad continued through a rocky wilderness dotted with the corpses of those who had gone too far in front of the column and were picked off by Ghilzai tribesmen. Akbar continued to insist that the British simply surrender to him. But he and his chiefs were, as one British civilian survivor later wrote, driven by such hatred of the British that all that would satisfy them was "extermination." A factor in all long wars, from the Punic Wars on, is such extreme hatred. Although they could be almost assured that the British government would retaliate, the Afghans wanted nothing but blood. Even though Elphinstone and many of his officers finally surrendered (to die in captivity), the rest of the Army of the Indus was methodically butchered as it struggled along.

After a last stand of twenty officers and forty-five men of the 44th Foot Regiment on a rocky hillside near Gandamak on January 13, six British officers escaped being slaughtered. Five of them were killed as they rode for Jalalabad. Only one man, a badly wounded army surgeon named Dr. William Brydon, survived to ride into Jalalabad late that afternoon.

ARMY OF RETRIBUTION

Of course, what the British were already calling the Army of Retribution was preparing itself to march into Afghanistan, free the British hostages, and deal a fatal blow to the tribesmen who had fought them so bitterly. Led by General George Pollock, the army, raised with troops rushed from India, attacked from Peshawar in April 1842, finally reaching Kabul in September after heavy fighting. For much of the journey, the British and Indian troops had to make their way through the skeletons of the Army of Indus soldiers and camp followers who had been killed on the retreat from Kabul. As a macabre joke, Afghan tribesmen often set up tableaus of these skeletons conversing with each other or embracing. Because many of the dead were friends and family members of those in the Army of Retribution, such desecration naturally stirred resentment. When the British reached villages whose tribes had taken part in the massacre, they destroyed them and indiscriminately slaughtered all inhabitants—men, women, and children. The cycle of violence, essential for long wars, therefore continued.

Arriving in Kabul, with all British hostages now freed (including the indomitable Lady Sale, who survived to be reunited with her husband and write a popular memoir of her experiences), the British systematically destroyed the Great Bazaar, held a victory celebration, and then simply departed the country. Most Afghans were puzzled by this behavior. What had the British won if they were leaving so soon?

Shah Shuja had already been murdered by forces loyal to Dost Mohammad, who was now returned to power in Kabul. He said to Lord Ellenborough, commander of the Army of Retribution: "I have been struck with the magnitude of your resources, your ships, your arsenals; but what I cannot understand is why the rulers of an empire so vast and flourishing should have come across the Indus to deprive me of my poor and barren country."

What the Afghans did understand was that the British were leaving—afraid to stay in Afghanistan—and this gave them great hope for the future. (As it did other people of the region who had once thought the British Raj invincible; the Sikhs were to rebel three years later and the Indians would stage their Great Mutiny within fifteen years.) However, the essential issue of the First Anglo-Afghan War for the British—keeping the Russians at bay—remained undecided. The spectacularly unsuccessful war had done little to stop the Russian Bear. In 1842, the Russians were on the other side of the Aral Sea, in Khiva, from Afghanistan. Thirty years later, they would arrive on the shores of the Oxus River, thus bringing their borders into direct contact with Afghanistan.

"MASTERLY INACTIVITY"

During the period between the First and Second Anglo-Afghan Wars, the British had been leery about becoming involved again in Afghanistan, despite the Russian advances in the north. They had pursued a policy that, in a phrase coined by a British scholar at the time, was called "masterly inactivity." There were numerous upheavals in Afghanistan during the thirty years after the First Anglo-Afghan War, during which

Dost Mohammad fought against rivals to consolidate his hold on the country, but the Liberal Party, which had taken over the British government in 1868, decided that any interference with the internal affairs of Afghanistan was unwise. British military planners at the time even began to understand that if Russia invaded Afghanistan, she would find herself in the same position as the British had in 1848—and that the British might even be able to act as liberators toward an Afghanistan under Russian thrall.

When Sher Ali, third son of Dost Mohammad, took over control of Afghanistan in 1868, he found that the British were unwilling to send troops to help him with the threat that the Russians posed on his northern borders. In 1872, Russia and Great Britain did sign a treaty in which each agreed to respect Afghanistan as a sovereign country, but Sher Ali was kept completely out of this process and did not trust either nation to have the best interests of Afghanistan in mind. However, in 1874, Benjamin Disraeli and the Conservative Party took over control of Great Britain and instituted a change in policy, the Forward Policy, the name of which actually harkened back to the pre-1848 days, when the British believed that the best protection against Russia was a strong British presence in at least part of Afghanistan, if not all of it.

Alarmed by this hawkish new British government, Russia decided (unasked by Sher Ali) to send a diplomatic mission to Kabul in the summer of 1878. Britain therefore told Sher Ali that he needed to accept a British mission; however, one of Sher Ali's sons had died, thus throwing the Afghan court into mourning, and he did not reply to the British. On September 21, the British sent a small number of troops to Afghanistan, along with an envoy, Sir Neville Chamberlain (no relation to Neville Chamberlain, the future British prime minister), but they were turned back at the entrance to the Khyber Pass by Afghan troops. The British, in fact, expected this—they were merely looking for a pretext for war against Afghanistan, and now they had found one.

Prepared, the British army invaded Afghanistan in November at three different points with a force of 45,000 men—much larger than their Army of the Indus in 1838. Troops poured through the Khyber Pass, another high pass known as the Camel's Neck, south of the Khyber, and then in the south through the Bolan Pass. The British were far more prepared and their forces included a unit known as the Corps of Guides, an elite frontier fighting force that traveled lightly, knew the mountains, and was a sort of Special Forces of its day.

At first, the British met with great success. Afghan tribesmen and ghazis would fight briefly and then melt away. Sher Ali appealed to the tsar for an alliance, but the Russian leader, unwilling to risk such direct confrontation with the British, refused him. Returning to Afghanistan, Sher Ali died of illness in February 1879, to be replaced by his son, Yakub Khan. Seeing the handwriting on the wall, Yakub agreed to sign a truce.

His meeting with the British took place, symbolically (from the British point of view) at Gandamak in May 1879—Gandamak was the village near the rocky hill where retreating British troops had made their last stand in 1842 (to this day, the hill there is still called Feringhee Ghunadi—the "mountain of the foreigners"). With little choice, Yakub relinquished control of Afghan foreign affairs to the British, gave them control of all the main passes into the country, and allowed British missions in Kabul and other Afghan towns. In return, the British paid him 600,000 rupees per year.

With a cholera epidemic sweeping through, the British then withdrew, thinking their job was done. However, in the way of Afghanistan and never-ending war, it was just beginning.

"A STATE OF FRENZY"

In the years since Shah Shuja had ordered the beheading of his black-shirted ghazi prisoners, the fundamentalist Islamic movement in Afghanistan (and in India) had grown. A member of the Corps of Guides wrote in his journal in 1879 that these warriors "are at all times ready for a jihad."

Most of the ghazis, as David Loyn writes in his book *In Afghanistan: Two Hundred Years of British, Russian and American Occupation*, drew their inspiration "from a single strain of Islam founded by Mohammad ibn Abd al-Wahhab." He was born in Arabia early in the eighteenth century and his teachings—which encouraged the leading an austere lifestyle while focusing on holy war against infidels—were highly influential in Afghanistan and the surrounding regions at this time. Those who followed Wahhabi principles set up their own schools and separated themselves from society, even mainstream Islamic society. Al-Qaeda and the Taliban, Loyn points out, are inspired "by the same Wahhabi vision," which included "religious police" who would stop workers during their daily labor and force them to pray; whippings would be meted out to those who refused.

As a British delegation, led by Sir Pierre Cavagnari, took up residence in Kabul, mullahs spread the rumor that the British were bringing in Bibles printed in Arabic to convert Muslims; another rumor had it that the British were flooding the region with Korans printed on paper from Europe—a sacrilege. "The Kabul Mullahs, who are renowned for their fanaticism, were in a state of frenzy" concerning all these stories, wrote one member of the British delegation. On September 3, the British embassy in Kabul was attacked by a mob of Muslims, many Afghan soldiers who had formerly been paid by the British. Sir Pierre Cavagnari was killed, along with all the members of the delegation except for one, who managed to flee at night in disguise.

The Second Anglo-Afghan War now began in earnest as Major General Frederick Roberts led a group of 2,500 soldiers, known as the Kabul Field Force, back into Afghanistan, vowing vengeance, despite pathetic missives from Yakub Khan in which he pleaded with the British not to attack ("Please God, the mutineers will soon meet the punishment they deserve, and my affairs will be arranged to the satisfaction of the British government").

In October, as British forces marched on Kabul, they were met near Charasiab, south of the city, by Afghan fighters who outnumbered them five to one and had taken the high ground. Nevertheless, the British charged and destroyed the surrounding enemy, who fled, leaving hundreds of dead. The British then marched into Kabul, took Yakub Khan captive, and sent him into exile in India. They then hung forty-nine Afghans whom they considered responsible for the September 3 uprising and placed Kabul under martial law.

"MOST TURBULENT AND UNTRACTABLE"

However, as imperial powers have learned in long wars, martial law and occupying forces cannot stifle resistance. Stirred up by a mullah named Mushk-i-Alam, Islamic radicals who called themselves mujahidin put up posters at night around Kabul, calling for jihad and the ouster of the British. Mushk-i-Alam (whose name the British ridiculed because it meant "fragrance of the world") had been able to stir up tribal forces outside of Kabul as well. In December, the British got word that a force of 100,000 Afghans was approaching. Roberts led his men out to engage them and in a desperate battle fought them off, but with heavy casualties. The Afghan tribesmen then surrounded the British in Kabul, making several assaults on the city before dispersing just before Christmas.

The British could not understand why the Afghans melted away, but the tribal leaders were using guerilla tactics of the kind that Afghans had used for hundreds of years against invading forces, dispersing to fight again later—their defeat at Charasiab had made them leery of confronting the British on open ground. By the spring of 1880, the British government was beginning to realize—once again—that victory in Afghanistan was going to be difficult. William Gladstone and his Liberal Party had replaced Benjamin Disraeli and his Conservatives; Gladstone had, in part, gotten himself elected by recounting a list of the atrocities the forces of General Roberts had committed when they first invaded Afghanistan, causing the British people to ask themselves whether the war was moral.

In the meantime, the British maneuvered to place Yakub Khan's cousin Abdur Rahman on the throne, something that did not sit well with Ayub Khan, Yakub's brother and nominally next in line. Ayub Khan advanced on the city of Kandahar, meeting a British army of 3,000 men near the small British outpost of Maiwand in July 1880. Ayub's army vastly outnumbered the British and his ranks were filled with fanatical ghazis, who attacked without care for their own lives. One thousand British and Indian soldiers were killed in the worst battlefield defeat suffered by the British in Afghanistan, one whose memory is revered to this day by the Taliban.

Once again, after a great defeat, came a British legend—this time the forced march of the troops of General Roberts (334 miles [534 km] in twenty-three days) to defeat Ayub Khan as he besieged Kandahar. With this rebellion at an end and Ayub Khan a fugitive, Abdur Rahman's position on the throne was solidified. At this point, in September 1880, the Second Anglo-Afghan War officially came to an end. In a sense, the British had achieved their goals—they now controlled Afghan foreign policy, thus ensuring no Afghan rapprochement could be made with Russia.

Although the British would rule the country in relative peace for the next forty years or so, they were never able to truly subdue Afghanistan, especially the tribes that lived in the extremely mountainous regions in the north and near the border with what would become Pakistan—tribes whose fanatical mullahs incited them against infidel occupation. Afghanistan finally received its independence in 1919, after a brief third war with the British, who were once again afraid the Afghans would conspire with the Russians (although this time with the new communist government after the Russian Revolution). The British finally withdrew, leaving Afghanistan on its own.

The country, while independent, would continue to remain one that foreign countries and competing ideologies fought over, however, and where the Afghan people remained undefeated and essentially unbeatable. As Abdur Rahman wrote to a British contact in late 1880: "The country is in a deplorable condition. Everything which belonged to the state is ruined and requires renewal. The people are, as you can see, most turbulent and untractable."

CHAPTER 10

THE VIETNAM WARS

"THE LIGHT AT THE END OF THE TUNNEL"

1945–1975

The Vietnamese under Ho Chi Minh won an epic war of independence against France and the United States, showing the durability of nationalist warfare.

On September 2, 1945, a slender, dark-haired Vietnamese man with a wispy black goatee stood on a platform in Hanoi's Ba Dinh Square, in front of thousands of people, and spoke the following words into a microphone:

"All men are created equal. The Creator has given us certain inviolable rights; the right to Life, the right to be Free, and the right to achieve Happiness. These immortal words are taken from the Declaration of Independence of the United States of America in 1776. In a larger sense, this means that: All the people on earth are born equal. All the people have the right to life, to be happy, to be free."

It is but one of the innumerable ironies of the Vietnam Wars that Ho Chi Minh, the slender man declaring the independence of the Democratic Republic of Vietnam, based his speech on the Declaration of Independence, even as the U.S. government was conspiring to make sure that Ho and his Viet Minh rebels did not, under any circumstances, become equal, free, or happy.

Like the American patriots in 1776, Ho was announcing independence when his forces could actually only hang on to a sliver of their country. Far larger and more powerful nations were at work to subsume any ambitions Ho might have for the freedom of Vietnam. It would take one long war divided into back-to-back conflicts against a fading colonial power and the most powerful country in the world for such independence to be achieved. The war would last thirty years, in part because the history of the Vietnamese, going all the way back to the first millennium, had taught them how to fight imperial powers and in part because the Vietnamese were highly adaptable, able to change and develop different tactics.

The long war in Vietnam cost millions of lives and became the classic struggle for national determination of the twentieth century, even though (ironically again) one of the reasons the war went on as long as it did is that the United States did not recognize early enough that the Vietnamese were fighting a struggle quite similar to the one that launched the American republic.

FROM FREE NATION TO COLONY

Vietnam is an ancient kingdom for which independence has long been elusive and its people have long been accustomed to fighting imperial powers. For more than a thousand years, until the middle of the tenth century, Vietnam was controlled by China, which considered the country a kind of southern Chinese province. The Chinese named Vietnam Annan, which means "pacified south," a name the fiercely proud and culturally homogenous Vietnamese people naturally resented. (Another ancient Chinese name for the country was Nam Viet—"Nam" meaning south, "Viet" being a derivation of a Chinese word meaning "beyond," as in beyond the boundaries of China—so that the name can be taken to mean "the people to the south.")

UNABLE TO STAND UP TO THESE FAR MORE NUMEROUS INVADING ARMIES IN PITCHED BATTLE, THE VIETNAMESE BEGAN TO PRACTICE GUERILLA WARFARE—HIT-AND-RUN ATTACKS, HIDING AMONG THE GENERAL POPULATION, NEVER FIGHTING WHEN OUTNUMBERED.

But when the Tang dynasty fell in 907, Vietnamese rebels seized the opportunity and by 939 were able to drive the Chinese out of the country. Even then they had to fight off repeated Chinese invasions, three of them carried out under the Mongol rulers who had taken over China. Unable to stand up to these far more numerous invading armies in pitched battle, the Vietnamese began to practice guerilla warfare—hit-and-run attacks, hiding among the general population, never fighting when outnumbered. This style of warfare took a long time, because decisive battles were avoided and small actions that chipped away at the enemy were preferred, and thus the Vietnamese became used to fighting wars that went on for years and years.

It took until the mid-fifteenth century for the Chinese to give up their designs on Vietnam, finally recognizing its independence. The first emperor of Vietnam, the rebel Prince Le Loi, named his newly free country Dai-Viet (Great Viet State) and established his capital city on the Red River, calling it Tong Kinh, a name that foreigners would pronounce "Tonkin." Tonkin was later renamed Hanoi.

Le Loi was the king of a country that roughly corresponds to the area North Vietnam covered from 1954 to 1975. Over the next two centuries, the Vietnamese expanded south, pushing out tribes such as the Khmers (native to Cambodia). By the early seventeenth century, however, the south and north of Vietnam had become divided between two families, with the north ruled by the Trinh dynasty and the south by the Nguyens, who established their capital at Hue, on the Perfume River.

In 1858, the French invaded Vietnam, seeking to add it to French colonial territories in Laos and Cambodia. The Vietnamese put up a bloody struggle, especially in the north, which the French were never able to entirely pacify. In 1883, the French finally set up a "protectorate" in Vietnam, called it Cochin China, and then combined it with Laos and Cambodia to form the French Indochinese Union in 1887. Saigon, in the southern part of the country, became the new capital city.

The French government forbade the Vietnamese from using the words *Vietnam* and *Vietnamese*, and had approval over all decisions made by Vietnamese rulers. Vietnamese armed resistance was sporadic and met with brutal repression from the French, who were now engaged in exploiting the natural resources of the country to the maximum. The French exported most of the rice from the rich Mekong Delta region in the south, leaving Vietnamese families starving, with few options but to work under brutal conditions in French rubber plantations.

In the north, and in Laos, the French encouraged the growing of poppy for opium—by 1903, according to historian Larry H. Addington, opium sales accounted for a third of the French government's income from Vietnam. More and more Vietnamese, who had once owned their own land, were turned into tenant farmers and became addicted to drugs. Educational standards for Vietnamese children fell. The nation that had fought off the Chinese for so many centuries was in danger of losing its identity.

Ho Chi Minh, pictured in Hanoi in 1955, kept a wary eye on history, not wanting to repeat mistakes of the past and also learning what tactics worked. These attacks, which included disappearing in the jungles, would sap the will of larger invading countries, such as France, and later, the United States.

"HE WHO ENLIGHTENS"

The man who would lead Vietnam back into nationhood was born Nguyen Sinh Cung in May 1890 in a village in central Vietnam. His mother was a concubine; his father, a Confucian scholar employed by the Imperial Vietnamese Court who grew tired of the court's subservience to the French and left to become an itinerant teacher. Nguyen followed in his father's footsteps, taking part in several tax revolts and earning a secret French police dossier for his activities.

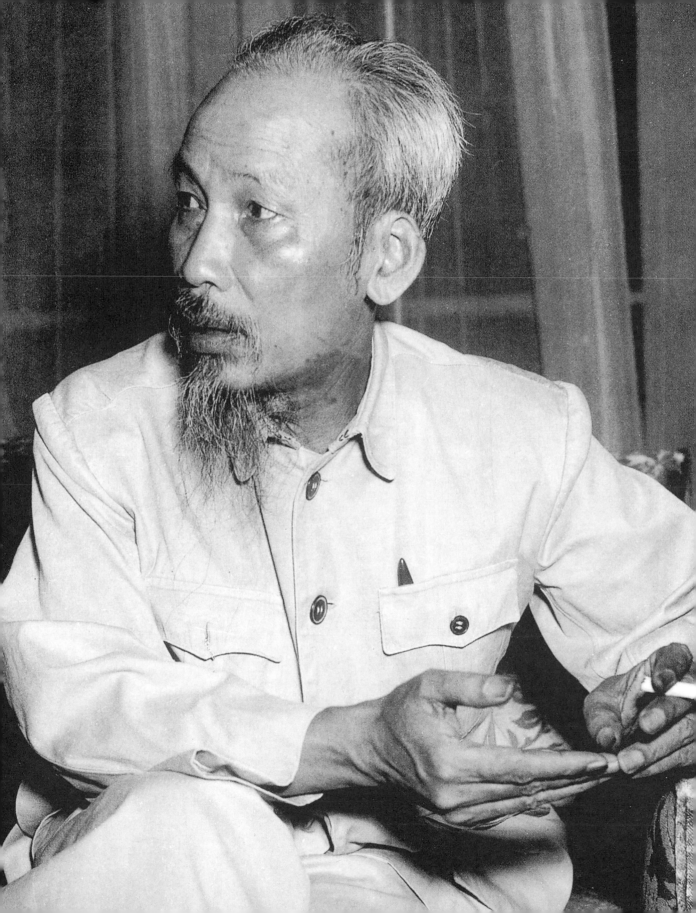

Despite the repressiveness of the French, Nguyen admired the principles of the French Revolution, just as he did those tenets of the American War for Independence of 1776. In 1911, at the age of twenty-one, the scarecrow-thin young man made his way to France, working as a galley boy on a passenger liner. In Paris he found work as a photo retoucher and continued to broaden his political thought. In 1919, when American president Woodrow Wilson arrived to sign the treaty that ended World War I, Nguyen tried to present him with a list of French abuses in Vietnam. Rebuffed, he joined the French Communist Party in 1920. "It was patriotism, not communism, that inspired me," he later wrote, but he began to work as an agent for Moscow, traveling to Russia, China, Thailand, and Hong Kong.

In 1930, while still in Hong Kong, Nguyen founded the small Communist Party of Vietnam—interestingly enough, a name that the Stalinists who controlled the Communist Party in Russia forced him to change to the Communist Party of Indochina, because the former smacked too much of nationalism. But it was only Vietnam, not international communism, that Ho truly cared about.

In 1940, with World War II beginning, Japan invaded Indochina; the French Vichy government, now loyal to the Germans, collaborated with them. Now Nguyen saw his chance. Sneaking back across the border from China into Vietnam in 1941—the first time he had been home to his native land in thirty years—he went deep into the wilderness with a small group of loyal followers, to the remote northern village of Pac Bo. There he founded the Viet Minh, an acronym for the Vietnam Independence League. The time had come, he told this band of men, to bring together "patriots of all ages and types, peasants, workers, merchants, and soldiers." Taking on a nom de guerre, Nguyen called himself Ho Chi Minh, which means "bringer of light" or "he who enlightens." He then began to wage jungle warfare against both the Japanese and the Vichy French.

In this he was aided by the Americans, who parachuted their agents into northern Vietnam and funneled arms and money to Ho's Viet Minh, who struck at the Japanese in hit-and-run raids wherever they could find them. Ho's primary general was Vo Nguyen Giap, born in Vietnam in 1912. He was ruthless in his jungle attacks, especially against the French, who had caught, tortured, and executed Giap's wife, sister, father, and sister-in-law.

Although the Viet Minh were initially a force of only about 200 fighters armed with ancient rifles, once supplied by the U.S. Office of Strategic Services (OSS), they had, as one U.S. agent recalled, "an uncanny ability to learn and adapt." Not only did they become expert in fighting with modern weapons, but also they were able to learn tactical maneuvers taught to them by the Americans with surprising swiftness.

This ability would become quite useful in the long years of war ahead, prolonging the conflict by allowing the Viet Minh and later the Viet Cong and North Vietnamese Army to strike hard and inflict damage while remaining flexible. They were also able to better understand the Western armies they were fighting. And Ho Chi Minh impressed the Americans as well, helping them recover downed pilots and escaped British and U.S. POWs. A team that included an OSS doctor saved Ho's life—another irony—when he was dying of dysentery and malaria and appeared "a pile of bones covered with dry yellow skin."

THE FIRST INDOCHINA WAR

By September 1945, with the Japanese and Vichy French defeated, Ho took over Hanoi with his fighters and proclaimed the Democratic Republic of Vietnam, using those ringing words derived from the American Declaration of Independence. Perhaps naively, he assumed that the Americans, who had allied themselves with him during the war, would now recognize his Democratic Republic of Vietnam.

Many OSS officers on the ground agreed, recognizing that colonialism was dead— one U.S. officer wrote in his official report: "Cochinchina [Vietnam] is burning, the French and British are finished here, and we [the United States] ought to clear out of Southeast Asia." The U.S. government, however, did not agree. In a secret agreement at their summit meeting in Potsdam, U.S. president Harry Truman, British prime minister Winston Churchill, and Soviet premier Joseph Stalin had decided that Vietnam would be temporarily occupied by the Chinese in the north and the British in the south, until France gathered the resources to come back in and take over the country again.

Before September was out, Vietnam descended into a hell of war and chaos, one it would not emerge from until 1975. At first, Ho and his advisors thought that organizing a mass peaceful protest would change the mind of the Allied Powers. But then the British (anxious to leave Vietnam) released and armed 1,400 French Foreign Legion troops that had been held as POWs by the Japanese. On September 22, 1945, these men, joined by angry French citizens, rampaged through Saigon, indiscriminately shooting and clubbing Vietnamese citizens.

Ho then called for a general strike on September 24, one that effectively paralyzed Saigon, shutting down water and electricity and shuttering shops. In tandem with this, Viet Minh squads attacked the airport and gunfire rang out across the city. Most awful of all, a group of Viet Minh terrorists attacked a French suburb, broke into private homes, and murdered some 150 French and Eurasian men, women, and children. Some were tortured and mutilated.

September 24, 1945, is the day that most historians assign as the beginning of the First Indochina War. The war began with both sides perpetrating terrible acts of violence against the innocent, a pattern that would repeat itself throughout the war and lengthen the conflict by hardening attitudes and making combatants exact retribution.

Quickly realizing that the country was in danger of falling to the Viet Minh, the French government sent 35,000 men to Vietnam in October under the command of General Jacques-Phillippe Leclerc, a brilliant Free French soldier and hero of the war against the Nazis in Europe. Leclerc pushed aside the Viet Minh forces blockading Saigon, placed the city firmly under French control, then spread out into the countryside, retaking the Mekong Delta and the Central Highlands, pushing Ho's forces back into the north. But the French—like the Americans after them—did not have the forces to hold the land they took, and they were harassed constantly by Viet Minh guerillas. Within five months, Ho Chi Minh was pushed back to Hanoi and Leclerc claimed victory in the south, but Vietnam was far from stable.

"THE WHITE MAN IS FINISHED IN ASIA"

Although the French were not in full control of Vietnam, Ho Chi Minh's first months since his declaration of independence were not necessarily successful ones. Despite his popularity in the north, he had to deal with the thousands of Chinese troops that poured into Hanoi and its surrounding regions, sent to "keep peace" under the Potsdam Agreement, but who quickly became a burden on the already overtaxed countryside, stealing and eating everything in sight. Forced to compromise with the French to get rid of the Chinese, Ho agreed to the presence of 25,000 French troops in Vietnam if France agreed to recognize Vietnam as a free state within the French Union.

Members of Ho's own party protested against this arrangement, which seemed to be giving in too much to the French, but Ho knew how important it was to send the Chinese home. He told one gathering of disgruntled Viet Minh advisors in Hanoi: "You fools! . . . Don't you remember your history? The last time the Chinese came, they stayed a thousand years. The French are foreigners. They are weak. Colonialism is dying. The white man is finished in Asia. But if the Chinese stay now, they will never go . . . I'd rather sniff French shit for five years than eat Chinese shit for the rest of my life."

Although expressed profanely, this type of careful calculation of the odds when faced with a situation where there was really no best choice was a hallmark of Ho Chi Minh's decision making. It also showed that he kept a wary eye on history, wanting, if at all possible, to avoid repeating mistakes of the past (just as what he learned from fighting the French would later help him in his struggle against the Americans, particularly when it came to sapping the will of large Western countries through lengthy war). Had Ho decided to allow the Chinese to stay, he might have ended up having to fight the Chinese as well as the French and the Americans.

In any event, the truce with the French was short-lived. Fierce fighting broke out in the fall of 1946 in Haiphong and Hanoi, forcing Ho Chi Minh to flee deep into the jungles. By February, French forces had taken most of the provincial capitals in north and central Vietnam and, in the fall of that year, marched north almost to the Chinese border. Once again, however, their victory was illusory.

HAD HO DECIDED TO ALLOW THE CHINESE TO STAY, THE LONG WAR FOR VIETNAMESE INDEPENDENCE MIGHT HAVE BEEN A VERY SHORT ONE INDEED.

The Viet Minh had not committed most of their forces to the field, preferring to regroup in their jungle hideouts, recruit new members, and wage hit-and-run attacks to harass the French. The Viet Minh were merely waiting until they were strong enough to strike—patience being a prime virtue of anyone engaged in long war. By 1950, General Vo Nguyen Giap had built up his guerilla forces into five conventional infantry divisions, armed in many cases with heavy U.S. weaponry the Red Chinese had captured from the Nationalists and provided to the Viet Minh. In February 1950, he began a massive offensive that in just ten months was able to push the French back from the Chinese border to a defensive line they had established from Hanoi to the Red River Delta.

Here, however, French resolve stiffened. In several battles, most notably the battles of Vinh Yen, Mao Khe, and Phu Ly, all taking place in early 1951, Giap completely abandoned guerilla tactics in his desire to crush his enemy. He sent line after line of his finest Viet Minh fighters against the French in human wave attacks, only to see them slaughtered with artillery, machine-gun fire, and napalm—the first time that weapon was used in Vietnam, but by no means the last. As many as 20,000 Viet Minh were killed in these assaults. Finally, Giap was forced to break off his attacks.

"THE LIGHT AT THE END OF THE TUNNEL"

Although the French were successful, the cost to them was great—by the end of 1952, the French armed forces had lost more than 90,000 men dead, wounded, missing, or captured. At the same time, the French public had begun to question the reason for

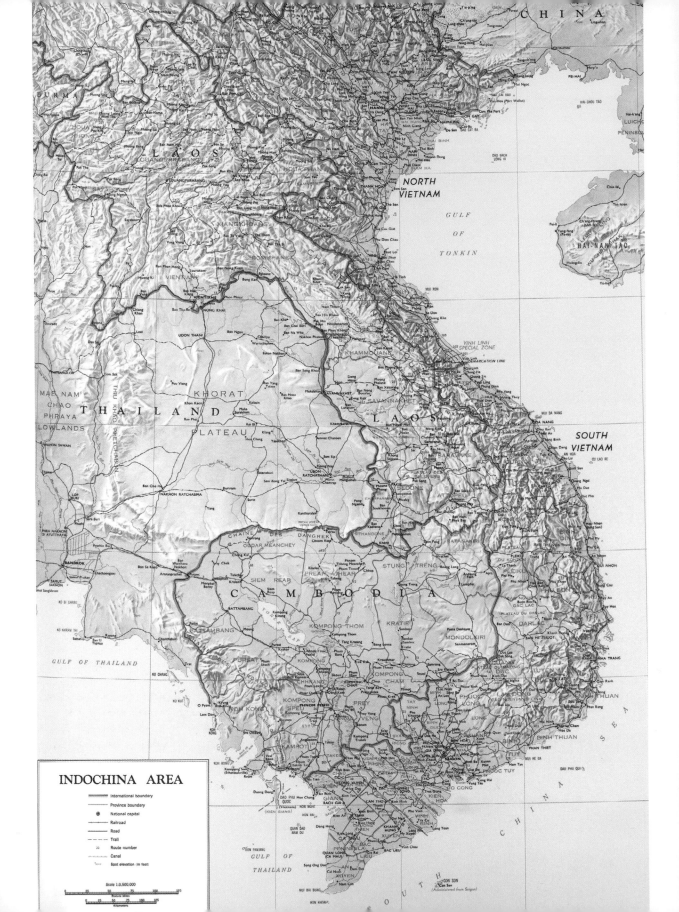

INDOCHINA AREA

	International boundary
	Province boundary
	National capital
	Railroad
	Road
	Trail
23	Route number
	Canal
	Spot elevation (in feet)

Scale 1:3,500,000

the war, because it was obvious to almost everyone that the French colonial empire was dead. The French government posed the fight in Vietnam as a crusade against communism—as did the U.S. government, which was heavily funding the French efforts. In 1950, the United States gave the French $150 million in military aid; by 1953, that figure had grown to $785 million. As the historian James William Gibson writes in *The Perfect War*: "The French became instruments of American foreign policy and their troops, mercenaries for hire."

A good deal of this was due to the fierce anticommunism sweeping the United States during the second half of the First Indochina War, which coincided almost exactly with the Korean War years. Top U.S. officials, including presidents Harry Truman and Dwight Eisenhower, were certain that the war in Vietnam was needed to stem the onslaught of communism. When the Soviet Union and the People's Republic of China gave diplomatic recognition to Ho's Republic of Vietnam, U.S. Secretary of State Dean Acheson sniffed that this should "remove any illusions as to the 'nationalist' nature of Ho Chi Minh's aims."

But it didn't. Ho was far more pragmatic. He didn't want to be a puppet state of the Chinese and Russians, nor was he a communist ideologue. But he took help wherever he could get it.

Building on their successes against the large-scale Viet Minh attacks, the French developed what they would dub the "hedgehog" strategy, which relied on creating heavily fortified emplacements in Viet Minh territory and then hoping to lure the Vietnamese to attack. This was partially successful, but then Giap, realizing he was bloodying his army needlessly, changed tactics.

He launched an attack into Laos, essentially a diversion to convince the French that he had designs on that country. The new French commander, General Henri Navarre, decided that he needed to fortify the valley of Dien Bien Phu, located in northwest Vietnam, near the Laos border, because it lay directly in the path of the Viet Minh movement into Laos. Fortifying Dien Bien Phu was also the grand culmination of the hedgehog strategy, for Navarre built a huge central base there, surrounding it with three auxiliary artillery bases, with an airbase close by for vital resupply. When the Viet Minh attacked in their human waves, Navarre would pulverize them.

"Now we can see clearly," Navarre told a French reporter, "like the light at the end of the tunnel."

This phrase would ultimately become infamous during the U.S. war with Vietnam as a symbol of futility, of failed hopes and foolish aspirations. And Giap would quickly show Navarre that all that lay at the end of the tunnel was darkness. After fortifying the valley in late 1953 and early 1954, the French expected Giap to attack. Indeed, Giap's

For more than 1,000 years, Vietnam was controlled by its neighbor to the north, China, which considered it a kind of southern Chinese province. Its history of internal strife and of pushing out neighboring tribes, such as the Khmers of Cambodia, created in its people a patience to fight out long, drawn-out wars.

Courtesy of the University of Texas Libraries, the University of Texas at Austin

forces, numbering around 50,000, surrounded Navarre's men on the hills overlooking Dien Bien Phu. And even Giap's Chinese advisors suggested he make a massive frontal attack, because he outnumbered the French four to one. But as Giap later said: "We came to the conclusion that we could not secure success if we struck swiftly. In consequence, we chose the other tactics: to strike surely and advance surely."

On March 13, 1954, the attack on Dien Bien Phu began in earnest, with the Viet Minh assaulting Firebase Beatrice, one of the artillery bases that were supposed to protect the main fortress of Dien Bien Phu itself. Giap had a surprise up his sleeve. His men had laboriously hauled forty-five 101mm howitzers and one hundred other big guns up the mountains surrounding the valley, assembled them, and now pointed them down the throats of the French. The artillery shells rained down on Beatrice, said one shell-shocked French survivor, "like a hailstorm on a fall evening. Bunker after bunker, trench after trench, collapsed, burying under them men and weapons."

Beatrice fell within one day—the French overall artillery commander killed himself immediately, muttering, "I am responsible! I am responsible!"—and the other supporting firebases were overrun shortly thereafter. This brought the main airstrip at Dien Bien Phu under heavy artillery fire, and the French were unable to resupply. After this, it was only a matter of time. The strain began to tell on senior French officers—one prominent French officer spent his days hiding in one of the deepest bunkers on the French base and had to be evacuated. General Christian de Castries, field commander in charge at Dien Bien Phu, had a nervous breakdown and was relieved of command by his subordinates.

Navarre, commanding from Saigon, knew that French forces were doomed. He and his superiors tried to convince the United States to come to their aid with a massive bombing attack. They were nearly successful in this effort; apparently, U.S. senior military officials considered the idea of using three tactical nuclear bombs that—"if properly employed," as their report read—would destroy the Viet Minh forces. Fortunately, President Dwight Eisenhower refused to intervene, either with conventional or nuclear weapons, and the French were forced to surrender on May 7, 1954.

"YOU KNOCK OVER THE FIRST ONE"

Dien Bien Phu was "another Waterloo" for the French, as one historian has said. Now anxious to find a face-saving way to leave Vietnam, they instituted talks in Geneva, which ended in June of 1954 with an agreement that the French would leave the northern part of the country and the Viet Minh would leave the south. Vietnam would be divided along the 17th parallel into the Democratic Republic of Vietnam (North Vietnam) and the Republic of South Vietnam. Elections, mandated to be held in 1956, would reunify the country.

However, the United States, the primary supporter of South Vietnam, understood that Ho Chi Minh was enormously popular in the country and would probably win any election. And this U.S. officials could not abide, as they were sure it meant a communist takeover of all of Vietnam. Just before Dien Bien Phu fell, President Dwight Eisenhower had given a pivotal speech about communism during a televised press conference. He explained to his audience that the Western democracies could not even let one country fall to communism. "You have broader considerations," Eisenhower said, "that might follow what you would call the 'falling domino' principle. . . . You have a row of dominoes set up, you knock over the first one, and what will happen to the last one is the certainty that it will go over very quickly."

THE UNITED STATES, THE PRIMARY SUPPORTER OF SOUTH VIETNAM, UNDERSTOOD THAT HO CHI MINH WAS ENORMOUSLY POPULAR IN THE COUNTRY AND WOULD PROBABLY WIN ANY ELECTION. AND THIS U.S. OFFICIALS COULD NOT ABIDE, AS THEY WERE SURE IT MEANT A COMMUNIST TAKEOVER OF ALL OF VIETNAM.

The loss of Vietnam, Eisenhower said, would lead to "the loss . . . of Burma, of Thailand, of the Peninsula, and Indonesia following." Even Japan, Eisenhower implied, might be at risk.

This so-called domino theory became a kind of guiding mission statement for Americans, both politicians and the public alike—the kind of firmly held (but little questioned) belief that contributes to people fighting blindly in long wars. U.S. officials immediately worked to subvert the Geneva Accords in Vietnam. They threw their weight behind a Vietnamese nationalist politician named Ngo Dinh Diem, who in 1956 rejected the tenets of the Geneva Accords and held a national referendum only in South Vietnam, a massively fraudulent and corrupt election in which Diem won 98 percent of the vote. The United States then sent money, military advisors and helicopter pilots to help build up the Army of the Republic of South Vietnam (ARVN).

In the years between 1956 and 1963, Diem's regime proved to be highly unpopular. Its officials were corrupt, Diem and his family uprooted peasants in order to confiscate their land, and the regime forcibly placed young men in the ARVN. Diem was also a

Catholic—a minority group representing only about 10 percent of the nation—and persecuted Buddhist citizens.

By the end of 1960, an insurgency movement calling itself the National Liberation Front (NLF) sprung up in South Vietnam, with help from the North. Diem disparagingly called them the Viet Cong (Vietnamese communists), and the name stuck. The Viet Cong quickly struck at the Diem government, carrying out assassinations against local policemen and hit-and-run raids against electrical and transportation facilities. Armed by North Vietnam, the Viet Cong grew stronger and stronger. Even so, U.S. advisors to ARVN units told reporters that they were certain they could destroy the Viet Cong if they would stand and fight.

They had a chance to test that hypothesis in January 1963 near a South Vietnam village called Ap Bac. There, three Viet Cong companies hidden in an irrigation ditch ambushed a far stronger ARVN attacking force, shooting down its helicopters and killing sixty-one ARVN troops and wounding more than a hundred. The ARVN forces were poorly led and performed badly, in many cases refusing to engage the Viet Cong. Three U.S. helicopter crew members were also killed. The Battle of Ap Bac had lessons for both the United States and the Viet Cong. It convinced many U.S. officials that the ARVN could not fend for themselves and that U.S. combat troops (rather than just advisors) were necessary to fight the war.

The Viet Cong—who, with their long memories, had set up their ambush on ground where they had also successfully ambushed the French a decade earlier—saw that they could win against the superior technology the enemy had to throw at them, if they prepared and stood their ground. As their commander wrote in his diary: "Better to fight and die than run and be slaughtered."

"GRAB THEM BY THE BELT"

President John F. Kennedy had kept the U.S. military presence in Vietnam mainly to an advisory capacity—although his administration had backed a coup in the fall of 1963 that saw Diem assassinated and replaced by an ARVN general named Duong Van Minh. When Kennedy himself was assassinated three weeks after Diem, Lyndon Johnson became president. By this time, it was amply evident that the Viet Cong, with backing from Ho's North Vietnamese military machine, were easily defeating the ARVN.

After North Vietnamese patrol boats clashed with a U.S. intelligence-gathering destroyer on August 2, 1964, in the Gulf of Tonkin, in a confused incident that has never been fully clarified, Johnson seized upon the encounter to prod Congress to pass the Gulf of Tonkin Resolution, which gave the president leeway to use "all necessary measures" to attack the enemy.

Indo-Chinese commandos are shown searching a village in Tonkin, now Hanoi, in Northern Vietnam. Fighting in small bands like these and disappearing into the jungle proved successful in wearing out the enemy.

U.S. troops immediately began pouring into South Vietnam, confident that they could defeat the enemy. Their doctrine was that of air mobility; the symbol of the U.S. presence in Vietnam became the helicopter, which carried troops to and from far-flung jungle battlefields and protected them by raining down fire from the air. To meet this threat, regular troops of the North Vietnamese Army (NVA) began to infiltrate the south. The first major meeting between these and the Americans came at the Battle of the Ia Drang Valley in November 1965, when the U.S. First Cavalry division made a combat assault directly into the assembly area of the NVA 33rd and 36th Regiments. In the bloody three-day battle that ensued, the First Cavalry destroyed the better part of an NVA division, inflicting 2,000 casualties, with 79 Americans killed and 121 wounded.

By most standards a U.S. victory, the Battle of the Ia Drang Valley did teach the North Vietnamese the important lesson that they had to fight quite close to the Americans to escape the withering power of their artillery and air strikes—to "grab them by the belt," as one North Vietnamese commander wrote.

The Americans were justly proud of the bravery with which their unseasoned troops had fought and at the power of their military killing machine. It was not yet apparent to them that the North Vietnamese were willing to suffer many, many more casualties than the Americans were to achieve their ends. Taking serious casualties— and continuing to fight, no matter what the cost—is often the determining factor in the ability of one side to be able to win long wars.

During the course of the U.S. war in Vietnam, the NVA and Viet Cong would lose 500,000 troops, a staggering number, but it only proved the truth of something Ho Chi Minh had told the French in the late 1940s: "You can kill ten of my men for every one I kill of yours. But even at those odds, you will lose and I will win."

"DESTROY THE TOWN"

Another big factor in the U.S. war against North Vietnam was the power of her air fleet— the big B-52 bombers that, starting in March 1965 with Operation Rolling Thunder, began to dump hundreds of thousands of tons of bombs on targets in North Vietnam. In fact, 864,000 tons of bombs were dropped, more than the United States rained down in the Pacific theater during all of World War II. The North Vietnamese took terrible casualties—possibly 90,000 during the three and a half years the bombing lasted, some 70,000 of these civilian. And yet they did not give up and come to the peace table, as Pentagon planners had predicted they would.

Had the Americans been students of history in the same way that the Vietnamese were, they would have noted that the worst bombing of World War II failed to break the morale of either the British or the German civilian populations—if anything, it heightened their willingness to continue the fight. And they might also have understood that the Vietnamese had survived attacks from imperial powers—China, France, and now the United States—by their willingness to take punishment.

U.S. military planners, heartened by the body counts they inflicted during the Ia Drang Valley attacks and others subsequent to it, instituted a policy that was in some respects similar to the failed French "hedgehog" plans. Americans were set up in remote "fire bases" inside enemy territory, from which they conducted extensive search-and-destroy missions to find and kill the enemy. Yet while thousands of Viet Cong and NVA soldiers were killed, U.S. casualties also rose, something that people back home simply found unacceptable. By 1967, with half a million troops fighting in Vietnam, almost half the U.S. public found the U.S. presence there unacceptable. It is difficult for a democracy to fight any war, but especially a long war, without support from its citizens, and support for the U.S. government was slowly dissolving.

Ironically, it would take what was ultimately a major U.S. victory to turn the country against Vietnam. In January 1968, the Viet Cong and North Vietnamese launched the Tet Offensive, a surprise attack against thirty-six cities in South Vietnam during the time of the Tet New Year festival. ARVN and U.S. forces were caught completely by surprise; Vietnam commando squads even entered the U.S. embassy compound in Saigon, killing five Americans before being killed themselves.

The NVA and Viet Cong captured the ancient South Vietnamese capital city of Hue on the Perfume River, executing 3,000 civilians whom they considered "reactionary elements" and burying them in shallow graves. It would take U.S. forces a month to drive them out of the city, at which point Hue was such a shambles that a U.S. Marine told a reporter that they had had to "destroy the town in order to save it."

It turned out that the Tet Offensive was a costly failure for the NVA and Viet Cong. An estimated 50,000 of them were killed and the Viet Cong infrastructure in South Vietnam was essentially destroyed. Yet the news and pictures pouring into the homes of Americans via television horrified the public and increased the calls to bring U.S. troops back home. At the same time, in March 1968, General William Westmoreland, commander of U.S. forces in Vietnam, made the enormous tactical error of asking for 200,000 more troops. His request was denied and he left Vietnam that spring, kicked upstairs to become army chief of staff.

The North Vietnamese, as usual, took the long view. General Vo Nguyen Giap, commander of all North Vietnamese forces, wrote a report in which he stated that, despite the Tet setback, the war could go on for twenty years or more. In the end, he was sure, North Vietnam would win.

North Vietnamese troops assault a
South Vietnamese paratroop base at
Laos during the Vietnam War in this
March 1971 photograph. More than
3 million people, including 58,000
Americans, died in the war, more than
half of them civilians.

Getty Images

"PEACE WITH HONOR"

Ho Chi Minh died in September 1969, but his nationalist revolution continued and increased in fervor just as protests against U.S. involvement in the war mounted in the United States. In 1969, news came out that a company of U.S. troops had massacred hundreds of Vietnamese men, women, and children in cold blood just after the Tet Offensive in what became known as the My Lai Massacre. For the first time, the majority of Americans wanted their government to abandon the war. By this time, Richard Nixon had become president, after Lyndon Johnson chose not to run again—the war had become his undoing. Nixon began to pursue a policy of negotiating with Hanoi while implementing what was called "Vietnamization"—supplying and training ARVN forces, but letting them do the fighting themselves. In the meantime, he gradually withdrew U.S. troops from Vietnam.

In October 1972, in Paris, U.S. Secretary of State Henry Kissinger and North Vietnam diplomat Le Duc Tho reached an agreement that called for U.S. ground troops to be withdrawn from Vietnam by March 1973. When the final agreement was signed in January 1973, Richard Nixon declared: "We have finally achieved peace with honor."

Although there may have been peace for U.S. ground troops, there would be little for the Vietnamese. Despite the armistice in place, the North Vietnamese, taking advantage of the fact that the Nixon administration was severely weakened by the Watergate scandal, began to move into South Vietnam in 1974. In March of 1975, they launched a major offensive against South Vietnam, which quickly collapsed demoralized ARVN opposition. They swept into Saigon on April 30. The South Vietnam government fell and U.S. officials, hastily fleeing on helicopters to U.S. ships stationed in the South China Sea, suffered one last ignominy.

The war was over. The North Vietnamese had been able to outlast the French and the Americans because of their tradition of not expecting quick victories and because they knew and believed in what they were fighting for, unlike their opponents.

The U.S. people, in particular, were conflicted. They were fighting a regime with strong ties to communist Russia and China, whose leader had avowed socialist goals, yet Vietnam was also bent on gaining its nationhood—just as the Americans had gained theirs in the Revolutionary War. Sympathy for nationalistic goals was combined with paranoia about communist takeovers. In the end, in Vietnam's thirty-year war, it would be the country with the clearest goals that came out the victor.

"ON THE BORDERS"
NATIONALIST STRUGGLES

Regions clash when countries struggle
to find their nationhood and
protect their cultures.

CHAPTER II

THE RUSSO-POLISH WARS

THE BATTLE FOR THE BALTIC AND SUPREMACY IN EASTERN EUROPE

1558–1667

Tsarist Russia's need to secure access to the rich
Baltic Sea trade, a long, disputed border with
the Polish-Lithuanian Commonwealth, and the dynastic
rivalries of the Baltic world all ensured more than
a century of bitter conflict.

At dawn, the enemy encampment was silent as Stanislaw Zolkiewski led his army of Poles and Lithuanians out of the trees and toward the palisade. It was July 4, 1610. He and his men were tired, having marched all night through the woods to arrive here, at Klushino, in what is today the center of far western Russia, where some 35,000 Muscovite and Swedish soldiers slept.

Zolkiewski was a *hetman*, or commander, of forces from the Commonwealth of Poland-Lithuania, who had just 4,000 to 6,000 men with him. If he was going to defeat the Muscovites and their Swedish allies, he would need to do so with surprise. Unfortunately, that plan disappeared not long after sunup when his army's efforts at breaking into the enemy palisade—a tall wattle fence supported by modest earthworks— alerted the slumbering encampment.

Suddenly, soldiers ran from their tents and hovels to man the palisade, including Muscovite *streltsy*, or elite musketeers, along with thousands of cavalry. The Swedish force came forward as well, including nearly 7,000 mercenaries from all over Western Europe, both infantry and cavalry. As defending infantrymen began to deliver volleys of musketry into the oncoming Poles and Lithuanians, tainting the early morning light with clouds of powder smoke, Zolkiewski's options began to run out. He could not flank the enemy, defended as they were by the fence, through which he had been able to make only a few breaches. Behind one of these on the far right waited the Muscovite cavalry, which had massed into a huge throng as if daring the Poles to come.

They came. Just 2,000 strong, Zolkiewski's finest regiment of *hussars*, or Polish lancers, charged their opposites beyond the palisade. The breach allowed only a handful to gallop through at a time, narrowing the front of their assault; however, the poorly trained Muscovite cavalry, packed in a mass that hampered their organization even as it enhanced the spread of their panic, proved no match for the hussars. The Muscovites wavered under the onslaught, then received the support of mercenary cavalry with arquebuses and pistols.

These veterans, delivering a desultory fire on the Poles before wheeling to reload in the rear, could not thwart the hussars, whose discipline and élan remained unbroken in one thundering charge after another. Many of them had shattered their lances and blown their mounts, but their expertise in the charge had broken the enemy. Although they were more skilled than their opposites, who preferred missile weapons and swordplay, it was their tactic of closing with the enemy in a savage burst of stabbing momentum—a practice so at odds with gunpowder tactics and unnerving to the uninitiated—that wrecked the Muscovites. A rout began in earnest.

The Swedes were next. To break them, with their excellent, Western-style infantry armed with pikes and muskets, Zolkiewski brought up a pair of cannon to start blowing gaps in the palisade. Soon the Polish infantry were joining in, keeping up a lively exchange with the foreigners until Zolkiewski thought the time was ripe to send in a fresh regiment of hussars. In they went, laying into the Swedish foot with lances and sabers, until the Swedes and their freelances could take no more and fled.

The Battle of Klushino, part of the Polish-Muscovite War of 1609–1619, served to highlight the strengths of Polish-Lithuanian tactics. But as dramatic as Zolkiewski's victory was, it could do little to help shape events in a decisive manner in this part of the world where war had become endemic.

This was a part of the world where perpetual war was all but unavoidable. To begin with, the Polish-Lithuanian Commonwealth, created to ensure the safety of its citizens in a volatile region, lay near the epicenter of a four-way grudge match for control of the Baltic world. Moreover, dynastic complexities and the rivalries they invariably sparked locked the commonwealth in power struggles that paid little heed to borders. Religion, an inflammatory issue in Early Modern Europe, also played a role in fueling conflict, as predominantly Catholic Poland found itself surrounded by Orthodox and Protestant powers.

Then there was the nature of Eastern Europe itself, a vast, sparsely populated region that dissipated the best efforts of invaders, ensuring that wars rarely, if ever, ended decisively. Finally, there was Muscovy—the tsars of which proved most dangerous of all to Poland for their unyielding desire to gain access to the Baltic and command the vast, almost fluid, frontier that separated the two countries. Its control ensured the upper hand in this tumultuous part of the world.

RICHES FOR THE TAKING

Eastern Europe was a tough place to carve out a nation in the sixteenth and seventeenth centuries. The rich trade of the Baltic Sea invited relentless competition. Grain, hides, furs, timber, pitch, and hemp drew merchants from all over Europe, who sustained a trade with the region that enriched Baltic ports such as Riga, Livonia (now Latvia); Danzig (Gdansk), Poland; Lubeck, in modern-day northern Germany; Reval (now Tallinn), Estonia; and Elbing (Elblag), Poland. Every great maritime nation participated in the Baltic carrying trade, including France, Great Britain, and the Netherlands, all of which were keen to keep the trade routes open at almost any cost.

Among those who benefited most from this situation was the king of Denmark, who levied a tax on every ship passing the narrows near his capital at Copenhagen before sailing into the Baltic. Known as the Sound Dues, these revenues went directly into the royal coffers, giving the crown a source of money that didn't depend on appealing to the Danish Diet, an advisory committee of aristocrats that historically represented a brake on royal ambitions. Should a Danish king find himself without widespread support for foreign adventures, he could always use the Sound Dues to fund his expeditions.

A popular target of those expeditions lay just across the sound. Sweden acquired its independence from Denmark in 1523 by force of arms, and immediately

The rich trade of the Baltic Sea invited relentless competition and underpinned the Russo-Polish Wars. Grain, hides, furs, timber, pitch, and hemp drew merchants from all over Europe, who sustained a trade with the region that made Baltic ports wealthy.

set its sights on dominating the Baltic. While the Oldenburg dynasty in Denmark had the Sound Dues to underwrite its ambitions, the ruling house of Vasa in Sweden had the support of a nobility that, while jealous of its liberties, was keenly aware that a strong throne had secured the kingdom's independence. Checks on the royal prerogative were frequent in Sweden, as they were in most early modern states, but the Vasas maintained a degree of control and support great enough to fund their imperial aspirations.

One state that had imperial ambitions that clashed with those of Sweden was Muscovy. Originally a regional power based around the city of Moscow and dwelling in the shadow of Mongol peoples to the east, the grand duchy expanded vigorously in the 1400s even as it endured a series of bloody dynastic conflicts. By the dawn of the sixteenth century, Muscovy had annexed Novgorod, Tver, and other principalities, establishing itself as the legitimate overlord of the Russian people. Just as important, its aristocracy had come to appreciate a centralized state as the surest safeguard against the sort of anarchy that characterized much of the previous century.

The man who exploited this new autocracy to its fullest was Ivan IV (r. 1533–1584), known to history as Ivan the Terrible. Ascending the throne at seventeen, he was the first Russian prince to be crowned tsar, and he set about reforming the military, streamlining the bureaucracy, and expanding his borders. This program, which tightened the bond between Ivan and the aristocratic houses of Russia and improved the training and equipment of the military, played a major role in prolonging the wars that were about to be fought in the Baltic world. For, unlike his predecessors, Ivan could now realize Muscovy's ambition to own a large piece of the Baltic coast—a goal for which he and his successors were willing to fight hard and long to achieve.

It was against these formidable players that Poland and Lithuania had to contend in the sixteenth century. Though linked by a dynastic union since the 1300s in the Jagiello family, whose members held the titles Grand Duke of Lithuania and King of Poland, the two nations remained administratively distinct. War changed that.

In 1558 Ivan, intent on securing greater access to the Baltic Sea, attacked Livonia (in modern-day Latvia), a region controlled by a branch of the Teutonic Knights known as the Livonian Order. Soon hard-pressed by the Muscovite armies, the knights sought protection from Sigismund Augustus, king of Poland and grand duke of Lithuania. The knights agreed to secularize the Livonian Order, becoming a Polish-Lithuanian vassal.

Under these circumstances, it wasn't long before the so-called "Livonian War" drew in Poland-Lithuania. As Denmark and Sweden sent troops to the Livonian region to protect their own interests, Ivan invaded Lithuania in 1563, then a vast state encompassing present-day Lithuania and much of what is now Ukraine and Belarus. In February he took the major city of Polock, opening the way to the Lithuanian capital, Wilno (modern-day Vilnius).

A NEW ERA

The war soon descended into a stalemate, largely because of a feature of the region that ensured wars would never be brief. Cities, few and far between in the expanses of Lithuania, Ukraine, and Poland, had to fall by way of siege. Once taken, the great distances between them prevented any rapid exploitation of the countryside; conquering armies had to limit their operations for fear of undertaking a long march to the next target only to be cut off by enemy forces or defeated by the onset of winter.

Nevertheless, Poland-Lithuania still had a serious problem on its hands. In addition to facing the aggression of a robust Muscovite empire, it had to deal with the inconvenient fact that the reigning monarch, Sigismund Augustus, had no heir.

The solution to both problems proved historic. In the 1569 Union of Lublin, Poland and Lithuania replaced their dynastic connection through the dying Jagiello family with a formalized partnership. Sigismund Augustus remained on the throne, but it was agreed that his successor—and all future kings—would be elected by the nobility. The result was a commonwealth that facilitated the coordination of the two nations' resources and responded to the Polish and Lithuanian penchant for a free, self-determining gentry.

What gradually emerged was a remarkable polity. The Polish-Lithuanian Commonwealth encompassed a vast range of ethnicities, including Slavs, Germans, Tatars, and Armenians. Religious diversity led to a unique degree of tolerance—Jews, Lutherans, Calvinists, Catholics, and members of the Eastern Orthodox churches lived in relative harmony almost unheard of throughout the rest of Christendom. The nobles formed an extremely numerous class—many were little better off than peasants—but cultivated a spirit of public and military service that underpinned the stability of the state even as it put serious checks on the king's autonomy.

The voting of a new monarch did not go smoothly in the wake of Sigismund Augustus's death in 1572, as the commonwealth stumbled to perfect the institutions required to find candidates and ease the transition while the war dragged on. By 1576, however, it had settled on an heir in Stefan Batory, prince of Transylvania, who turned out to be an excellent choice if only because he was an accomplished soldier.

With Swedish help he went on the offensive in Livonia and defeated the Muscovites at Wenden, then relied on the commonwealth's generous resources to take the war into

Muscovy itself. In 1579 he recaptured Polock, then took Velikie Luki the following year. Pskov, the vital stronghold that guarded Muscovy's Livonian frontier, was next. Batory subjected it to five months of siege as the Swedes kicked the Russians out of Narva and Ivangorod. Forced to the negotiating table to save Pskov, Ivan was compelled to give up all the gains he'd made in Livonia.

Sapped by the wars in Livonia and Lithuania, Ivan the Terrible's military reforms, though impressive, did not stand up to the quagmire he had gotten himself into. The tsar had created a service-based structure in which those who fought for him were rewarded with newly won territories. But when stalemate choked off his supply of new estates to reward, the system broke down.

Exhaustion of troops and resources did the rest. Increasingly hysterical, Ivan responded with characteristic ruthlessness, turning his own streltsy musketeers against disloyal opponents both real and imagined, and immersing the realm in terror and bloodshed. He died in 1584, just two years after the Treaty of Iam Zapolskii, in which he signed away all that he'd fought to win in the Livonian War.

GUNPOWDER REVOLUTION

By contrast, the system of war making employed by the commonwealth had proven not only useful but also durable. Space defined Eastern Europe. Cities were few, winters were long, and vast stretches of forest and steppe meant food and fodder were hard to come by and had to be brought along in supply trains. Under such circumstances, everything depended on the ability to cross distances quickly and efficiently, making cavalry all-important.

To be sure, infantry were still vital; both Muscovy and Poland-Lithuania had embraced the gunpowder revolution with a vengeance, favoring musketeers over pikemen, which appeared in large numbers in Western armies. But local terrain, as well as constant conflict with the hard-riding Tatars (fifteenth-century descendants of the Mongols who had conquered Asia) on the southern frontier, had driven both nations to cultivate cavalry as the bedrock of their armies.

While Muscovite horsemen were poorly equipped and trained at state expense according to Ivan's top-down authoritarian regime, Polish-Lithuania, its royal government incapable of funding the army on its own, relied on its nobles to make up the difference. Tradition dictated that Poland's celebrated hussars fight in impressive regalia, including a wing of feathers on the back and leopard-skin adornment, most of which were paid for by the nobles themselves as part of the system of rights and liberties that defined their freedom from the crown and its abuses.

The superbly trained winged Polish hussars were more than capable of holding their own against the Muscovite cavalry and their Swedish allies, even in moments of dire peril, further lengthening the duration of its wars.

Fashioned into informal retinues, these high-quality horsemen could be employed by commanders, or *hetmans*, in a wide variety of formations depending on the needs of the moment, their flexibility perfectly suited to the broad scope of Eastern warfare. The quality of this vast pool of noble horsemen would prove more than capable of offsetting the advantages of the commonwealth's enemies again and again, even in moments of dire peril, further lengthening the duration of its wars.

Complementing the hussars was a force of infantry levied from the peasantry, Cossacks from the southern Ukraine, and groups of foreign and domestic arquebusiers, or cavalry equipped with firearms. Mercenary groups from throughout Europe, always drawn to the strife of the East, were an invariable complement as well.

The Sejm, being the supreme representative body of the commonwealth, voted the taxes to pay the army, which was further subsidized by funds from the king's personal demesne. It was an unwieldy system compared to many, but it worked through the Polish-Lithuanian system of traditional obligations alongside legal checks and balances.

ROYAL AMBITION

It was fortunate that Stefan Batory built an effective military establishment, for the commonwealth was going to need it. In his successor, Sigismund III (r. 1587–1632), Poland-Lithuania got a perfect example of one of the many causes of long wars: an ambitious dynast.

Sigismund was a Vasa, a fact the commonwealth was hoping would galvanize the recent rapprochement with Sweden into an alliance. In 1592 he ascended the throne of Sweden (he was officially crowned in 1594) upon the death of his relation John III, making him monarch of both nations. But his Catholicism was viewed with suspicion in Sweden, which was overwhelmingly Protestant, making it easy for his uncle, Duke Charles, to organize an effort to throw him back across the Baltic. Civil war ensued, climaxing in the Battle of Stångebro, which went disastrously for Sigismund. Having banished his rival to Poland, Duke Charles ultimately took the throne as Charles IX.

Sigismund would never rescind his claim on the Swedish throne, but he would also never again lead an army north to seize it. Charles, however, wasn't through beating up his nephew, and in 1600 invaded Livonia. One by one, the towns of the region fell; by December he had taken the northern cities of Pernau, Fellin, and Dorpat. The following year, the Sejm of the commonwealth, goaded by Sigismund, agreed to raise funds for a Livonian expedition, which headed north in the late spring of 1601 under Lithuanian hetman Christoph Radziwill.

The commonwealth forces caught up with Charles's army in late June at Koken-hausen, where a Polish garrison had been chased from the town into the local castle. Radziwill routed the Swedes in a fierce battle in which Lithuanian cavalry were used to devastating effect.

Almost exactly a year later, the Polish-Lithuanians, this time under the command of Stanislaw Zolkiewski, again used their superior mobility to smash the Swedes outside Reval, Estonia. While launching a series of frontal assaults against the entrenched enemy position with his hussars, Zolkiewski sent his Cossack cavalry on a 10-mile (16 km) journey to strike the Swedes unexpectedly in the rear.

These victories in Livonia against the Swedish invader, however, were merely a prelude to the stunning bloodbath of Kircholm. On the morning of September 27, 1605, a small Lithuanian force under Jan Karol Chodkiewicz came up against a much larger army under the personal command of Charles IX. With just 2,600 cavalry and 1,000 infantry, Chodkiewicz had to take on an enemy 10,800 strong deployed along a ridge between the Dvina River and a wooded hill. Employing the ruse of a feigned retreat, Chodkiewicz lured the enemy into a rash advance and slaughtered them.

In the following days the citizens of nearby Riga, enlisted to clean up the battlefield, buried more than 8,900 soldiers of Charles's army, some 80 percent of the Swedish force.

THE TIME OF TROUBLES

By the time the commonwealth was giving Charles IX cause to question his invasion of Livonia, things were starting to fall apart on the eastern frontier once again. Ivan the Terrible may have been a nightmare in life, but in death he was a catastrophe, a fact that Muscovy's long border with the commonwealth turned into yet another war.

IVAN THE TERRIBLE MAY HAVE BEEN
A NIGHTMARE IN LIFE, BUT IN DEATH HE WAS
A CATASTROPHE, A FACT THAT MUSCOVY'S
LONG BORDER WITH THE COMMONWEALTH
TURNED INTO YET ANOTHER WAR.

Ivan IV, in one of his many fits of pique, allegedly struck his eldest son with a staff during a fierce argument, killing him. Whatever the true cause of Ivan Ivanovitch's death, it left the tsar's half-witted son as the only heir. Fedor I took the throne in 1584, ushering in a period of utter chaos that came to be known as the Time of Troubles.

The sickly Fedor carried on with the help of his chief minister, Boris Godunov, who was proclaimed tsar upon Fedor's death in 1598. But without unimpeachable legitimacy, and facing a state that had been in decline since the Livonian War, Godunov struggled against resistance to his rule. Ironically, his greatest threat came from a corpse: a series of three pretenders claiming to be Dmitry, a son of Ivan the Terrible who had supposedly died in 1591, bedeviled the stability of Muscovy.

When Godunov died in 1605, he had failed to defeat the "first Dmitry," whose followers placed him on the throne and then murdered him in 1606 for marrying a Pole and filling the capital with unsavory foreign influences. Vasilii Shuiskii, a *boyar*, or Russian aristocrat, was elevated to tsar, his first order of business being the destruction of no less than two other Dmitrys and their enthusiastic followers. Bedlam reigned in Muscovy.

From Sigismund III's perspective, the situation was delicate. The commonwealth was already at war with Sweden, after all. But the troubles in Moscow were drawing in Poles and Lithuanians who had devoted themselves to one or another of the Dmitrys and who now, thanks to increasing Russian consternation and xenophobia, were being killed in the chaos. The first Dmitry had been a Catholic and therefore was seen by Orthodox Russians as an interloper backed by Poland, a largely Catholic nation. Matters in Muscovy were taking an ugly sectarian direction.

Driven by this, as well as the signing of a new Russo-Swedish alliance, Sigismund opted for war against Muscovy in 1609. Chief on his list of priorities was Smolensk, the mighty fortress near Muscovy's border with Lithuania, the conquest of which would place the commonwealth in an ideal bargaining position. He began siege operations against it in 1609, the year before his hetman Stanislaw Zolkiewski won his spectacular victory at Klushino against enormous odds. Matters took a decisive turn when a group of boyars in Moscow, having defeated Vasilii Shuiskii, elected Sigismund's son Wladyslaw as tsar.

Smolensk, along with Danzig, Poland's largest city, was one of the most heavily fortified places in Europe. Between 1595 and 1602, the Russians had undertaken the modernization of the city's defenses, embarking on one of the grandest construction projects in European history. The result was a stronghold that Sigismund, with 22,000 men and some thirty heavy guns, could not take in less than two years.

Poland-Lithuania got a perfect example of one of the many causes of long wars in the form of Sigismund III—an ambitious dynast. He focused his energies on taking Smolensk, the fortress on the Lithanian-Muscovy border. Once taken, it opened all of Muscovy to invasion.

But take it he did, opening all Muscovy to invasion. In one of the most notorious chapters of Russian history, a garrison of Poles occupied Moscow until 1612. Although they were ultimately starved into submission by an angry populace, the event served as the high-water mark of Poland's interminable fight against Muscovy.

SIGISMVNDVS III DEI
POLONIAE SVECIE
TIAE VANDALI
REX

A STORM FROM THE NORTH

Wladyslaw would never sit on the throne of the tsars, despite leading an army against Moscow in 1618 that helped secure the Truce of Deulino, in which Muscovy was forced to cede Smolensk to the commonwealth. But he and his father Sigismund soon had bigger things to worry about—namely, Sweden. Again. For the Scandinavian heavyweight now produced a king who dragged out Poland's long agony of perpetual war through nothing but sheer expansionism.

In 1611, Gustav Adolf had succeeded his father Charles IX to the Swedish throne. Brilliant and charismatic, Gustav Adolf (often referred to as Gustavus Adolphus) was prudent and methodical where Charles had been rash and impulsive. One of his signature achievements was bringing the most cutting-edge theories on warfare then current in Western Europe to his native Sweden, creating a military revolution in the north. Borrowing from the Dutch school, which favored linear tactics over squares and more firepower over the pike, the king struck a balance, based on lessons learned against Poland in the past, between powerful infantry and cavalry capable of fending off the most formidable horsemen.

In 1621, Gustav Adolf invaded Livonia, sweeping out the Polish, whose finest troops were busy at the other end of the commonwealth defending against an army of Ottoman invaders. He then descended on Royal Prussia, the northernmost region of Poland around the wealthy city of Danzig. In a three-day battle before the town of Mewe in Prussia at the end of September 1626, Gustav's immaculately trained army consistently drew the commonwealth forces into situations favorable to the Swedish infantry, whose firepower proved devastating. A similar fate awaited the Polish-Lithuanian forces at Dirschau, also in northern Poland, where even the Swedish cavalry gave a good accounting of themselves against the famously implacable hussars.

The loser of Dirschau, hetman Stanislaw Koniecpolski, withdrew to lick his wounds and revamp his strategy. Clearly the Swedes had the tactical advantage: their well-drilled infantry with state-of-the-art muskets, gift for quick and sturdy fieldworks, and hard-charging cavalry (the Swedes favored the saber over the lance) had changed the balance of power in the Baltic.

Koniecpolski turned to raiding the countryside, relying on his horsemen to deny the occupying Swedes any safe haven and burning the crops on which Gustav Adolf relied to feed his troops locally. Through 1627 and 1628 the armies danced about each other, the Swedes scoring minor victories and expanding their bridgehead in Prussia but gradually losing numbers to attrition, ambush, and desertion.

Then, in 1629, events took a decisive turn. Ferdinand, the Habsburg emperor in Vienna, saddled with his own war but eager to strike a blow against rival Sweden, sent 5,000 reinforcements to Koniecpolski. Gustav Adolf was caught trying to attempt a withdrawal to the north in June near a place called Honigfelde on the Leibe River, precipitating a running battle that ended climactically in a savage hand-to-hand melee. After dreadful losses, the defeated Swedes broke off and retreated. Like a lightning bolt, Koniecpolski's victory rejuvenated Polish-Lithuanian pride, proving that the Swedes were not invincible. The following September, Sweden and the commonwealth signed the truce of Altmark, ensuring a grudging peace between the two nations.

The breather would not last long. For Muscovy, the archenemy in the east, was stirring once again. Still smarting from the 1619 Treaty of Deulino in which Muscovy had been forced to give away Smolensk and other possessions along the Lithuanian frontier, Tsar Michael (r. 1613–1645, the first of the Romanov dynasty that would endure until 1917) prepared for war with the commonwealth. As had been the case since the previous century, the massive territorial fault line between Poland and Russia served to lure an ambitious ruler into a military gambit. The death of Sigismund III in 1632 presented an opportunity too good to pass up, and Michael soon invaded. By the end of October his army was outside Smolensk.

Wladyslaw IV (r. 1632–1648), son and elected heir of Sigismund, acted swiftly to amass a relief army. Supported by the Sejm, which voted him an army of more than 23,000, the new king began smuggling troops into Smolensk to buttress the city's defense and, in September, marched east with 14,000 men. As reinforcements trickled in, the force grew to more than twice that.

To take the city, Michael had built an army around Western instructors. The Time of Troubles had shaken the Muscovite state to its core, requiring bold new initiatives. Michael turned to the West, welcoming foreigners in droves to train his streltsy and teach his cavalry the latest tactics. Artillery, made by royal foundries around Moscow, employed the best technology, and now poured ruin on the bastions of Smolensk.

The Polish-Lithuanians launched concerted attacks throughout September 1633 on the fortified Muscovite positions encircling the city, gradually forcing them to withdraw back into the Russian main camp. In October, after raiders destroyed a huge Muscovite supply dump, the Polish-Lithuanians launched a series of desperate assaults to take a hill overlooking the Muscovite camp, using it as an artillery platform to threaten the whole Russia position. A siege of the besiegers ensued, with the encircled and harried Muscovites waiting for a relief force that never came.

It was a hard winter. On March 1 the Muscovites surrendered. Their commander, Mikhail Borisovich Shein, was forced to prostrate himself before the Polish king. Not long afterward, the so-called Smolensk War petered out. Poland was allowed to keep Smolensk while Wladyslaw renounced his claim to the Russian throne.

THE DELUGE

Peace came to the commonwealth, whether King Wladyslaw wanted it or not. While hoping to launch further offensives, he was thwarted by the Sejm, who refused to authorize any more taxes.

The tranquility, of course, was short-lived. And when war came, it was from an unlikely quarter. In 1648 the Cossacks of the Ukraine exploded into the commonwealth in open revolt. The Cossacks were a group of semiautonomous military communities based on the Don and Dnieper rivers, and their skills in infantry and cavalry fighting made them a rich source of recruitment for both the Russian and the Polish states.

Although their ethnic origins are disputed, the Cossack hosts had by the seventeenth century become a vast, loosely organized, stateless nation with the ability to shape events through threat of violence. Poland-Lithuania, having routinely kept thousands of Cossacks on the registers as paid fighters for generations, was nevertheless eager to limit their role, especially in peacetime. After the conclusion of the Smolensk War, the Sejm cut their numbers further, spreading discontent through Cossack communities that had long relied on Polish service for their livelihood.

Moreover, the commonwealth's peculiar manner of funding its wars had inadvertently exacerbated the problem. The royal demesne of the Vasa kings, traditionally used as a means of supporting military units, had for decades been divvied out as currency to powerful magnates by a crown with little else in the way of political leverage. The result was an increasing reliance on extraordinary taxation by the Sejm, which ultimately broke the back of the gentry. Many of the petty nobles who could neither bear the increased taxation nor find employment in a magnate's retinue joined the Cossacks, attracted by their fierce egalitarianism and solidarity. The Cossack communities had been growing for years, swelled by malcontents, and their very presence and increasing agitation became a new factor in dragging out the Russo-Polish Wars.

Their fury now bore down on a hapless commonwealth whose army, thanks to peacetime reductions, had never been smaller. It was the beginning of a period known as the Deluge—a flood of invasions that all but destroyed Poland-Lithuania and began the state's decline.

Wladyslaw IV Vasa died in May 1648, shackling the state with the further burden of choosing a successor. The commonwealth chose the late king's brother, John Casimir, who set about picking up the pieces of his nation after the November election. A desperate struggle ensued, with the Cossack forces appealing for help to Tsar Alexis (r. 1645–1676) for direct aid.

It took a while, but Alexis eventually joined the fray in 1654, commencing the Thirteen Years' War between his empire and the commonwealth. Religion had already come to frame the revolt: the Cossacks, overwhelmingly Orthodox, grew to see their revolt against a callous commonwealth as a righteous crusade against Catholic oppressors, a fact that Alexis was all too eager to exploit. As fellow Orthodox believers, the Muscovites quickly formed a bond with their new Cossack allies. The Russians invaded in three great columns, the center of which, the largest at 41,000 strong, headed straight for Smolensk, which fell in October 1654. Much of the Grand Duchy of Lithuania followed as hetman Janusz Radziwill retreated before the onslaught, too weak to do anything.

By spring of 1655 the Swedes, under Charles X (r. 1654–1660), had invaded commonwealth territory from Livonia and Pomerania, in northern Germany, in the hopes of grabbing as much as they could before it was all gone, the refusal of John Casimir to give up his claim on the Swedish throne offering Charles a foolproof excuse. That year, as the Swedish tide swept south through Poland, the Muscovites conquered the Lithuanian capital of Wilno.

The following year was even worse for the commonwealth. Frederick William, Elector of Brandenburg and Duke of Prussia, was convinced by Charles to nullify his feudal relationship to Poland-Lithuania and become instead a vassal of Sweden. It wasn't long before his troops were fighting alongside Sweden's. In the two-day Battle of Warsaw, in July 1656, a combined Swedish-Brandenburg army managed to pin a commonwealth force against the banks of the Vistula River and deal it a major defeat.

The commonwealth was crumbling like a broken levy in the rainy season. Even the Transylvanians joined the beating, their prince, George Rakoczi, drawn by Swedish inducements in December 1656 to lead an army of 25,000 against the desperate Poles. Only a miracle, it seemed, could save them now.

"TO PERISH CORPSE UPON CORPSE"

The situation, however, wasn't quite what it seemed. The Swedes and Muscovites, having come so far so fast, found themselves overstretched in a country that quickly came to loathe their presence. Poland, in effect, had become a perfect storm of unending conflict in which religious strife, despoilment of the countryside, and the sheer size of the commonwealth itself conspired to prevent anything like a peaceful resolution. Fueled by the confessional differences between Lutheran, Orthodox, and Catholic, the occupation gradually descended into a cycle of violence and retribution. Such an environment proved ideal for fomenting resistance, allowing the faltering commonwealth army to find its footing while the enemy scrambled to control an increasingly explosive situation.

Moreover, the Cossack rebels, whose grievances had inspired the conflict, had grown disillusioned with their Muscovite allies. Unlike the informal society that governed politics in Poland and Lithuania, the Russians and their tsar dictated from above in a fashion wholly at odds with Cossack freedoms. It wasn't long before the Cossacks felt duped into becoming little better than slaves to Alexis and his plans of conquest. Divisions appeared in Cossack communities, undermining the war effort.

The year 1657 had yet more surprises in store. In May, King John Casimir received some 12,000 reinforcements from the Habsburgs. But even more important, Denmark saw its window of opportunity and, in June, declared war against Sweden.

In a virtual flash, the situation changed. Charles departed with much of his army to lead a series of bold strikes against Copenhagen, leaving Rakoczi and his Transylvanians to deal as best they could alongside the Muscovites. Before long, the resurgent commonwealth forces had routed Rakoczi and even compelled Frederick William of Brandenburg to reinstate his vassalage to Poland-Lithuania as Duke of Prussia. Three years later, the commonwealth settled a series of treaties with Sweden, Brandenburg, and Austria. Peace at last reigned in the north.

But not in the east. The war with Muscovy still raged, compelling John Casimir to send a pair of armies eastward into the heart of Lithuania. At Polanka, they met like a pincer to battle a larger Muscovite force. What ensued on June 27 was classic Polish-Lithuanian tactics. Attacking from the flanks and rear, the Polish-Lithuanian cavalry, with the support of a pair of guns, forced the enemy infantry out of its defenses and drove off the enemy horse. The commonwealth infantry and artillery then surrounded the exposed enemy foot in a small wood and methodically reduced it, producing a massacre. "Hard it was to look upon so much human blood as there was in that throng," wrote an eyewitness, "the soldiers being packed close together and so to perish corpse upon corpse."

Further victories followed. Soon the commonwealth had purged itself of the enemies that had fueled the Deluge. The cost, however, was high: in the 1667 Truce of Andrusovo, Muscovy kept Smolensk and gained Kiev. The Ukranian Cossacks were divided along the Dnieper between Russia and Poland, the deep divisions with Cossack leadership preventing anything more ambitious.

A deeper price had been paid, as well. The Deluge had weakened the foundations of the commonwealth, exposing the weaknesses in Poland-Lithuania's consensual form of government during wartime. How many more wars could it survive? As Russia and the other great states of the Baltic centralized, Poland-Lithuania remained a fascinating and noble curiosity—one that found it difficult to endure in such a relentlessly combative environment.

During the eighteenth century its neighbors would undertake the dismantling of Poland, condemning to history the once mighty, multiethnic experiment that had defied so many assaults. Not until the twentieth century would Poland reemerge as an independent state—one whose identity began three hundred years previously in a glorious, albeit blood-soaked, era, when virtually everything about Poland's situation guaranteed war without end.

CHAPTER 12

THE BALKAN WARS

THE FIELD OF THE BLACKBIRDS

1912–2001

The religious, national, and ethnic tensions that convulsed this entire region began with a battle that took place in 1389. The Balkan Wars continued into the twentieth century when Bulgaria, Greece, Montenegro, and Serbia attacked the crumbling Ottoman Empire, and ended, for the time being, with a bloody civil war in the 1990s.

And she alone walks out before the tower.

Thus she speaks and asks the two black birds:

"Ravens! In the name of God Almighty

Tell me where you come from this bright morning.

Could it be you come from Kosovo?

Have you seen two mighty armies there?

And did those armies join in furious combat?

Great black birds: Which army won the battle?"

—"The Battle of Kosovo," Serbian traditional poem
Translated by John Matthias and Vladeta Vuckovic

The mountainous peninsula that forms southeastern Europe wasn't called the Balkans until the beginning of the nineteenth century—the name *balkan* is a Turkish word referring to a wooded ridge or series of low mountains—but that name has stuck, carrying with it connotations of bloodlust, chaos, and never-ending ethnic, religious, and nationalist warfare that dates back for centuries. It is a region of the world that, if not experiencing outright conflict, is simmering with repressed violence.

There are numerous reasons for this. The Balkan countries are a mixing ground of three different religions—Roman Catholicism, Eastern Orthodox Christianity, and Islam—and the strife that can historically accompany these faiths. Because the Balkans lie astride traditional trade and invasion routes between Central Asia and Europe, they are lands that have often been occupied or vied over by empires—the Ottomans, the Habsburgs, and the Soviet Union. But a primary reason for the long war in the Balkans has been a battle that took place on June 28, 1389, on a desolate plain high in the mountains known as Kosovo Polje—the Field of the Blackbirds.

The Serbs, in fact, lost this battle to the Ottoman Turks, but in one sense it doesn't matter. Remarkably, writes the historian André Gerolymatos, "in the kaleidoscope that is Balkan history, success and failure have almost the same significance. Both have provided the justification for future conflict. Great defeats are fodder for revenge and spectacular victories the prelude to further conquest."

THE GREAT DEFEAT

The Field of the Blackbirds lies in the self-proclaimed Republic of Kosovo (formerly a province of modern-day Serbia, which disputes Kosovo's claims of independence), about 5 miles (8 km) northwest of the capital city of Pristina. The mountains break open here on the wide flat area that in 1389 was bordered by Serbia, Bosnia, Herzegovina, and Albania. What we know about the battle that took place there that year owes more to legend than history, but a few bare facts are present.

The Ottoman Turks, in their movements toward empire (see chapter 4), already occupied territory from Asia Minor to the southern part of the Balkans. They had caused such deterioration in the once-powerful Byzantine Empire that it basically controlled only the area immediately surrounding its grand capital city of Constantinople. In the spring of 1389, Sultan Murad I marched on the Balkans with an army comprised of Ottomans and Christian vassals. Countering them was an army of Christians—Serbians, Hungarians, and Albanians—raised by the Serbian prince Lazar Hrebeljanovic.

In the thirteenth century, a powerful Serbian leader named King Stefan Uroš I had consolidated the feudal Serbian kingdom. His successors had expanded it southward at the expense of the Byzantines, who were still reeling from the sack of Constantinople in 1204 by the armies of the Fourth Crusade, which controlled the city until 1261. The Serbs might have reached far enough south to ally with the

Greeks and overthrow the Byzantines, but after the death of the great Serbian king Stephan Dusan in 1355, the Serbs fell prey to internecine strife and feuding. Prince Lazar was able to temporarily unite them to ride out and meet the Ottoman threat. According to the epic series of Kosovo poems—an oral tradition that arose after the battle—Lazar warned the Serbs:

Whoever is a Serb and of Serbian birth,
And who does not come to Kosovo Polje
to do battle against the Turks,
Let him have neither a male
nor a female offspring,
Let him have no crop. . . .

However, Lazar himself fell prey to the type of feuding that had so crippled the Serbs in the past. Although his army probably outnumbered that of Murad, Lazar allowed himself to be convinced that his son-in-law Milosh Obravich was going to betray him to the Turks. According to legend, an enraged Milosh decided to prove his loyalty by assassinating Murad and so, before the battle, he came to the Ottoman camp under the guise of pretending to defect and stabbed the sultan to death before being killed by Murad's bodyguards. Another story has that he played dead on the battlefield and stabbed the sultan as the latter toured the grisly scene after the battle. Or he didn't even exist, as some historians believe.

The real traitor actually may have been the Serb leader Vuk Brankovic, who possibly conspired with Murad for his 12,000 soldiers to retreat at a strategic moment, thus ensuring an Ottoman victory. On the other hand, it is also possible that Vuk made a wise decision to retreat and save his forces after the Ottoman army broke through the Serb lines. We'll never know for sure. What is known is that Murad was killed that day—

An eighteenth-century copper engraving depicts the 1389 Battle of Kosovo at Polje in which the Ottoman Turks defeated Serbia and its allies. The battle would come to be the Serbs' reason for future wars. "Great defeats are fodder for revenge and spectacular victories the prelude to further conquest," one historian wrote of the Balkans.

ullstein bild / The Granger Collection

whether in battle or by Milosh or a nameless assassin—and that Lazar was captured and executed by the Ottomans. The Ottomans won, named a new sultan in Bayezid I, and continued their conquest of the Balkans.

The Serbs lost—but gained forever what André Gerolymatos calls their national "themes of self-sacrifice, betrayal, and assassination," which resonated not just under the centuries of Ottoman domination to come but also under the domination of the Habsburgs and the Soviet Union. Something had been stolen from the Serbs—by treachery, and despite Serbian heroism—and they would always be determined to get it back.

"I AM SULTAN HERE"

The Ottoman Empire held sway over the Balkan Peninsula for five long centuries. "The coming of the Turks," writes historian Mark Mazower, "is often seen as ushering in a new dark age from which Balkan Christians never fully recovered." In fact, as Mazower points out, the Ottoman Empire, at first, brought advantages that included a better system of roads, better security in the heretofore lawless parts of the peninsula, and, surprisingly, relative freedom of religion. The Ottomans had learned to allow people to worship as they chose, for the most part, although these captive peoples were not allowed to build churches that were higher than mosques, or to wear green (the color of Islam), and Christians were also taxed at a higher rate.

Too, under the Ottoman model of empire, all land belonged to the state, not individual aristocrats, so that peasant farmers who had previously been in thrall to petty feudal dictators tended to have their lot in life bettered, at least to some extent. (The fact that Balkan aristocrats could not pass on their land to their children also kept dynasties from arising that might challenge the Turks.)

However, there were obviously drawbacks. Some children were expected to be provided to Turkish janissary armies, Muslims tended to get all the good jobs in the bureaucracies, and—most galling of all—those with a belief in national self-determination were thwarted everywhere they turned. What would become the Balkan states—Serbia, Croatia, Montenegro, Albania, Bosnia, Herzegovina, Macedonia, and Bulgaria—were no more than provinces in the Turkish Balkan possessions.

By the beginning of the nineteenth century, however, the Ottoman Empire was well on its way to falling apart. The Ottoman collapse started as early as 1683 when the Austrians and Russians began to push back the empire, and continued throughout the eighteenth century. As the Ottomans faced strong military threats from the British, Russians, and Austrians, and as the borders of their territory constricted, they began to tax Balkan peasants more and more. The result was that many of these hardy and

The Balkan countries, shown here, are a mixing ground of three different religions—Roman Catholicism, Eastern Orthodox Christianity, and Islam—and the strife that can historically accompany these faiths. Because the Balkans lie astride traditional trade and invasion routes between Central Asia and Europe, they are lands that have often been occupied or vied over by empires—the Ottomans, the Habsburgs, and the Soviet Union.

Library of Congress

independent people retreated to mountainous refuges where imperial armies could not reach them. Here they lived with something very like complete autonomy, many of them making a living as robbers and brigands. One British traveler through Albania in the late eighteenth century found himself the unwilling guest of one such robber, who told him: "Your coffee is ours, your money is ours, and your blood is ours. I am sultan here. I am king of England here."

In 1804, what is generally called the First Serbian Uprising broke out. Ironically, it began when Serbians fought on behalf of the Ottoman sultan to attack a group of rogue janissaries who had massacred numerous Christian supporters of the sultan. However, the sultan refused to aid these Serbs—it would not do for him to arm Christians against Muslims, even Muslims who were his enemies. Even so, the Serbs were able to fight off the forces the sultan sent against them for nine long years, using guerilla tactics they learned from the brigands among them, who had fought Ottoman army patrols sent out to capture them. By 1813, the Ottomans were finally able to bring Serbia under control, but the long war was not a good sign. A ragged, poorly armed group of peasant farmers and bandits had fought them to a standstill—in the main because the peasants used their rugged terrain against the Ottomans, but also because they were instilled with a fighting spirit that came of the burgeoning sense of themselves as a people.

THE SEEDS OF REVOLUTION

As ideas from the French Revolution filtered into Balkan cities and the War of Greek Independence (1821–1832) ended with the Greeks completely throwing off Ottoman rule, the Serbs and other Balkan nationalities continued to lobby for freedom. With the Ottoman Empire—famously called by Tsar Nicholas I "the sick man of Europe"— crumbling from internal corruption and external enemies, it seemed that independence was an attainable goal. After the Russo-Turkish War of 1877–1878, the Turks were forced by the Treaty of Berlin to recognize Bulgaria, Serbia, Montenegro, and Romania as independent states, while Austria-Hungary occupied Bosnia-Herzegovina.

However, the Balkan states were still the playthings of the great powers of the time, which only supported independence for them as a way of further weakening the Ottomans while at the same time strengthening their own positions. For instance, the Habsburgs of Austria merely wanted Bosnia as a way to keep what they considered aggressive Serbian expansion in check, while the British sought independent Balkan states to force the Russians away from Crimea and the Mediterranean. As André Gerolymatos writes: "The Balkan communities under Ottoman rule received support for their struggles for emancipation only when it was in the strategic interests of the Europeans."

None of the European powers held a high opinion of the region. Archduke Franz Ferdinand, heir to the Austrian Habsburg throne, once described Serbia as a land of "thieves and murderers and bandits and a few plum trees." The great German chancellor Otto von Bismarck wrote that "the Balkans are not worth the bones of a single Pomeranian grenadier."

But Balkan states themselves had their own ideas about their worth. In 1893, radicals in Macedonia founded the Internal Macedonian Revolutionary Organization (IMRO), which used guerilla tactics involving rebel soldiers called *chetas* to unsuccessfully overthrow the Turkish government. When the IMRO rose up in a general revolution in the spring of 1903, the Ottomans threw 175,000 soldiers into Macedonia to put it down; the chetas responded by attacking small Ottoman units, massacring Muslim settlements, and hitting Ottoman supply trains. However, the sheer number of Ottoman forces was too much for them and the IMRO was finally defeated by the fall of 1903. As an example of the conflicting forces at play in the region, when the IMRO was diminished, other guerilla bands—Serbians, Bulgarians, Romanians, and Greeks—stepped in, fighting each other and the Ottomans for control of Macedonia.

Serbia had achieved its independence, but radicals there were fueled by dreams of what they had lost so many years ago on the Field of the Blackbirds. Serbia wanted more than just independence—it wanted the ancient Serbia of Prince Lazar, land that now included Kosovo, Bosnia-Herzegovina, Slovenia, and Croatia. A successful revolution in Albania in 1911—in which radicals demanded to be identified not as Muslims or non-Muslims (i.e., Christians or Jews), as they were on Ottoman census roles, but as Albanians—showed that armed revolt could work.

THE BALKAN WARS

In 1912, with the backing of the Russian government, which wished to use the Balkans as a buffer against the Austro-Hungarian Empire, Serbia and Bulgaria made a secret agreement to attack the Ottoman Empire. Joining them were Macedonia and Greece.

The war began in mid-October with Serbian and Bulgarian forces moving on Turkish forces in Thrace. These were no guerilla actions, but massed armies, with artillery and machine guns, meeting in battles involving hundreds of thousands of men on both sides. The Bulgarians took immense losses—in one battle, 16,000 men—in their attempt to destroy the Ottoman army. Ultimately weakened by overextended supply lines and a cholera epidemic that killed or weakened an additional 1,600 troops, they were unable to break through their enemy's lines. However, in the spring of 1913, they were able to besiege and capture the strategic Ottoman city of

Adrianople, their ancient capital (before Constantinople), which sits close to the borders of Greece and Bulgaria.

The fighting was fierce, with the Bulgarians attacking out of anger and national feeling and the Ottomans digging in, fighting back with desperation. In Macedonia, the Serbian army destroyed Ottoman opposition and swept through the province, while Greeks and Montenegrins also scored pivotal victories. The Ottoman government, which had been toppled in the middle of the war by the Young Turks' coup d'état, sued for peace. Finally, the Ottoman Empire was crushed in Europe.

The Serbs took Kosovo as their reward, while the Greeks also scored impressive gains, taking territory in Macedonia. Bulgaria, despite doing a lion's share of the fighting, was rewarded with much less; in the summer of 1913, Bulgaria declared war on its former allies, and was soundly defeated. Even more land went to Serbia, which was rapidly becoming the most powerful country in the Balkans, which frightened Austria-Hungary.

Austria then began to plot with Albania and a growing and powerful Germany under Kaiser Wilhelm II to crush Serbia. Naturally, various Serbian nationalist groups did not take kindly to this. On June 28, 1914—the 525th anniversary of the mythical Serbian defeat at the Field of the Blackbirds—a young Serbian nationalist named Gavrilo Princip played his role as the nation's assassin. He fatally shot Archduke Franz Ferdinand—first in line to the Austria-Hungary throne—and his wife, Sophie, as they visited the Bosnian capital of Sarajevo.

Because of the interlocking alliances between nations, the shooting set off a chain of events that resulted in the beginning of World War I—Austria-Hungary invaded Serbia; France and Russia came to the aid of Serbia, which was their ally; and Germany came to the aid of Austria-Hungary. Fierce fighting took place in Serbia and the Balkans throughout the war. Afterward, however, the victorious Allied Powers dismembered the Austria-Hungarian Empire and—tone-deaf to some of the actual tensions in the region—created what was clumsily called the Kingdom of the Serbs, Croats, and Slovenes, which eventually became known as Yugoslavia (which means "Land of the Southern Slavs").

The Croats—Roman Catholics who were age-old enemies of the mainly Eastern Orthodox Serbs—were concerned that the far larger Serbia would rule this new kingdom from its capital of Belgrade, which turned out to be true. Serbians would fill almost all positions in the Yugoslav army, government, and civil service.

"NOBODY HAS THE RIGHT TO BEAT YOU"

With the coming of World War II, violence in the region reached a new high. The Balkans were occupied by the Nazis, with whom Albania, Hungary, and Bulgaria were allied.

The June 28, 1989, rally at Polje, Kosovo, by Serbians marked the 600th anniversary of their defeat during the Battle of Kosovo. Two million Serbs gathered, some shown here carrying portraits of Serbian leaders Slobodan Milošević (right), and Borisav Jović (left). Milošević used the event as a rallying cry to war against the Muslims in the Balkan region.

Associated Press

After a lightning-fast invasion in April 1941, the Yugoslav army surrendered. The Nazis dismembered the country, turning most of it into the so-called "Independent Kingdom of the Croats," which were Nazi sympathizers.

As is always the case in the endless wars of the Balkans, age-old animosities sprang forth anew. The Croats were now in a position of power over the Serbs and used it to perpetrate almost unimaginable violence on their Eastern Orthodox adversaries. The fascist Croat Ustase regime, using the Nazi concentration camp model, set up extermination camps, the largest of which was Jasenovac, a huge complex of five different camps spread out over 150 square miles (388 square km) on the banks of the Sava River. There, anywhere from 70,000 to 400,000 (depending on which figure you believe) ethnic Serbs were butchered—shot, gassed, cremated alive, hung from cranes, stabbed, or pounded to death with mallets.

Partisan armies fought back against the Nazis in Yugoslavia. The most successful of groups was led by the charismatic communist leader Josip Broz, known by the nickname Tito, who, with assistance from the Allies, including Russia, was able to keep thousands of German forces tied down in Yugoslavia.

At the end of World War II, Tito became prime minister and later president for life of Yugoslavia. Although he was socialist in his sympathies and Yugoslavia was part of the Communist Bloc directly after the war, Tito was able through sheer willpower and charisma to steer the country on a relatively independent course. From 1945 to 1980, when Tito died, Yugoslavia was comparatively quiet internally, thanks to Tito's control. But the unity was superficial. The majority Serbs were in control in the country, something the Croats, Muslim Bosnians, and Albanians resented. Many Serbs, in the meantime, longed to gain revenge for Croatian atrocities during the war.

After Tito's death, Yugoslavia was governed by a so-called "collective presidency," with members from each of the country's six republics and two autonomous provinces, but this did not take long to unravel. During the 1980s, an ambitious Serbian Communist Party politician named Slobodan Milošević found an issue that would help him gain power in the country. Milošević claimed that in Kosovo, one of Yugoslavia's autonomous provinces, minority Serbs were being oppressed by majority (and mainly Muslim) Albanians. In part because of the Field of the Blackbirds, nationalist-minded Serbs had always considered Kosovo to be the center of their homeland, and it struck a chord that here, in the very place where the Serb national dream was defeated 600 years before, it was being oppressed again.

Or so Milošević claimed. In fact, it mainly appears that he was seeking to grab power in any way he could get it, and he hit upon the idea of bringing up the age-old

Ottoman defeat of the Serbs in a new guise—as that of Muslims keeping modern-day Serbs from getting their due. On June 28, 1989—the 600th anniversary of the battle—Milošević traveled to a well-publicized speaking engagement at the Field of the Blackbirds. More than 2 million Serbs showed up on a brilliantly sunny day on the huge flat battlefield, chanting the name "Slobodan! Slobodan!" over and over again (Slobodan means "freedom" in Serbo-Croatian). Arriving by helicopter, surrounded by Orthodox priests and girls in Serbian folk costumes, Milošević made a stirring speech. He told the crowd: "Nobody, either now or in the future, has the right to beat you . . . After six centuries, we are again waging struggle and confronting battles." These battles were not yet military ones, Milošević said—"although armed struggle cannot be ruled out"—but battles against discrimination by Muslims.

The crowd easily picked up on the theme and shouted back to Milošević in verse form, comparing him to the martyred Prince Lazar:

> Oh Tsar Lazar, you didn't have the fortune
> To walk shoulder to shoulder with Slobo.

It was an extraordinary scene. Millions of contemporary Serbians standing on an ancient battlefield in the ecstatic grip of a historical myth, and embracing another myth at the same time—the myth of ancient Serbia (what Milošević called "Greater Serbia") whole at last, as it supposedly was just before it was destroyed by its enemies and the perfidy of traitors.

THE HORROR OF THE BOSNIAN WAR

Two years after the Soviet Union fell apart in late 1989, civil war began in the former Yugoslavia as Slovenia and Croatia declared their independence. Slobodan Miloševi´c, by this time president (in reality, virtual dictator) of Serbia, sent troops to intervene in Slovenia in June 1991, but the fighting lasted only ten days, as the international community quickly recognized Slovenia's independence. Even so, dozens of soldiers on either side were killed and the internecine nature of the conflict was clear as Slovenian soldiers in the Yugoslav People's Army (the JNA), mainly the rank and file, deserted to the Slovenian side, while Serbian officers tried to hold them in check.

The conflict in Croatia was a far bloodier matter. Croatia contained a large number of ethnic Serbs who opposed its independence from Serbia; at first the conflict inside Croatia was between this population and the native Croatians. Soon, however, the JNA invaded Croatia and savage fighting broke out. Huge numbers of refugees were displaced on both sides and the term *ethnic cleansing* was used for the first time to describe driving people from their home areas and/or murdering them. During the battle for the Croatian city of Vukovar in the fall of 1991, more than 300 Croatian military prisoners and civilians were murdered and buried in mass graves by Serbian paramilitary units. Many others were transported to the Sremska Mitrovica prison camp in Serbia, where they were abused, raped, and sometimes executed, with many Serbian prison guards using as their excuse for such brutality the Croatian Ustase camps during World War II.

From the beginning of the war, history was always present, showing that age-old conflicts were never truly resolved. One journalist who interviewed both Serbs and Croatians wrote, "The answer to an artillery attack yesterday will begin in the year 925, illustrated with maps [of that year]." A cease-fire was finally arranged between Croatia and Serbia with the help of the United Nations in 1992, but not before 10,000 people on both sides were killed. Hostilities would later resume between Serbia and Croatia, but for now, both sides had something different in mind. Serbian president Milošević and Croatian president Franjo Tudjman had made a secret deal to divide Bosnia, which would declare independence in August 1992, between them, thus creating a "Greater Serbia" and a "Greater Croatia."

THE MOTIVE FOR ALL THESE KILLINGS WAS REVENGE—BUT A REVENGE ROOTED DEEP IN THE PAST, IN WHAT HAD HAPPENED AT THE FIELD OF THE BLACKBIRDS, AND AFTERWARD.

The war in Bosnia was a true ethnic conflict, in which Serbs and Croatians sought to link up with enclaves of their own nationalities, while fighting Muslim Bosnians. The UN had declared an arms embargo, but this simply favored the Serbs, because they had all the heavy weaponry of the army of the former Yugoslav Republic.

In the spring of 1992, the Serbs began to besiege the Bosnian capital of Sarajevo, where Gavrilo Princip had assassinated Archduke Franz Ferdinand so many years before. Sarajevo, once a beautiful city (where the 1984 Winter Olympics were held), was devastated by the surrounding Serb forces, which, over the course of a four-year siege—one of the longest in the history of modern warfare—fired 350 shells into the city every day. Snipers nested in high-rises and in the woods on the hills surrounding the city and shot civilians at random, for no reason but terror. The main boulevard of the city became known as "Sniper Alley," with Serbian sharpshooters accounting for 260 dead civilians, sixty of them children.

In central Bosnia, the mainly Muslim Bosnian army was fighting a separate war against the Bosnian Croatians, who wished to become a part of Croatia. In the meantime, Serbian irregular troops, Bosnian Serbs armed by Serbia, and the Serbian National Army (formerly the JNA) began a campaign to wipe out Muslims in Bosnia.

It is chilling that, despite growing international awareness of the level of ethnic cleansing happening and UN intervention in certain areas, the Serbs managed to set up numerous concentration camps (such as Brcko, where 3,000 Serbs were executed in 1992), as well as "rape camps," where hundreds of Bosnian women of all ages were held captive and repeatedly raped. These actions were condoned by Serbian leaders such as Radovan Karadžić and General Ratko Mladić. Countless other murders took place on a smaller, more informal scale, usually perpetrated by Serb paramilitary groups such as the Serbian Tigers, a murderous force run by Željko Ražnatović (nicknamed Arkan).

The motive for all these killings was revenge—but a revenge rooted deep in the past, in what had happened at the Field of the Blackbirds, and afterward. The Muslims being killed by Milošević and his commanders were killed because of the actions of their ancestors hundreds of years before. As in the conflicts between the Arabs and the Israelis (see chapter 7), history, in a very real sense, was always present.

"PREPARE FOR MARTYRDOM"

Despite massacres that would be classified as genocides, including the killing of 8,000 Muslims at Srebrenica in July 1995, the UN and the United States did not act decisively until Serbian forces finally overstepped in Sarajevo in August of that year, firing mortars into a crowded marketplace and killing and wounding dozens of civilians. Unlike the concentration camps, these killings happened in front of the world, as if the Serbs thought that no one would dare to stop them. On August 30, the United States began bombing the Serbian army, which quickly brought the Serbs to the peace table. In November 1995, they signed the Dayton Accords, a peace treaty that ended the war with a Bosnia divided among Serbs, Croats, and Bosnians—and one that is, as of early 2010, still patrolled by NATO peacekeeping forces.

Slobodan Milošević's plan for a Greater Serbia was temporarily thwarted and he was, in fact, unpopular in his own country. Serbia's economy was devastated by the war and her borders were flooded with Serbian refugees from Bosnia and Croatia. Some people in international agencies such as the UN, and even within the U.S. government (U.S. Secretary of State Lawrence Eagleburger was one), publicly called Milošević a war criminal. But like many leaders with a long view of history, Milošević bided his time, waiting for a crisis that would once again allow him to convince his people that they were being violated yet another time, just as they were at the Field of the Blackbirds.

The bodies of 45 ethnic Albanians lie in a mosque in the village of Racak, in southern Kosovo, in January 1999. That year, Serb leader Slobodan Milošević's top general told his troops to "prepare for martyrdom" and proceeded, under the eyes of NATO observers, to expel upwards of 800,000 Albanians from their homes in Kosovo. Serb forces finally capitulated after a ten-week NATO bombing campaign.

Associated Press

He found such a crisis in Kosovo. The Dayton Accords had brought the world's attention to the plight of the Muslims in Bosnia, but the agreement had failed to address the very real animosity the Serbs heaped upon the Albanians in Kosovo. Back in 1990, Milošević had revoked Kosovo's status as an autonomous province and ignored it when it declared its own independence in 1991. In 1997, frustrated young Albanians formed the Kosovo Liberation Army, fighting a shadowy guerilla war against Serbian forces in Kosovo. It was just what Milošević was looking for. In 1998, telling his people that the Muslims were threatening to overwhelm them once again, he launched a massive counterinsurgency effort, using police, regular Serbian army troops, and paramilitary troops.

Thus began the greatest episode of ethnic cleansing in the wars of the former Yugoslavia. U.S. Secretary of State Madeleine Albright and U.S. chief negotiator Richard Holbrooke, who had brokered the Dayton Accords, told Milošević that he needed to accept a cease-fire in Kosovo and a peace agreement that would lead, in a few years, to Kosovo independence—or his forces would be bombed. Albright privately confided that Milošević was nothing but "a schoolyard bully" whose forces in Bosnia had been dispelled with military action. One simply had to stand up to him.

But this was a misreading of the situation and of Serbian history. Milošević and other Serbs considered Kosovo to be the very heart of the Serbian nation, and Milošević could not simply hand it over to Muslim Albanians without a fight. As historians Dusko Doder and Louise Branson have written, "Milošević calculated . . . that the spectacle of a leader uncompromisingly rejecting a foreign ultimatum fitted the nation's psyche, much as [Prince] Lazar had refused to accommodate the Turks in 1389. There arose a wave of patriotic euphoria which projected Milošević as the leader of a united people embarked on a holy cause."

Milošević's top general told his troops to "prepare for martyrdom" and proceeded, under the eyes of NATO observers, to expel upwards of 500,000 Albanians from their homes in Kosovo. On March 24, 1999, NATO began a ten-week bombing campaign directed at Serbian forces. At first the Serbs resisted, but with their forces taking steady losses and their military infrastructure receiving serious damage, they finally capitulated.

Milošević finally signed an agreement on June 10, 1999, in which he agreed to withdraw his forces from Kosovo, which then became an international protectorate under NATO control. Even so, that very night, he made a television address to the Serbian nation, telling them that "we never lost Kosovo" and that "we have survived and we have defended the country" against foreign forces that now included NATO and the United States.

Six hundred years after events at the Field of the Blackbirds, Serbs were still fighting the same war—a war against those who sought to steal the soul of their nation. The most senseless thing about the recent installment of their long war was that it brought ruin on them. Serbia was suspended from the UN (although the suspension was lifted in 2001). The NATO bombings destroyed factories containing thousands of tons of toxic chemicals, which were released into the soil and ecosystem, with future results uncertain.

Slobodan Milošević was indicted as a war criminal in 2000 and died in a prison cell at The Hague in 2006, of natural causes, though rumors persist that he was poisoned. Other Serbian leaders wound up dead or serving long jail sentences. Kosovo declared its independence in 2008 and since then has been recognized by sixty countries and has joined the International Monetary Fund and World Bank.

Serbia continues to reject Kosovo's claim—to them it is unthinkable that the Field of the Blackbirds should lie outside Serbian borders—and so far has made its protests in the International Court of Justice, following international procedures. However, if another Milošević arises, the legend of Prince Lazar and the Field of the Blackbirds may arise as well.

"CRY HAVOC"

WARS OF CHAOS

Wars go on for long periods because
events go spinning out of control.

CHAPTER 13

GUATEMALA CIVIL WARS

THE BITTER FRUIT OF OPPRESSION

1944–1996

Ages of exploitation, beginning with some
three hundred years of Spanish imperialism and
culminating in a corrupt pseudo-independence
that sold out the Guatemalan peasantry to U.S.
business interests, transformed a mostly impoverished
Central American nation into a Cold War pawn,
igniting and fueling nearly fifty years of
civil war that ended in a mixture of exhaustion,
national reconciliation, and hope.

From at least six hundred years before the birth of Christ, the Maya K'iche' lived freely in the lush green highlands of Guatemala until the early thirteenth century, when invaders from the Gulf of Mexico conquered them and made them subjects of a powerful new kingdom that endured until 1524.

That year, the Spanish conquistador Pedro de Alvarado fought the native army and triumphed, the K'iche' corpses from a single battle numbering nearly 10,000. When the surviving K'iche' and their former overlords surrendered, inviting Alvarado to the capital city of Q'umarkaj, the conquistador smelled an ambush and preemptively put the forsaken city to the torch.

Centuries later, in 1980, the descendants of the K'iche' and another Mayan people, the Ixil, sought refuge in the embassy of Spain in the heart of Guatemala City. For they believed the Spanish, their original conquerors, were now sympathetic to the cause of indigenous Guatemalans, who for some thirty years and more had been killed as a matter of nearly casual routine by those who governed their country.

A FIRE IN THE EMBASSY

These K'iche' and Ixil people had marched to Guatemala City in January 1980 to protest the abduction and murder of peasants in the Mayan municipality of Uspantán at the hands of the Guatemalan army. The protestors were farmers, not political people, but they were joined by members of the Comité de Unidad Campesina (Committee of Peasant Unity), a band of radical students who called themselves the Robin García Revolutionary Student Front, and people who claimed to be soldiers in the Ejército Guerrillero de los Pobres (the Guerrilla Army of the Poor, or EGP). Together, they marched to Congress, seeking to be heard. Congress refused to hear them. Then someone killed their legal adviser. Denied a voice, they stormed two radio stations on January 28, and briefly held them before marching on to the Spanish embassy, which they entered at 9:30 on the morning of January 31.

They carried handguns and Molotov cocktails in addition to the broad-bladed machetes traditional in the highlands. However, they told Spanish ambassador Máximo Cajal y López that they had come in peace and wanted nothing more than to use the embassy as a safe place to hold a press conference. They wanted the world to hear them. One of them handed the ambassador a letter, beseeching the Spanish, as "honorable people," to "tell the truth about the criminal repression suffered by the peasants of Guatemala."

The ambassador appealed to President Fernando Romeo Lucas García to meet with the protestors, but he met instead with Chief Germán Chupina Barahona of the Guatemala City Police Department and Minister of the Interior Donaldo Álvarez Ruíz. Emerging from this meeting, the president decided not only to deny them an audience, but also to force them out of the embassy. He issued no warning but, just before noon, deployed a contingent of fifty riot-equipped police officers around the embassy. At noon sharp, the officers rushed the embassy and took up positions on the first and third floors, above and below the occupiers. Over the scuffle of police boots, the ambassador's shouts could be heard protesting the violation of sovereign Spanish soil.

In the meantime, the occupiers took hold of the embassy staff and the Guatemalan officials with whom Ambassador Cajal y López had been meeting and barricaded everyone, including themselves, in the ambassador's second-floor office suite.

Then someone outside issued an order to storm the office. The clatter up and down the stairs was followed by the explosion of axes through heavy wooden doors and a succession of blinding silver flashes. The Spanish ambassador later reported that highly volatile white phosphorus had been thrown through one of the shattered doors. On contact with the air, it burst into a sheet of flame, igniting the protestors' Molotov cocktails. Others, including two prominent academic historians, believe

The conquest of Guatemala by Pedro de Alvarado in 1523 is shown in this mid–fifteenth century color print. The Spanish conquistador conquered the native peoples, including the Maya K'iche', beginning ages of exploitation and setting the stage for years of warfare.

that the Molotov cocktails had ignited on their own, either accidentally or as a result of deliberate, desperate action by the protestors. However the fire began, it quickly swallowed up the entire second floor and, with it, the occupiers and their hostages.

Outside, firemen were barred from entering the embassy by police officers who refused to step away from the doors. Of thirty-eight persons on the second floor, only Ambassador Cajal y López and Gregorio Yujá Xona, a protestor, survived. Both were rushed to Herrera Llerandi Hospital. Early on the morning of February 1, someone gave the order for the withdrawal of the police assigned to guard the hospital. Twenty men, masked with bandanas and heavily armed, quietly entered the hospital, abducted the badly burned Yujá Xona, took him—somewhere—tortured him, and shot him to death, dumping his body on the campus of the University of San Carlos.

OCTOPUS AGENDA

Long civil wars disrupt a nation's life, then become that nation's way of life. After many years, the abductions, the torture, the killings, the terror—no matter how relentless, how horrific—become the background noise of daily existence. The people suffer. The rest of the world, most of it, hardly takes notice until an event such as that of January 31, 1980, happens and suddenly the background snaps front and center. People look back, then look ahead, positions harden, the war gains a new momentum, but this time, the world watches.

Looking back, perhaps it all began with Alvarado and his conquistadors, in their broad-brimmed helmets and gleaming cuirasses, who first robbed the people of their land, their wealth, and any possibility of self-determination. Most historians, however, trace the long civil war to 1944, when the so-called October Revolutionaries gained a foothold in the government and introduced liberal reforms that elevated—or proposed to elevate—both the urban working classes and the rural peasantry. This national movement to the left soon found homegrown leaders in Juan José Arévalo—who billed himself as a "spiritual socialist," dedicated to the "psychological liberation" of Guatemalans—and Jacobo Árbenz Guzmán, a reformer of a more pragmatic turn of mind.

Arévalo was elected president in 1944 and served from 1945 to 1951, an interval of remarkably enlightened and peaceful government. His successor, Defense Minister Árbenz, transformed Arévalo's spiritual socialism into something more practical: a drive to end Guatemala's quasi-colonial status as what he and other reformers considered an economic and political puppet of the United States and U.S. business interests. The legislative centerpiece of this drive was Decree 900, a 1952 law Arévalo sponsored, which empowered the government to expropriate uncultivated portions of large plantations and redistribute the land to individual peasant families. Not surprisingly, the peasant majority—in Guatemala, the arable land at this time was owned by just 1.6 percent of the population—welcomed the Árbenz reforms while the landowning minority opposed them.

The peasants had numbers on their side, but the landowners could count on elements of the Guatemalan military and U.S. corporate interests, paramount among them the United Fruit Company, long criticized throughout Central America as "el pulpo," the octopus, for its bribing of government officials and propping up of repressive regimes in exchange for preferential treatment regarding taxes and land ownership and limitless license to exploit cheap agricultural labor. The single biggest landowner in Guatemala, United Fruit suddenly found its holdings in as-yet uncultivated jungle plantation real estate directly threatened by Decree 900.

Not that Árbenz proposed simply to seize the land. He offered to purchase it—at the rate United Fruit itself had valued it for taxation purposes: $3 per acre. The company responded to the proposal by claiming a true per-acre value of $75, but was silent when asked to explain the yawning gulf between this figure and what it had already furnished to the Guatemalan tax assessors. The company did, however, loudly join the growing chorus of those who were now accusing Árbenz of leading Guatemala into the communist camp.

As World War II ended and morphed into the Cold War, U.S. president Harry S. Truman announced a policy of "containing" the spread of communism wherever and whenever it threatened governments struggling toward democratic self-determination. The policy grew from the administration's understanding of the Monroe Doctrine, by which the nation's fifth president had in 1823 effectively proclaimed the United States guardian of the Western Hemisphere against foreign interference.

Whereas the Guatemalan right wing had been willing to tolerate Arévalo's spiritual socialism, the far more concrete reforms of Árbenz threatened U.S. business interests and investments, including United Fruit with its potent Washington lobby, and provoked what the U.S. government characterized as "increasing political instability." The CIA, created in 1947 to cope with the emerging realities of the Cold War, responded in the spirit of the containment policy and Monroe Doctrine by preparing, in 1951, Operation PBFORTUNE (the prefix "PB" was the CIA cryptogram for Guatemala). It was conceived as a contingency plan for the removal of Árbenz if and when he was determined to have become an outright communist threat.

THE CIA ACTS

Without doubt, under the Árbenz regime, the communists gained influence, but they remained a minority among the political parties. Nevertheless, United Fruit pressed

The reforms of Jacobo Árbenz Gúzman, pictured in 1945, before he became president, would threaten Guatemala's largest landowner, U.S. magnate United Fruit. The company pressed for CIA intervention, which was eventually green lighted by President Dwight Eisenhower.

for the CIA to take action. Truman withheld his authorization, but his successor, Dwight D. Eisenhower, took the advice of his vehemently anticommunist secretary of state, John Foster Dulles, and green-lighted on February 19, 1954, the CIA's Operation WASHTUB.

It was a "false flag," or disinformation, scheme in which arms, purportedly from the Soviet Union, were to be planted in neighboring Nicaragua as proof of a direct Soviet supply line from Moscow to Central America. While WASHTUB got under way, Dulles proposed to a March meeting of the Organization of American States (OAS) a resolution echoing the Monroe Doctrine. It called for OAS members to take "appropriate action in accordance with existing treaties" against agents of "the international communist movement" who attempted to dominate "the political institutions of any American state."

When some OAS members objected that the resolution gave the United States a blank check for intervening anywhere at will, Dulles sugared it until the pill was more palatable. Privately, however, he preserved the original language and considered it the foundation of U.S. foreign policy in Latin America.

Operation WASHTUB was never implemented. It didn't have to be. In May 1954, actual events made it unnecessary. A Swedish freighter docked in a Guatemalan port. Something about its cargo manifest looked fishy, and inspection of the vessel's hold revealed weapons shipped from Czechoslovakia. Never mind that they were no more than a handful of captured World War II German infantry arms, obsolete and barely functional; it was enough that they had arrived clandestinely, not from the Soviet Union, to be sure, but from an Iron Curtain country nevertheless.

Secretary Dulles professed outrage and alarm, claiming that the weapons were undeniable proof of Soviet ties to Árbenz. President Eisenhower covertly authorized the CIA to foment a coup d'état in Guatemala. Operation PBFORTUNE was taken off the shelf, dusted, tweaked, and implemented as Operation PBSUCCESS. (Among those tapped to lead the operation was CIA agent E. Howard Hunt, who would become infamous during the 1970s as one of President Richard Nixon's "plumbers," the covert unit that broke into Democratic National Headquarters in Washington and triggered the Watergate scandal that forced the president's resignation.)

Operation PBSUCCESS combined an economic embargo and a naval blockade with the creation and dissemination of anti-Árbenz propaganda and, most important, the recruiting, organizing, equipping, and training of local right-wing rebels for a coup d'etat. In the distant past, foreign invasion and occupation had permanently disrupted Mayan Guatemala. Now, however, the CIA sought to disguise its intervention by orchestrating what appeared to be a grassroots rebellion. The propaganda it broadcast emanated from a radio station dubbed *La Voz de la Liberación* ("The Voice of Liberation"), said to be located deep in the jungle. In truth, like the arms and CIA trainers, the source of the broadcasts was purely American. The Voice of Liberation transmitted from a nondescript building in Miami, Florida.

The CIA chose to back Carlos Castillo Armas to lead the coup. He was the son of a wealthy, Spanish-born Guatemalan landowner, who had nevertheless abandoned his family, leaving young Castillo Armas and his brother to be raised by their suddenly impoverished mother. Bright and eager, Castillo Armas gained entrance into the Escuela Politécnica, the Guatemalan military academy, and was subsequently sent to Fort Leavenworth, Kansas, for special training. There he became friendly with many influential members of the U.S. military. A rightist, he had opposed the liberal reforms of Arévalo and led an abortive attempt to overthrow his successor Árbenz in 1951. Wounded and arrested in the attempt, he escaped into Honduras, where the CIA found and groomed him.

INVASION, 1954

At eight o'clock on the evening of June 18, 1954, Castillo Armas sent some 480 rebels into Guatemala across five points along the country's border with Honduras and El Salvador. His CIA mentors had taught him that dividing his force in this manner would give the impression of a much larger invasion. In advance of the main force, saboteurs and sappers blew up key bridges and cut telegraph and telephone lines to disrupt the government's ability to communicate. The object was to create panic and confusion, so that the people would rise up to follow whichever leader seemed to offer control and stability.

But despite the CIA's best advice, the invaders fared poorly. Coordination among the five groups was nonexistent, and the divided forces were a poor match against the well-trained and well-equipped Guatemalan army. At this point, Árbenz could well have crushed the invasion, but understanding that the United States was behind the rebellion, he ordered restraint, lest the total defeat of the rebels provoke a full-scale invasion by U.S. troops. Neither the invasion nor the propaganda and disinformation broadcast via the Voice of Liberation incited the national panic the CIA had promised; however, Árbenz's own strategy of restraint did the trick, quickly demoralizing the army and prompting the government units to surrender to the far inferior forces of Castillo Armas. Stunned, Árbenz convened a meeting of his cabinet, announced to them that the army had mutinied, and on June 27, resigned. In a military sense, the CIA–Castillo Armas coup had failed and yet the Árbenz government was overthrown.

Two insurgent soldiers stand in a sodden field during the Guatemala Revolution in 1954, the year the United States sent armed rebels into the country to create an uprising. The move led to leader Jacobo Árbenz Gúzman's voluntary resignation—and years of civil war.

Still, the army "mutiny" was by no means universal. Many officers remained reluctant to pledge allegiance to Castillo Armas. The CIA quickly stepped in with bribes. This tactic succeeded in winning over the army, but the allegiance of the Guatemalan people was ambivalent. During the first eleven days following Árbenz's resignation, five different military juntas successively moved in and out of the presidential palace. Each professed more compliance with U.S. demands than the last. Finally, on September 1, after the fifth junta resigned en masse, Castillo Armas himself was proclaimed provisional president, and a subsequent plebiscite confirmed him in office.

"A BETTER HAND AT PULLING DOWN THAN BUILDING"

When, in 1776, a friend wrote to the American revolutionary John Adams to describe the sensation created by Thomas Paine's pamphlet *Common Sense*, which galvanized the popular resolve for independence, Adams remarked to his wife, Abigail, that Paine had "a better hand at pulling down than building." In this homely phrase, Adams summed up the fatal flaw of most revolutions. Whatever else he was, Castillo Armas was no builder. Immediately upon assuming office, he declared literacy as a requirement for voting, thereby effectively disenfranchising the peasantry, Guatemala's illiterate majority. Shortly after this, he summarily reversed Decree 900, which forced those same peasants off the lands they had just acquired. He then conducted an internal purge, sweeping out of office anyone suspected of leftist sentiments. All political parties and political, labor, and peasant organizations were summarily banned.

Castillo Armas reconstituted the secret police force that Arévalo had abolished, and upon the request of the CIA, created the National Committee of Defense against Communism. Historians overwhelmingly believe this was neither more nor less than a death squad, probably the first in Latin American history, assigned to covertly and efficiently eliminate leftist leaders, dissidents, and peasant organizers. The activities of a death squad are by definition extrajudicial, but Castillo Armas also promulgated the Preventive Penal Law Against Communism, which provided harsh judicial penalties for so-called communist activities, including virtually all forms of labor organizing. Although Castillo Armas postponed the 1955 presidential election, he allowed the congressional elections to proceed—albeit with the participation of a single party: his National Liberation Movement (MLN).

Visiting Guatemala in 1955, Vice President Richard Nixon pronounced the regime of Castillo Armas "the first instance in history where a Communist government has been replaced by a free one." The following year, Castillo Armas engineered a four-year extension of his presidency, but he was assassinated by one of his own guards, Romeo Vásquez, on

July 26, 1957. For the next forty years, Guatemala would know nothing but repression and civil war as a series of military dictators conducted a nonstop counterinsurgency in which more than 140,000 Guatemalans—some say more than 250,000—would die.

GUERRILLA WAR

Pulling down without building up deepened the lethal divisions within the country. Government repression did not destroy the left, but irreversibly radicalized it. Moreover, whereas a certain percentage of the Mayan peasants had not been pleased by the land reforms under Árbenz—because they were often among those forced off uncultivated tracts—the brutal policies of Castillo Armas and his successors created common cause between the indigenous peasants and the radical left laboring and student classes. Seeking to wipe out the opposition, the right wing both deepened and expanded it.

Vice President Luis González replaced the slain Castillo Armas. After disputed elections and months of instability, the legislature named General José Miguel Ramón Ydígoras Fuentes president. He took up where Castillo Armas had left off, using his predecessor's assassination to justify abandoning even the pretense of democracy and embracing more openly the country's status as a U.S. client. Responding to Ydígoras Fuentes's embrace, the U.S. Army and CIA trained and equipped an army that was directly under his control. These events did not stop a group of zealously patriotic junior military officers, all products of the Escuela Politécnica (national military academy), from rising up against Ydígoras Fuentes in 1960. They were joined by certain members of the educated classes and university students, loosely united as the now-outlawed Guatemalan Party of Labor (PGT). But government forces quickly suppressed their initial action of November 13, 1960. Those who escaped capture or death went underground and, drawing on Fidel Castro's Cuba for financial support and strategic advice, formed Revolutionary Movement 13th November (MR-13), a guerrilla group headquartered in the rugged and remote eastern mountains in Izabal, Puerto Barrios, and Zacapa.

The guerrillas organized peasant support in the countryside, attacked army outposts to steal arms, and raised money by means of kidnapping and bank robbery. In the meantime, in Guatemala City, thousands took to the streets in March 1962 to protest the Ydígoras Fuentes government. Violence flared and was accompanied by a general strike, which alarmed the U.S. military mission now permanently stationed in the capital. Accustomed to such outbursts, Ydígoras Fuentes himself was less perturbed—or at least less so than his U.S. military backers thought he should be.

In May, the U.S. government established in Izabal a base for counterinsurgency training and staffed it with Green Berets (the recently established U.S. Special Forces), all carefully selected from among U.S. soldiers of Puerto Rican and Mexican descent, so that they would not obviously look like Yankees. In addition to the Green Berets, fifteen Guatemalan officers, who had been trained in counterinsurgency at the U.S. School of the Americas at Fort Gulick, Panama Canal Zone, served on the base.

The U.S. counterinsurgency strategy was founded on a schizophrenic philosophy that combined punishment with reward and, if anything, tended to prolong rather than resolve conflict. Even as the U.S. military trained and equipped Guatemalan government forces in brutal counterinsurgency methods, U.S. "civil action" troops dug wells, provided medical care, furnished certain food supplies, and provided other services. Locals took advantage of these benefits, but could not forget that they came from the same people who were enabling the government soldiers to kill them; even as they accepted the aid, they believed (with good reason) that the civil affairs officers were really on the hunt for insurgents.

Combat, concentrated in the northeast, consisted not of "set" battles, but of guerrilla actions (ranging from the ambush of government soldiers and officials to the looting of military supplies and the robbing of banks and other sources of funds) followed by disproportionate government reprisals. Although the guerrillas killed people, between 1960 and 1996, of 37,255 fully documented fatal casualties of the civil war, fewer than 1 percent were attributable to guerrillas; more than 99 percent were the result of government action.

During the period from October 1966 to March 1968, Amnesty International estimated that 3,000 to 8,000 Guatemalans, most of them of indigenous Mayan origin, were killed by the police, the military, or death squads. By 1972, the total reached 13,000, and by 1976, climbed to more than 20,000. The fact was that killing those even remotely suspected of organizing a union or a peasant group, or of supporting guerrillas, was quicker, easier, and more certain than taking the time and effort to investigate the suspects.

Death squads simply broke into suspects' homes, took people away, and killed them. Some disappeared and were never seen or heard from again. More, however, were burned or mutilated—amputation, castration, the gouging out of eyes, and decapitation were death squad calling cards—the bodies (what was left of them) disposed of in graves so shallow that they were clearly intended to be found to serve as a warning to others. In many cases, bodies were dumped into rivers and lakes. Native fishermen abandoned familiar waterways when they became choked with bloated corpses. Most terrifying of all were the bodies that fell out of the sky, pushed out of aircraft, hands tied behind backs. Although some mutilation was postmortem, many bodies showed unmistakable evidence of torture, doubtless inflicted in the course of interrogation. Favored methods included inducing extreme illness by tying a hood saturated with insecticide over a victim's head, or applying electric shock to the genitals using the current from hand-cranked magneto-powered field telephones made, of course, in the United States.

U.S. civilian pilots contracted with the CIA flew unmarked Korean War–era F-51(D) Mustang fighter planes specially modified for anti-insurgency patrol with six .50-caliber machine guns for ground strafing and wing hard points for dropping napalm and launching small air-to-ground rockets. The aircraft and their pilots were based in Panama and flew their missions, roundtrip, to and from those bases without ever landing in the country. The Guatemalan government designated large tracts of the northeast as *zonas libres*—free zones—which meant that pilots were free to bomb them at will, heavily, and indiscriminately.

In the cities, especially the capital, the U.S. Agency for International Development (USAID)—under the auspices of the Alliance for Progress begun by President John F. Kennedy to improve U.S.–Latin American relations—expanded, trained, and equipped Guatemala's national police force. Up to 1964, senior officers were trained at the Inter-American Police Academy in Panama; from 1964 on, they were sent directly to Washington, D.C., home of the newly created International Police Academy, where their instructors were CIA officers. By 1970, the United States had trained and equipped more than 30,000 Guatemalan police officers. This gave the government sufficient muscle to keep fighting the insurgency, but not to destroy it, and thereby ensured that civil war would become chronic or, at least, prolonged beyond rapid resolution.

OPERATION CLEANUP

The main phase of Guatemalan counterinsurgency began in 1965 under the direction of CIA officer John P. Longan and was called Operation CLEANUP. At first, the operation targeted major insurgent leaders, but it was soon expanded so that, by the end of 1968, the campaign had pretty thoroughly disrupted rural guerrilla activities, sending the insurgents into Guatemala City, where they targeted leading figures of the government. These included U.S. Ambassador John Gordon Mein, who was gunned down on August 28, 1968, by members of the Fuerzas Armadas Rebeldes (Rebel Armed Forces) a block from the U.S. embassy.

In the countryside, the war did not resume at full intensity until about 1976, when a new guerrilla movement, the Guatemalan Army of the Poor (EGP), joined more established groups (especially the Rebel Armed Forces) in renewed attacks on government forces. Funded and trained by Cubans (who, in turn, were supported by the Soviet Union), the insurgents also raided government military outposts to obtain weapons and other equipment. In the meantime, urban warfare not only continued but also intensified so greatly that Colonel Carlos Manuel Arana Osorio, a veteran of counterinsurgency in the department of Zacapa (they called him "the butcher of Zacapa") who became president in 1970, entered office by declaring Guatemala City to be under a "state of siege." This designation gave him license to crack down whenever and wherever he wanted. During the state of siege, which lasted two years, an estimated 7,000 Guatemalans were killed or disappeared. Foreign diplomats based in the capital estimated that for every political assassination by leftists, government or pro-government forces killed fifteen people.

FROM CARTER TO REAGAN

Elected in 1976, President Jimmy Carter declared that human rights would be the top priority of his administration's agenda. Both executive orders and congressional legislation sharply reduced military aid to nations, including Guatemala, accused of flagrant violations of human rights. Yet although U.S. arms shipments were embargoed, the Guatemalan government continued to purchase weapons and other military equipment from Israel, and at least a portion of these shipments was covertly underwritten by Washington. Also, although the controversial military training schools in the United States were now closed to Guatemalan government officers, the country's security forces continued to receive training in clandestine CIA sites maintained in Chile and Argentina.

THE CARTER PRESIDENCY DREW ATTENTION NOT ONLY TO THE ABUSES AND ATROCITIES OF THE GUATEMALAN GOVERNMENT BUT ALSO TO U.S. COMPLICITY IN THEM AND THE U.S. ROLE IN PROLONGING THE CIVIL WAR.

Still, for all the loopholes in its human rights policies, the Carter presidency drew attention not only to the abuses and atrocities of the Guatemalan government but also to U.S. complicity in them and the U.S. role in prolonging the civil war. As a result, many people in both Guatemala and the United States became hopeful that the United States would at last begin to play a healing role in the war, especially after the horrific spectacle of the Spanish embassy fire. Die-hard anticommunist Cold War warriors, however, were not chastened. Fred Sherwood, who was a CIA contract pilot during the anti-Árbenz coup of 1954 and who became president of the American Chamber of Commerce in Guatemala, addressed a Guatemalan audience during the 1980 U.S. presidential campaign, in which Carter ran for reelection against Ronald Reagan. "Why should we be worried about the death squads?" he asked. "They're bumping off the commies, our enemies. I'd give them more power. Hell, I'd get some cartridges if I could, and everyone else would too. . . . Why should we criticize them? The death squad—I'm for it. . . . Shit! There's no question we can't wait until Reagan gets in. We hope Carter falls in the ocean real quick. . . . We all feel that he [Reagan] is our savior."

Ronald Reagan defeated Jimmy Carter and, although he voiced continued support for the Carter human rights agenda, he shifted the focus from that subject to Central America as a critical Cold War battlefield. Just two months after he took office, President Reagan sent his secretary of state, Alexander Haig, to testify to Congress that the Soviet Union maintained a four-phase "hit list . . . for the ultimate takeover of Central America." Phase one had already been carried out: communist takeover of Nicaragua. El Salvador, he said, was slated as phase two, to be followed by Honduras and—phase four—Guatemala. The testimony was intended to reengage Congress in the Guatemalan anti-insurgency.

During the Reagan years, Congress again began funding anti-insurgency efforts, but even before it did, the Guatemalan government was sufficiently encouraged by the mere fact of Reagan's election to resume aggressive action in the countryside without fear of criticism. By the end of 1981, an estimated 2,000 Mayan peasants had been killed, along with seventy-six leaders of the opposition Christian Democratic Party, many labor activists, and at least six Catholic priests—for members of the Catholic clergy had begun to take an active role in the antigovernment resistance.

Throughout its first two years, Reagan administration officials found ways around the Carter embargo without formally rescinding it. Washington investigative journalist Jack Anderson revealed in August 1981 that the U.S. government was employing CIA-trained Cuban exiles to train Guatemalan security forces, with an emphasis on what Anderson called "the finer points of assassination." In 1982, Anderson reported that Green Berets were still engaged in training Guatemalan army officers, and in 1983 it was revealed that the United States was supplying Guatemala with helicopters and that the U.S. School of the Americas in Panama, closed to Guatemalan officers during the Carter presidency, had reopened.

On March 23, 1982, junior Guatemalan army officers staged a coup d'état to bar from office Ángel Aníbal Guevara, anointed by outgoing president General Romeo Lucas García as his successor. As an alternative to Aníbal Guevara, the officers asked General

Efraín Ríos Montt, widely respected for his membership in the Christian Democracy Party and his position as a lay minister of the evangelical Protestant "Church of the Word," to negotiate the peaceful removal of both Lucas García and Aníbal Guevara.

Instead of negotiating, however, Ríos Montt proclaimed it the "will of God" that he assume the presidency—an event the Reagan administration, which had received strong support from U.S. Christian conservatives, enthusiastically approved. In April, one month after Ríos Montt took office, President Reagan cited improvements in the Guatemalan human rights record and, based on this, openly resumed military aid shipments. Three months later, on July 1, 1982, Ríos Montt proclaimed a "state of siege" and assumed "emergency" powers.

It was the culmination of an anti-insurgent campaign combining military action and economic reforms—what Ríos Montt described as a campaign of "rifles and beans" but a Guatemalan army officer put more bluntly: "If you are with us, we'll feed you; if not, we'll kill you." That statement was made to an assembly of indigenous—mostly Mayan—Guatemalans on July 18, 1982, the very day on which more than 250 ethnic Achi Maya, almost all of them women and children, were massacred by members of the Guatemalan army and paramilitary forces at Plan de Sánchez, a village in the Baja Verapaz department in central Guatemala. It was the bloodiest and most notorious episode in Ríos Montt's campaign of genocidal intimidation.

The Plan de Sánchez massacre began a rapid erosion of support for Ríos Montt within his own administration, but not before he had instituted a program of recruiting local civilian defense patrols (PACs). Membership in these PACs was voluntary, but, throughout the northwest region, the assumption was that anyone who did not join the local PAC was a guerrilla and therefore subject to shooting (or worse), no questions asked. In effect, Ríos Montt had institutionalized the absolute division of the countryside, as if to ensure that the civil war would be fought to the death of one side or the other.

THE END OF MILITARY GOVERNMENT

With the support of the United States during the first term of President Ronald Reagan, Ríos Montt served for thirty-six months—the most violent period of the Guatemalan Civil War. In 1982 alone, the state killed 18,000 Guatemalans. From March to August of that year, hardly a day went by without newspaper reports of a political "disappearance" or the discovery of a mutilated corpse in or near the capital. Security forces descended upon the annual May Day march through the center of Guatemala City, abducting in the broad light of day thirty-one marchers, some of whose mutilated bodies later showed up. Others just vanished. None survived.

At last, on August 8, 1983, Ríos Montt's own minister of defense, General Óscar Humberto Mejía Victores, overthrew him and assumed the presidency in his place. He announced the return of democracy, and on July 1, 1984, sanctioned the election of members of a Constituent Assembly tasked with drafting a new, democratic constitution. The document was completed on May 30, 1985, and immediately put into effect.

Vinicio Cerezo, of the Guatemalan Christian Democratic Party, was the first president elected under the new constitution and the first civilian president of Guatemala elected since 1944. The Reagan State Department hailed the election as a vindication of the policies it claimed to have fostered; nevertheless, the civil war continued for another ten years, and it became apparent to most outside observers that the succession of civilian presidents from 1986 through 1995 were still subject to heavy-handed influence from the military.

Undeniably, however, the Cerezo government was an improvement. It reintroduced habeas corpus, created a legislative human rights committee, and eventually established an Office of Human Rights Ombudsman. The entire Guatemalan legal system was revamped and to a significant (if incomplete) degree, cleansed of corruption. Although the military remained powerful—and twice, in May 1988 and May 1989, attempted to overthrow the civilian government—the annual rate of killing dropped precipitously, into the hundreds rather than the thousands.

Although the first two years of Cerezo's presidency were notable for improvement in Guatemalan life, the last two years marked a renewed deterioration as the nation's economy hovered near collapse. Poverty drove a resurgence of violence, resulting in the election of a more left-leaning president, Jorge Antonio Serrano Elías, inaugurated on January 14, 1991. Serrano was able to gain fuller—though by no means total—control over the military, and he managed to bring significant economic improvements, but, frustrated by the difficulty of dealing with a congressional majority from an opposition party, he took the blatantly unconstitutional step, on May 25, 1993, of unilaterally dissolving both Congress and the Supreme Court and, in an effort (he said) to fight corruption, also abridged civil liberties.

This so-called *autogolpe* ("auto coup") backfired badly on Serrano, who, faced with the army's declared determination to enforce the decisions of the Court of Constitutionality, which ruled against the autogolpe, summarily resigned his office and fled the country. If the idea of the Guatemalan military, long accustomed to behaving as a power unto itself, actually enforcing the Guatemalan constitution was in itself stunning, even more so was the strong evidence that the CIA had been instrumental in ending the autogolpe in the interests of preserving a democracy that seemed to be on course for an unprecedented degree of stability.

"TO ENCOURAGE PEACE AND NATIONAL HARMONY"

On June 5, 1993, the Guatemalan Congress elected the Human Rights Ombudsman, Ramiro de León Carpio, to serve out Serrano's unfinished presidential term, and both Congress and the Supreme Court were swept by reforms that, with the assistance of Catholic Church clergy who served as observers, significantly reduced corruption and promoted peace talks mediated by the United Nations. In March 1994, landmark human rights agreements were signed, and in June, tens of thousands of persons displaced by civil war were resettled. That same month, the Comisión para el Esclarecimiento Histórico (CEH), or Historical Clarification Commission, was created and tasked with three extraordinary missions designed to serve as the basis of a lasting peace:

- To objectively investigate and clarify all human rights violations and acts of violence since January 1962.
- To publish the findings of its investigations.
- To make recommendations "to encourage peace and national harmony in Guatemala." This mandate emphasized creating "measures to preserve the memory of the victims, to foster a culture of mutual respect and observance of human rights and to strengthen the democratic process."

The establishment of the Historical Clarification Commission was augmented in March 1995 by legislation defining and permanently guaranteeing the rights of Guatemala's indigenous population.

In November 1995, national elections, once restricted to a single party, were crowded with contenders from twenty parties. Nevertheless, they proceeded in an orderly fashion, and Álvaro Arzú Irigoyen edged out his nearest rival by just 2 percent of the vote. He presided over the conclusion of peace negotiations, which included the legalization of what had been the leading guerrilla organization as a legitimate political party. The accords of December 1996 formally ended a transgenerational war that, depending on how one reckons it, had begun in 1960, 1954, 1944—or perhaps even in 1524.

CHAPTER 14

THE SUDANESE CIVIL WAR

EVIL HORSEMEN, SNAKE VENOM, PROXY WAR, AND GENOCIDE

1955–2005

Centuries of outside interference by imperialist powers combined with internal religious division and staggering economic inequality culminated in fifty years of civil war in Sudan that killed 2.5 million people, made refugees of another 4 million, and created a legacy of genocidal suffering in a place called Darfur.

The pounding swept across the powdery Saharan sand into the little Darfur farming village of Furawiyah, outside of El Fasher, on a January afternoon in 2004. It was pounding from horses ridden by the *janjaweed*—an Arabic word meaning, roughly, "evil horsemen." Sometimes they stormed into towns like Furawiyah after government air force bombing and in the wake of ground sweeps by the regular army. Sometimes they came on their own, without warning.

They wanted livestock, and they saw cows, horses, camels, and human beings all as livestock. Cattle, slaves—there was good money in both. The Sudanese government tolerated, encouraged, supported, and even deployed the janjaweed because, when they stole the animals, they killed the people they didn't take, shooting them, beating them, beheading them, sometimes leaving the bodies where they fell, but more often stuffing the corpses into the local wells, forcing parents to drink the water in which their sons and daughters had died.

The raid at Furawiyah was no different from many others in the region marking the division between southern and northern Sudan—even though the long civil war, seemingly a war without end, was clearly coming to an end. Yet the killing was far from over. Even today, in Darfur, the killing is not over.

CAULDRON OF CONFLICT

The Sudanese Civil War—or civil *wars*; some see one war, others two—burned up half a century of Sudanese history and killed about 2.5 million people, few of whom ever raised a weapon. Long and terrible though it was, the civil war was only a moment in the multi-millennial span during which people have lived—or struggled to live—in Sudan. Archaeologists say that the region has been settled for at least 60,000 years, and, for every one of them, Sudan has been a hard place, often a killing place.

Much of the land is baked and desiccated, yet vast; in area it is the largest African country today, the tenth biggest in the world. Sudan is bordered by Egypt, the Red Sea, Eritrea, Ethiopia, Kenya, Uganda, the Democratic Republic of the Congo, the Central African Republic, Chad, and Libya. It debuted into written history about 5,000 years ago in an Egyptian record that describes in a single word the Sudanese kingdom of Kush, at the confluences of the Blue and White Nile with the River Atbara. That word is *wretched*.

POVERTY, THE TERRITORIAL AMBITIONS OF NEIGHBORS,
THE FORMER IMPERIAL ASPIRATIONS OF GREAT BRITAIN, THE
COLD WAR MANEUVERINGS OF THE SOVIET UNION
AND THE UNITED STATES, AND, MOST INTRACTABLE OF ALL,
RELIGIOUS STRIFE, HAVE PROVIDED WHAT SEEMS
TO BE AN INEXHAUSTIBLE SOURCE OF COMBUSTION
IN PERPETUATING THIS CONFLICT.

The historical regions of Sudan—Kush, Darfur, the three kingdoms of Nubia—have been dominated by their neighbors, especially Egypt, and by distant powers. They have also been guided, led, goaded, pulled, and punished by the tides of conflicting religions, mainly Christianity and Islam. Poverty, the territorial ambitions of neighbors—who in recent years have coveted Sudan's one great natural resource, oil—the former imperial aspirations of Great Britain, the Cold War maneuverings of the Soviet Union and the United States, and, most intractable of all, religious strife, have provided what seems to be an inexhaustible source of combustion in perpetuating this conflict.

By the sixth century, the Nubian kingdoms of northern Sudan were largely Christianized, but after Islam came to Egypt in the mid-seventh century, that religion entered Sudan, in both the north and the south. From that time forward, religious conflicts have occurred, at times relatively quietly, at other times violently.

During 1820–1821, a large Ottoman force swept down from Turkey and established *Turkiyah*—Ottoman rule—over the north, even as Egypt (at the time a *pashalyk* or province of the Ottoman Empire) gathered to itself most of the rest of the region. Ostensibly, then, all of Sudan had been swallowed up by the Ottoman Empire; however, whereas the Turkiyah region became fairly unified, the Egyptian Sudan, especially the south, remained fragmented, divided among indigenous tribes. This gave Europeans an opening and an incentive to intervene. Beginning before mid-century, British missionaries traveled from what is today Kenya to convert Sudanese tribes to Christianity. By the 1870s, the European powers were sponsoring initiatives to end the slave trade, which was rampant in Sudan. These efforts enlarged the influence of the missionaries and suppressed slavery, yet it soon became apparent that much of Sudan produced little for export other than slaves, and the region sank into a severe economic depression.

THE RISE OF THE ANSARS

Ungoverned yet oppressed, the disparate tribes found in Muhammad Ahmad Ibn As-Sayyid 'abd Allah (or Muhammad Ahmad) the leadership both Egypt and the Ottoman Empire had failed to provide. Calling himself "the Mahdi"—or "enlightened one"—ibn-Ahmad commenced in 1881 a war that brought together tribes throughout the western and central portions of Sudan. Followers—that is what they called themselves, using the Arabic word *Ansars*—were eager to slip the yoke of oppressive and incompetent Ottoman and Egyptian misrule. On January 26, 1885, the Mahdi led the conquest and occupation of Khartoum, principal city of Sudan, slaughtering thousands, including British Major General Charles George "Chinese" Gordon, who, employed in the service of the Egyptian khedive, Ismail Pasha, served as Egypt's governor-general of Sudan.

This led Britain to war against the Mahdi's successor, the Khalifah Abdullah Ibn-Mohammed (or Abdullah al-Taaisha). Defeated in 1899, the Khalifah's Mahdists yielded control of Sudan to an Anglo-Egyptian "condominium" government, which actually meant that, by the start of the twentieth century, Sudan was governed, for all intents and purposes, as a province of the British Empire. The imperial administration recognized that the north and south of Sudan were very different in culture, religion, and economy, and it set about reinforcing those differences to make governing the huge territory more manageable. By the early 1920s, the regions were effectively different countries, travel between them regulated by passport. In the north, only Arabic and English were recognized as official languages, and virtually all British-sponsored enterprises and economic development were focused on this region.

In the south, a variety of tribal languages—in addition to English—were deemed official, economic development was deliberately neglected, and the region was thrown open to Christian missionaries. Whereas Islam was encouraged in the north, it was discouraged in the south. The idea was to bond the north as a cohesive whole closely to the condominium government, while allowing the south to be politically fragmented and different in religion from the north, so that it could be easily broken off from the condominium and attached instead to British East Africa, where it would fall under more absolute imperial governance. Apart from the social injustice of this arrangement, it hardened the divisions, virtually ensuring the eruption of a chronic state of civil war.

Even within the north, the imperial administration created conflict by playing off the Ansars—former "followers" of the Mahdi—against another sect, the Khatmiyya, which supported union with Egypt. This divide-and-conquer administrative approach was intended to make it easier to exert control over the region, but, in the long run, it promoted the founding of two rival political parties, the Umma Party (which developed from the Ansars) and the Democratic Unionist Party (DUP, which grew from the Khatmiyya). Versions of these parties would endure, creating the opposing poles around which the major warring factions organized themselves year after year.

During World War II, the British began dismantling their empire in India and Africa and in 1943 established a North Sudan Advisory Council to guide in the creation of government for the Khartoum, Kordofan, Darfur, and Eastern, Northern, and Blue Nile provinces. After the war, however, Britain reversed its long-standing policy of strictly dividing north from south and announced instead a single government for Sudan.

The southerners, who had anticipated self-government independent from both the British Empire and northern Sudan, were effectively excluded from the new "unified" administration. For one thing, the official language of the new government was Arabic, whereas that of the south was English; for another, while 800 administrative positions opened up when the British completed their withdrawal from Sudan in 1953, all but four were filled by northerners. In the south, therefore, "self-government" was a cruel joke, and the alienated, disenfranchised south now had a freshly urgent reason for fighting a civil war.

THE BEGINNING OF CIVIL WAR

Back in 1925, the British military administration of Sudan had created the Sudan Defense Force (SDF), a native Sudanese army of about 4,500 men under British command assigned to augment the British regulars who garrisoned frontier outposts. In August 1955, elements of the British Equatorial Corps, a southern-based battalion of the SDF, joined forces with local indigenous police in the southern provincial capital of Torit—which erupted into revolt on August 18—and other, smaller towns in the south to stage a series of mutinies. Poorly coordinated, they were readily suppressed, but marked the beginning of five decades of civil war.

Although the mutinies were put down, neither the outgoing British administration nor the incoming northern-dominated Sudanese government did anything to address the main issue behind them: the virtual exclusion of the south from the independent Sudanese government. What is more, the mutineers who survived the military action taken against them fled the towns and began a guerrilla movement in the countryside. Before the close of 1955, these elements had banded together with southern student groups to become a full-fledged secessionist insurgency known as the Anya Nya guerrilla army.

Sudanese independence was officially declared on January 1, 1956. The Anya Nya insurgency in the south was active, but, torn by internal dissension, vulnerable. Had the new independent government been any more unified than the insurgents, it probably could have nipped the civil war in the bud. But it, too, was fragmented by factionalism. Ismail al-Azhari, a northerner who received his education at British-funded Gordon Memorial College in Khartoum (named after Charles Gordon) and U.S.-funded American University in Beirut, Lebanon, struggled to create a parliamentary government. The Umma Party opposed the parliament, instead favoring a strong executive—a system al-Azhari feared would be tantamount to dictatorship.

Even as the basic structure of government remained unresolved, al-Azhari faced the great problem of Sudan: how to unite the black, non-Muslim southerners with the Muslim Arab northerners. It was a labor for which the well-meaning al-Azhari was utterly unequipped. He lacked both an understanding of and an empathy with the values and desires of the southerners. He announced his willingness to engage in dialogue with the south, even as he used the army and police to suppress incipient uprisings there.

As support for the al-Azhari government disintegrated in the south, the alliance his National Unionist Party (NUP) had forged with the Khatmiyya sect eroded, leaving him vulnerable to opposition by the Umma Party. He tried to create a new coalition government, only to have the Khatmiyya jump ship by founding its own People's Democratic Party in June 1956. The next month, a no-confidence vote in parliament forced al-Azhari to resign. Abdullah Khalil rushed in to fill the vacuum left by al-Azhari's departure, but the fractious conservative coalition he tried to head was quickly overthrown in a coup d'etat led, on November 16, 1958, by the commander-in-chief

This map shows the division between northern Sudan, with its Islamic majority, and the south, dominated by non-Arabs. The religious, cultural, and economic differences between the two regions underpin the violence and civil war that continues today.

Courtesy of the University of Texas Libraries, the University of Texas at Austin

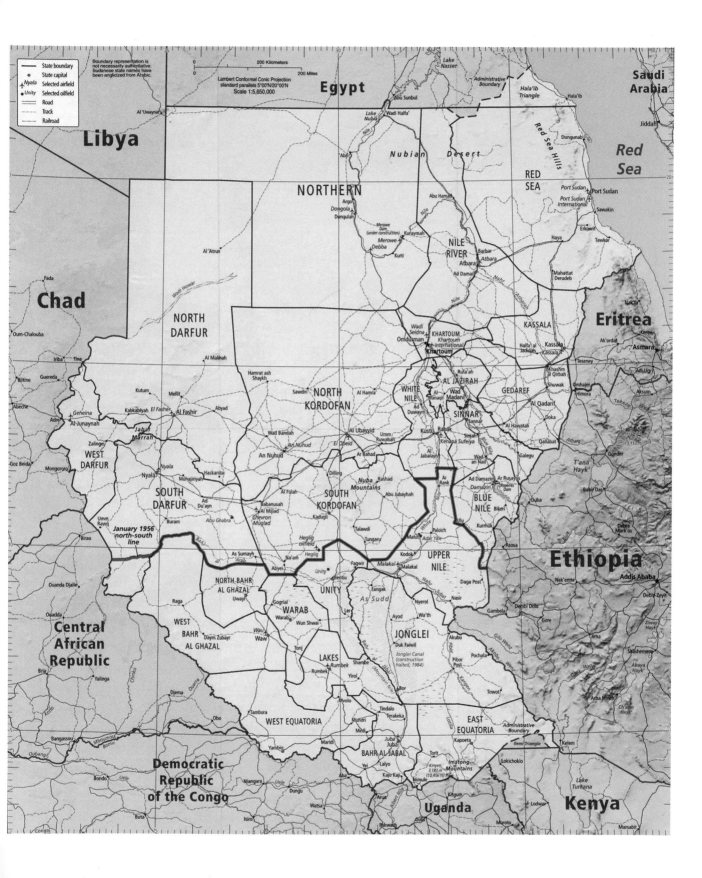

of the Sudanese military, General El Ferik Ibrahim Abbud. (Some believe that Khalil himself orchestrated the coup in conjunction with Abbud and another general to block the formation of a new coalition that would exclude his party.)

ABBUD'S ASCENSION

Trained as an engineer at Gordon Memorial College and in Khartoum's military college, Abbud was commissioned in the Egyptian army in 1918, then joined the SDF at its founding in 1925. He served with the SDF in World War II and by 1956 was commander-in-chief of all Sudanese military forces. Throughout his military career, he had scrupulously avoided politics until (he said) he could no longer allow Sudan to wallow in "degeneration, chaos, and instability." Clearly driven by a spirit of reform, Abbud enjoyed an unprecedented degree of popular and political support, but opposition developed within the military, as senior officers fell to arguing over policy, and younger officers, including the cadet corps, actively rose up against him.

These challenges prompted Abbud to assume broad dictatorial authority. He suspended the provisional constitution, abolished all political parties, and ordered a drastic reduction in the wholesale price of Sudan's chief non-petroleum export, cotton. This brought into the country a desperately needed influx of cash, which, in turn, delivered to Abbud a renewed measure of popular support, as did his rapid resolution of a dispute with Egypt over apportionment of the Nile waters. With this, simmering tensions between Egypt and Sudan ended, and Egypt formally recognized the nation's full independence.

From this base of stability, Abbud launched an ambitious, even visionary, economic development program, yet refused to make the transition from dictator to constitutional president. He did authorize local governing councils throughout the country, but these created as much dissent as they resolved. As urban dwellers saw it, the councils gave the people in the countryside too great a voice in the direction of the nation.

Predictably, the greatest upheaval was in the south, which rose up against Abbud's attempts to introduce Arab language and Islamic religion into the region. Students went on strike, and farmers rebelled. When Abbud sent in the army to suppress the uprising, the southern insurgency coalesced around a guerilla army that called itself the Anya Nya (or Anyanya), which, on September 9, 1963, attacked the Pachala administrative post. In Madi, a principal language of southern Sudan, *anyanya* means "snake venom." It spread during 1963–1969, and expanded from Equatoria, where it had begun, into Sudan's other two southern provinces, Upper Nile and Bahr al-Ghazal.

No great battles marked what the Anya Nya leaders characterized as a "defensive war" during this period. The insurgents deployed in small units to inflict what they called "venomous bites" against the northern government troops. The Anya Nya warned that they were, like the snake, small, but deadly if stepped on. Attacks were ambushes, either targeting isolated government patrols or the rearguard of larger units. An ambush might consist of a firefight by day or a murder by night, as two or three Anya Nya guerrillas would infiltrate a government camp or bivouac, steal into a tent, and cut the throats of soldiers while they slept. Throughout the south, insurgents yielded the towns and cities to Abbud's army, sometimes even withdrawing into neighboring nations before returning to raid the Sudanese countryside. The Anya Nya strategy was to cede the towns and cities to the Khartoum government while denying it control of the rural areas, forcing Abbud to maintain a costly military presence in the south in what amounted to a war of attrition, a war of sudden, violent shoot-outs and stealthy murders on moonless nights.

Abbud quickly grasped the futility of trying to suppress an insurgency by military means alone. In August 1964, therefore, he created a special commission to study the "southern question" and recommend solutions. But if Abbud expected his twenty-five-man commission to dictate an answer, he was mistaken. Instead, the commission called for free public debate on the issue, which, spearheaded by students at Khartoum University, quickly led to the popular denunciation of the Abbud regime. This, in turn, prompted Abbud to ban the very debates that agents of his government had called for. Predictably, the ban served only to incite further dissent, and when a student was killed in an anti-Abbud demonstration, Khartoum erupted in violent mass strikes of civil service and transport workers, paralyzing the capital and resulting in scores of deaths and hundreds of injuries. Both the work stoppages and the rioting soon spread to the provinces in what was called the October Revolution of 1964.

Abbud realized that he was facing a moment of truth. He could now turn the army loose on the capital to suppress the rebellion there or he could attempt to reset the government and get a fresh start. Unlike the stereotypical military dictator, he chose the latter, dissolving his own government on October 26, 1964, and calling for the creation of a provisional cabinet to replace the Supreme Council. On November 15, he stepped down, making way for a provisional civilian government. Abbud would never reenter Sudanese public life.

THE COLONEL ASSUMES COMMAND

At this point, Ismail al-Azhari, who had stepped down as prime minister in 1956, reentered the political arena and became president of the Republic of Sudan in March 1965. In contrast to prime minister, however, the office of president was little more

Thousands of Sudanese take to the streets of Khartoum on June 2, 1969, supporting democratic reforms. The demonstration came after yet another coup, staged the previous month, installed Colonel Gaafar Nimeiry, into office. However, the coup, like others in Sudan, overrated a weak leader who was unable to stop the civil war.

than that of a figurehead in a government controlled by an Umma-Nuf coalition, and al-Azhari found himself unable to use it as a springboard to real governing power before a new military figure, Colonel Gaafar Nimeiry, led four other officers in a coup d'état on May 25, 1969.

Although the coup itself was bloodless—the government was so shaky that little was required to bring about its collapse—Nimeiry immediately assumed dictatorial powers, sealed off Sudan's airports, pointedly warned against all foreign interference, banned political parties, and summarily nationalized all banks and businesses. Modeling himself on Egypt's dynamic Gamal Abdel Nasser, he connected Sudan with the region's pan-Arab movement, thereby instantly alienating the predominantly non-Arab south.

In 1970, Sadiq al-Mahdi, a charismatic Ansar imam (religious leader) and head of the Umma Party, led a coup d'etat by which he briefly replaced Nimeiry as prime minister before he himself was ousted and Nimeiry returned to office.

In the meantime, the civil war, now in its fifteenth year, raged on, mainly in the south. Idi Amin Dada, the commander of the Ugandan army who would go on to become the most infamous dictator on the African continent, began in the late 1960s recruiting a paramilitary force made up of members of Kakwa, Lugbara, Nubian, and other ethnic groups from the West Nile area of Uganda bordering Sudan. In 1970, seeking to build his military power base by extending his influence across the Sudanese border, Amin began funding the Anya Nya.

He was approached at this time by a German-born soldier of fortune named Rolf Steiner. Born in Munich in 1933, Steiner was sixteen when he decided to enter the priesthood, deliberately choosing not to follow in the footsteps of his father, who had been one of "Red Baron" Manfred von Richthofen's squadron pilots in World War I. He began his studies, but, within a year, an affair with a nun pushed him in a new direction. Now seventeen, he joined the French Foreign Legion.

While serving in Algeria, he met the woman he would later marry, an Algerian who turned him against French imperialism and prompted his enrollment in the anti-de Gaulle Organisation de l'Armée Secrète (OAS), which got him drummed out of the Legion. In 1967, while living in Paris, Steiner organized a mercenary army and took it to Africa, where he worked for the newly independent Republic of Biafra. In 1970, he offered his services to Amin, who quickly dispatched him to southern Sudan, where he trained the Anya Nya in the small-unit tactics he had learned as a French Foreign Legionnaire and served as a mediator among the disputatious southern tribes that contributed members to the Anya Nya. A charismatic figure whom the tribal people saw as a kind of knight or pure warrior, Steiner was able to forge the guerrilla army into a unified and therefore truly formidable antigovernment force. The pace of ambush and harassment of government forces accelerated, yet no sooner had Steiner resolved tribal disputes than dissent broke out between Marxist and anti-Marxist elements within the Anya Nya before the insurgency could mount anything like a major offensive.

In 1971, Steiner was taken out of the picture when he became a prisoner of the Nimeiry government, which deported him to West Germany, after three years of confinement and torture. Although Nimeiry saw Steiner as an enemy of the state, the German mercenary's efforts at unifying the Anya Nya were actually instrumental in ending what some historians call the First Sudanese Civil War and others consider merely the first phase of one continuous war.

Thanks to the preliminary work of Steiner, in 1971, Joseph Lagu, formerly a young Sudanese military officer, was able to gather under his leadership the fragmented southern Sudanese guerilla bands into the Southern Sudan Liberation Movement (SSLM). Although this enhanced the military might of the rebels, it also created for the first time since the war had begun in 1955 a single organization with which Khartoum could negotiate. The Nimeiry government and the SSLM entered into the Addis Ababa Agreement of February 1972, which made southern Sudan a single administrative region with a certain degree of autonomous authority. In exchange for this, the SSLM agreed to end the guerrilla war.

It had been, up to this point, a conflict of no great battles but almost continuous strife, in which an estimated half million Sudanese had perished. Only 20 percent of these casualties were armed combatants, or fighters by choice; the rest were civilians, farmers, and farm families mostly caught in the crossfire or subjected to starvation and privation when they were forced to leave their homes.

HOPE AND ITS COLLAPSE

For eleven years following the Addis Ababa Agreement, Sudan settled into a period of relative peace, during which Nimeiry sought to increase the nation's economic well-being by improving relations with the West. The banks and most businesses were returned to private ownership, and foreign investment was both encouraged and actively sought. This embrace of capitalism led Marxist military officers to stage a short-lived coup in 1975.

While the communists had their reasons for opposing Nimeiry's overtures to the capitalist West, Sadiq al-Mahdi, who saw himself as the nationalist heir to *the* Mahdi who had killed "Chinese" Gordon in 1885, wanted Sudan returned to the splendid isolation of total religious and political disengagement from the West. In 1976, he led a thousand Darfuri Arab raiders, who had been armed and trained in Muammar al-Gaddafi's Libya, through Darfur and Kordofan, and into Khartoum and Omdurman. More than a guerrilla insurgency, this was an invasion, which exploded into three days of urban warfare. Armed by Gaddafi with AK-47 assault rifles, the raiders fought street-to-street and house-to-house, with civilian noncombatants caught in the crossfire. Nimeiry could successfully apply against insurgents in a city what never worked well in the countryside: superior firepower. He rolled all of the government army's available tanks into Khartoum and Omdurman, suppressing the insurgents by main strength and brute force.

Although defeated, Sadiq al-Mahdi remained an important political power in Sudan, and in 1977 Nimeiry agreed to a much publicized "national reconciliation" with him. Sadiq al-Mahdi and his political allies were permitted to join the legislature to form the Sudan Socialist Union. Despite this, relations between the Nimeiry government and the leadership in southern Sudan deteriorated, and the national reconciliation, so filled with hope, soon dissolved.

By 1981, the Khartoum government was rapidly reversing its tolerant and inclusive policy toward the south. In an appeal to his power base, Nimeiry bowed to Islamist pressure to transform Sudan into a monolithic Muslim Arab state. In 1983, he announced that he would redivide the south into three regions—clearly a move to undermine the south's capacity for united action against the north. Moreover, he further declared his intention to impose on the entire Sudanese nation Sharia law—a judicial code that would place criminal and civil justice, as well as individual conduct, under traditional Islamic law.

WAR REIGNITED

Some historians believe that Nimeiry's announcement restarted a dormant civil war; others think it touched off a *second* Sudanese civil war. Either way, the cost in lives and suffering would be even greater than that during 1955–1972.

By early 1984, Sudan was again in turmoil, and on April 26, Nimeiry declared a state of emergency, hastening the imposition of stringent Sharia, which replaced constitutional rights. Throughout the north, ad hoc "decisive justice courts" dispensed instant Sharia justice, which included amputation of a hand (or hands) and/or a foot (or feet) for theft; in the case of repeat offenders, the amputations might be the prelude to summary execution. Brutal though these penalties were, even more controversial were judgments against women in cases of adultery, for which the prescribed penalties ranged from public flogging (an often lethal seventy-five lashes) to death by stoning.

Although Nimeiry refrained from setting up the "decisive justice courts" in the south, Sharia nevertheless applied there as well as in the north and represented to many non-Muslims the most hated aspect of the religion that was being forced upon them. Largely in response to the new religious decree, John Garang, a Christian, U.S.-educated agricultural economist from the southern Sudanese Dinka tribe, founded the Sudan People's Liberation Army (SPLA) in 1983. After the Addis Ababa Agreement, Garang, who opposed the government, had been absorbed into the Sudanese army as a colonel. In 1983, however, he fomented an army mutiny in the south and incorporated nearly 3,000 mutineers into the SPLA.

The creation of the SPLA greatly alarmed President Nimeiry, who hoped to placate the south by ending the state of emergency in September 1984 and issuing assurances that the rights of non-Muslims would be (in his somewhat ambiguous word) "respected." Yet even as he disbanded the decisive justice courts, he approved a new judiciary act, which made many of the features of those courts a permanent part of the regular judicial system. Outraged by this cynical sleight of hand, southern dissidents intensified their hit-and-run attacks against government forces in the southern countryside.

WAR BY PROXY

In the best of times a poor place, Sudan suffered catastrophic economic disruption during the renewal of war. In Khartoum, 1985 began with critical shortages of food and fuel, while much of the countryside was swept by famine. As the cost of the barest of essentials skyrocketed, violent demonstrations broke out in the capital and in many towns.

In contrast to acute shortages of subsistence staples among Sudanese civilians, both the government military forces and the guerrillas who opposed it were remarkably well armed. As the world had meddled in the region's affairs throughout much of its history, so now nations far from Sudan sold it mountains of arms. Britain, the United States, and West Germany had supplied the nation's military needs throughout most of the 1960s, until the Six-Day Arab-Israeli War of 1967 prompted these countries to distance themselves from Sudan and other Arab powers.

The Soviet Union, however, soon took up the slack, not only equipping Sudanese forces, but also training them. Between 1968 and 1972, during the height of the first civil war, Soviet arms and assistance allowed Sudan's army to expand from 18,000 to more than 50,000 men. But following the communist coup attempt in 1972, the Khartoum government backed away from the Soviets and turned instead to Egypt, which not only furnished arms but also developed pan-Arabic programs of full military cooperation.

In response to Soviet and Egyptian arms supplies, the United States and U.S.-aligned countries, especially Israel, resumed supplying Sudan in the mid-1970s. From roughly 1976 to 1987, in fact, the United States sold particularly large amounts of materiel to Sudan specifically to counteract the Soviet Union's funding and equipping of Marxists in Ethiopia and Libya. In 1982 alone, U.S. arms sales to Sudan reached $101 million, a staggering sum for such a poor nation.

BLOOD FROM A "BLOODLESS COUP"

On April 6, 1985, General Abdul Rahman Suwar ad-Dahhab led a coup d'état that toppled the Nimeiry government. Dahhab immediately rescinded Nimeiry's decreed intention of making all Sudan an Islamic state, and his Sudanese Socialist Union Party was ordered disbanded. Nevertheless, the Sharia laws remained in effect. Dahhab in the meantime headed a military junta, or "transitional military council," which consulted with a variety of political parties and trade unions to assemble a temporary civilian cabinet, pending elections, which were held in April 1986 and returned to power the Umma Party's Sadiq al-Mahdi as prime minister. He assembled a coalition government in which southern interests played a major role, and in May 1986 opened peace negotiations with John Garang's Sudan People's Liberation Army (SPLA). These talks produced the Koka Dam Declaration, which called for a new constitutional convention and the abolition of Sharia. By 1988, plans were in place to pave the way for a new constitution by terminating the military agreements with Egypt and Libya that drove the war, ending the government-imposed state of emergency, suspending Sharia, and imposing a strict cease-fire.

It was a noble plan, but it served only to intensify the fighting, as all sides jockeyed for political and military advantage prior to the commencement of cease-fire negotiations and a constitutional convention. With the intensified combat came greater disruption of commerce and the economy. This, in turn, brought sharp price increases for the most basic goods, which, predictably, triggered riots and popular uprisings in Khartoum as well as the countryside. In November 1988, the Democratic Unionist Party agreed on a peace plan with Garang's SPLA and presented it to Prime Minister Sadiq al-Mahdi, who rejected it out of hand.

With this, the DUP, the oldest political party in Sudan and the only party that had ever governed the country through unchallenged democratic elections—back in 1953—left the coalition government. Now only the Umma and the Islamic fundamentalist National Islamic Front (NIF) remained. This prompted the army in February 1989 to warn the prime minister of the military's intention of mounting a coup d'etat unless he took positive steps toward ending the war. Al-Mahdi responded by reaching out to the DUP, inviting its members back into the government, and approving the SPLA-DUP peace agreement he had rejected. This cleared the way for a constitutional convention, which was slated for September 1989.

Once again, hope seemed to be reborn in this most hopeless of places. Then, on June 30, 1989, Sudanese army Colonel Omar Hassan Bashir, backed by the NIF, overthrew al-Mahdi in what was hailed as a bloodless coup.

Born in a northern Sudanese village, Bashir was raised mostly in Khartoum, joined the Sudanese army in 1960, and was sent to the Egyptian Military Academy in Cairo. He then returned to the Sudan Military Academy in Khartoum, from which he graduated in 1966. He served with the Egyptian army during the Yom Kippur War against Israel in 1973 and rose rapidly through the ranks of the Sudanese army. A staunch Islamic nationalist, he immediately replaced the coalition government with a military junta called the Revolutionary Command Council for National Salvation (RCC), which he chaired. The junta, assisted by a handpicked civilian cabinet, issued a blanket ban on political parties, trade unions, and all secular institutions. The junta then turned to the government itself, purging from it nearly 80,000 military officers, police personnel, and civil servants who were (or seemed) unwilling to cooperate in the creation of a new Islamic Sudanese government.

In March 1991, the regime promulgated the Criminal Act of 1991, which reversed the retreat from Sharia by incorporating traditional Islamic law into the national penal code, with punishments that included flogging, amputation, and lethal stoning. Recognizing the inflammatory nature of Sharia in the south, the Criminal Act exempted the southern states from a number of Islamic prohibitions and penalties, but nevertheless provided for the possibility of *future* application of Sharia in the south. Just two years after enactment of the new penal code, all non-Muslim judges were transferred from the south to the north, where they were replaced by Muslims. In addition, a new law enforcement agency, the Public Order Police, was created specifically to enforce Sharia. Although the operations of these officers were restricted to the north, they had full authority over non-Muslims, including southerners, living in or visiting the north.

The Bashir government used more than the law to attempt to gain control of the south. The National Islamic Government of the Sudan (GOS), as the Bashir regime officially styled itself, used a combination of regular Sudanese army forces and a militia—the People's Defense Forces (PDF)—to raid southern villages. These raids were often carried out in conjunction with government-sanctioned janjaweed bandits, who looted cattle, slaughtered men, and abducted women and children to be sold into slavery, mainly in northern Sudan. The raids, which began in 1991, continued through at least 2001, a ten-year period during which an estimated 200,000 people from the south and the Nuba Mountain region were enslaved. In Darfur, janjaweed raids continue still, and the raiders, fearing little in the way of retaliation, can be seen in almost any village marketplace, casually strolling, AK-47s slung over their shoulders, among the people they victimize.

When Bashir launched his major operations in the south, beginning in 1991, the SPLA held most of the rural areas of the Equatoria, Bahr al-Ghazal, and Upper Nile provinces in the south and had a strong presence in rural parts of Darfur, Kordofan, and the Blue Nile provinces. Government forces quickly came to control the major southern cities and towns, however, and by the summer of 1991, Garang suffered a series of challenges to his leadership from dissident elements within the SPLA. Some of these SPLA groups split off into what was called the Nasir faction, which attempted to oust Garang.

Into the growing chaos of government raids and challenged rebel leadership stepped Osama bin Laden. The Saudi-born extremist led al-Qaeda ("the Base"), which was dedicated to waging jihad ("holy war") for the ultimate purpose of reestablishing throughout the Middle East and North Africa the "caliphate," the great Islamic spiritual and political hegemony that had existed during the early Middle Ages. The Sudanese government quietly welcomed bin Laden because of the funding he brought with him, and did nothing to interfere with his exportation of terrorist attacks beyond the borders of Sudan. This, together with Bashir's outspoken support for Saddam Hussein in the Persian Gulf War of 1990–1991, turned U.S. political and popular opinion against Sudan. Early in his administration, which began in 1993, President Bill Clinton cut off aid to Sudan and prohibited private investment in the country while his administration obtained from Congress funding for the military efforts of neighboring nations to secure their borders against Sudanese incursions.

THE SUDANESE GOVERNMENT QUIETLY WELCOMED OSAMA BIN LADEN BECAUSE OF THE FUNDING HE BROUGHT WITH HIM, AND DID NOTHING TO INTERFERE WITH HIS EXPORTATION OF TERRORIST ATTACKS BEYOND THE BORDERS OF SUDAN.

Yet the antigovernment rebels had little credibility among Americans or in the West generally. The SPLA continued to fragment, and competing rebel factions sprang up in September 1992 (under SPLA officer William Nyuon Bany) and in February

1993 (under another disaffected SPLA leader, Kerubino Kwanyin Bol). There emerged from the violent clashes among the rebel factions no single identifiable leader who was palatable to the West, and Sudan—north as well as south—came to be increasingly regarded in the United States as a lawless, isolated, rogue presence in the world. Without leadership and without the presence of either journalists or international observers, the world knew little of Sudan other than its seemingly inexhaustible capacity to generate violent death.

> WITHOUT LEADERSHIP AND WITHOUT THE PRESENCE OF EITHER
> JOURNALISTS OR INTERNATIONAL OBSERVERS, THE WORLD KNEW
> LITTLE OF SUDAN OTHER THAN ITS SEEMINGLY INEXHAUSTIBLE
> CAPACITY TO GENERATE VIOLENT DEATH.

THE WAR ENDS . . .

The world might well have been willing simply to turn its back on Sudan were it not for the fact that, throughout the 1990s, the ongoing civil war often spilled across the nation's porous borders with Eritrea, Ethiopia, Uganda, and Kenya. In a bid to protect their own peoples, the leaders of these nations created in 1993 the Intergovernmental Authority on Development (IGAD), hoping to broker peace. The first step was an attempt to reduce the raw chaos of religious, ethnic, and tribal enmities to a clear list of conditions on which all sides could agree to peaceful coexistence. In 1994, this effort resulted in a Declaration of Principles (DOP), which included a plan for equitable political power sharing between the two regions of Sudan, a permanent and just definition of the relationship of religion to state, a plan for economic equity, and a blueprint for southern self-determination.

The Bashir government made a show of welcoming the DOP but refused to sign it—and continued to refuse as long as its regular and militia forces were successful in wreaking havoc throughout the south. In 1995, however, the fractious rebels began to coalesce in the south and, even more important, opposition political parties and movements in both the south and the north joined forces as the National Democratic Alliance (NDA). Suddenly, the government found itself facing increasingly coordinated opposition in the south as well as on an entirely new front in *northeast* Sudan. The geography of the war radically changed, as the longstanding north-south opposition became complicated by conflict between government-controlled central Sudan and the increasingly dissident northeastern periphery. Moreover, the NDA was not regionally limited. Its major constituents included the SPLA in the south but also the DUP and Umma parties, which were strong in the northeast.

Feeling itself increasingly imperiled and in a move to end its international isolation, the Bashir government sought to appease the United States and the West by expelling Osama bin Laden and al-Qaeda from Sudan in 1996 and, the following year, by finally signing the DOP as well as related agreements with various rebel factions. These steps began a gradual thaw in relations with the United States, and in September 2001, President George W. Bush sent former U.S. senator John Danforth to Sudan as his peace envoy. Danforth's brief was to explore with all sides an intermediary role for the United States, which had, in addition to genuine humanitarian motives for ending the war, a more urgent imperative to ensure that Osama bin Laden, who had just taken credit for the terrorist attacks against the United States of September 11, 2001, would be denied reentry into Sudan and that the country would not become the kind of failed state in which al-Qaeda and similar terrorist organizations found safe haven and an abundance of desperate recruits.

In 2002, the U.S. Congress passed the Sudan Peace Act (P.L 107-245), signed into law by George W. Bush on October 21, which identified and condemned human rights violations on all sides of the Second Sudanese Civil War, but focused most directly on the Bashir government's genocidal policies ranging from the aerial bombardment of civilian targets to the use of militia and other forces, especially the janjaweed, to carry out mass killing and enslavement. Funding was appropriated to assist those areas of Sudan outside of government control to resist Bashir's oppression. Thus, for the first time in the long conflict, the United States sided with the rebels against the government; however, the U.S. president was required to certify every six months that both the Sudanese government and the SPLA were negotiating in good faith. Good behavior on the part of the Bashir regime would be guaranteed with the threat of a UN Security Council resolution for an arms embargo and other economic sanctions.

Growing isolation from the West and the increased unity and effectiveness of internal opposition, including the opening of a second front in the war, plus the U.S. sanctions threatened by the Sudan Peace Act of 2002, spurred negotiations throughout 2003 and 2004, leading to the Comprehensive Peace Agreement, which was signed on January 9, 2005, in Nairobi, Kenya. Major terms of the agreement include southern autonomy for a period of six years, followed by a referendum on secession; merger and limitation of national military forces; a fifty/fifty division of oil income north and south; equitable division of national employment; and the continuation of Sharia in the north, with its application in the south is to be decided by the elected assembly.

. . . BUT THE KILLING CONTINUES

Civil war in Sudan cost 500,000 lives between 1955 and 1972 and nearly 2 million more between 1983 and 2005. Most of the deaths in both phases of the conflict were among civilian noncombatants. Although many died in raids, far more succumbed to the economic effects of prolonged warfare, including famine and starvation, compounded by severe drought, which the conditions of chronic war prevented any group from dealing with adequately. In addition, some 4 million southerners were displaced from their farms. Some became internal exiles, crowding into impoverished southern cities or into the slums of Khartoum in the north; others fled the country, seeking refuge in neighboring Ethiopia, Kenya, Uganda, Egypt, and elsewhere.

Although the 2005 peace agreement greatly reduced the fighting throughout most of Sudan, it did not end the conflict in the Darfur region. Resistance movements continue to oppose government-sponsored militias and the janjaweed, which have periodically carried out a government policy of displacing non-Muslim black Africans with Muslim Arabs. The U.S. government has consistently accused the Sudanese government of genocide in the region, although the United Nations has refused to label as genocide what it nevertheless calls government-sponsored acts of atrocity. Although the Hague-based International Criminal Court prosecutor filed ten war crimes charges against President Omar Bashir on July 14, 2008, including three counts of genocide, the arrest warrant, issued in March 2009, dropped the genocide counts for lack of sufficient evidence. As of March 2010, Bashir remains free and in power. (He stepped down as commander of the armed forces in January to comply with constitutional requirements regarding presidential eligibility, as he planned to stand as National Congress candidate for president in April 2010.) He has consistently opposed the United Nations mission in Darfur, calling the UN peacekeeping troops sent there "invaders." The situation in the region remains one of great danger and even greater suffering.

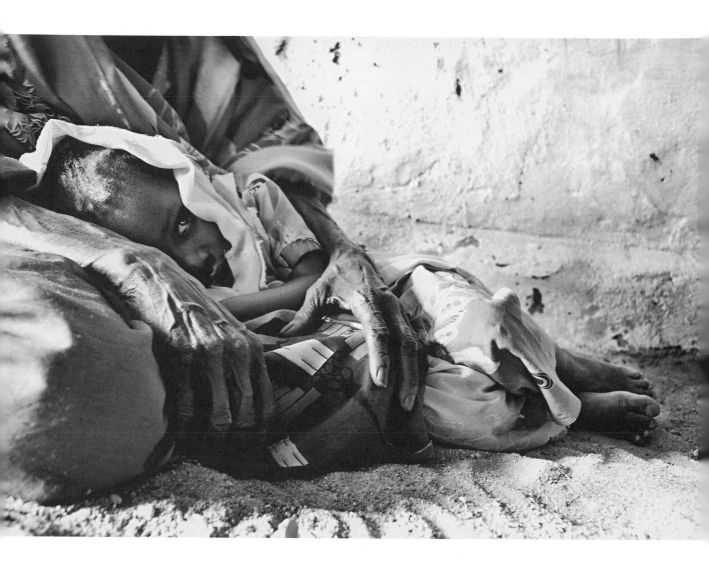

Refugees from Darfur, including this sick child being cradled by a parent, rest in Iriba, Chad, in this September 2008 image. The war in Sudan has made refugees of 4 million people.

Edit by Getty Images

AFTERWORD: THE LONGEST WAR—THE U.S. IN AFGHANISTAN, 2001–?

A s *Why Some Wars Never End* went to print, numerous press stories appeared declaring the United States's war in Afghanistan the nation's longest conflict, surpassing the war in Vietnam. That is, if you count the U.S. War in Vietnam as having begun with the Gulf of Tonkin Resolution in August 1964, which is controversial: The Department of Defense counts the first American casualties in Vietnam from 1955, and there were 4,000 U.S. military advisors in Vietnam as early as 1962.

However, it is probably fair to say that the first major U.S. effort in Vietnam came in 1964, and by this standard, the war in Afghanistan has become the U.S's longest fight. The war began with a provocation far more deadly than that of the confused Gulf of Tonkin incident—the terrorist attacks on the World Trade Center and the Pentagon on September 11, 2001, when thousands of Americans lost their lives in what the 9/11 Commission called "a day of unprecedented shock and suffering in the history of the United States."

Blame for the attacks quickly fell on Osama bin Laden, the charismatic Saudi terrorist leader whom American intelligence officials had also implicated in a string of deadly terrorist attacks, from the first bombing of the World Trade Center in 1993, to the bombing of American embassies in Tanzania and Kenya in 1998, and the October 2000 suicide attack on the destroyer USS *Cole* while it was refueling in the Yemeni port of Aden, in which seventeen American sailors died. Bin Laden, the founder and funder of a worldwide Islamic terrorist organization known as *al-Qaeda*—"the Base"— had taken refuge in Afghanistan with his longtime friend, Mullah Mohammed Omar, who had founded the fundamentalist Taliban (*Taliban* means "student") regime, which had taken over control of most of the country in the 1990s.

When the Taliban refused to give up bin Laden to the Americans, the United States, under the administration of President George W. Bush, attacked. This was meant not to be the United States's longest war, but one of its shortest—a surgical strike that would disable the Taliban and the al-Qaeda forces fighting with them, and capture or kill bin Laden. For a number of reasons, it didn't quite turn out that way.

OPERATION ENDURING FREEDOM

On September 20, 2001, the Bush administration gave the Taliban regime in Afghanistan a five-point ultimatum, demanding that it turn over all al-Qaeda leaders to the

United States, release imprisoned foreign nationals, close terrorist training camps, hand over terrorists to U.S. or international authorities, and give the United States full access to terrorist training camps.

The Taliban rejected this ultimatum the very next day and continued to reject demands that it turn over bin Laden to the United States for trial. On October 7, the United States and its British allies began bombing Taliban and al-Qaeda forces with a mix of air strikes from B-52 bombers, attacks from carrier-based fighter planes, and assaults from cruise missiles fired from U.S. and British ships and submarines. It was the beginning of an attack the United States called Operation Enduring Freedom. The first American forces on the ground were so-called Special Operations Forces: Green Berets, Navy SEALs, and Delta Force operators, trained to fight in small units with indigenous forces—in this case, with the Northern Alliance fighters who had been combating the Taliban for years.

In the first few months of the war, the Americans reigned supreme. American Special Ops forces called down the might of U.S. firepower on poorly prepared Taliban

An Afghan solider in 2004 trains with a recoilless rifle near the mountainous border with Pakistan. Such soldiers, along with U.S. Special Forces troops, have attempted with mixed success to capture al-Qaeda and Taliban fugitives.

Associated Press

The controversial decision by the Bush Administration to attack Saddam Hussein and Iraq not only caused huge protests in the United States but took crucial attention and resources away from the war in Afghanistan, thus lengthening the conflict.

Getty Images

armies that massed in the open, a perfect target for mammoth 15,000-pound (6,804 kg) "daisy cutter" bombs that obliterated thousands of Taliban off the face of the earth. The first pictures released to the American public showed Green Berets making charges on Afghan ponies with their Northern Alliance allies; this war of retribution had a romantic feel to the American public, a sense that the country had returned to the days of the cavalry charge and frontier justice.

As the U.S. Army and Marines joined the fight, Taliban-held cities began to fall, first Mazar-e-Sharif on November 9, followed by Herat on November 11, and Kabul, the capital city, on November 13. At the end of November, Konduz, the last remaining Taliban stronghold in northern Afghanistan, fell to the Americans and British. By mid-December, almost all of the enemy resistance was reduced to isolated pockets, although these put up fierce resistance. Most of these pockets were located in the eastern and southeastern parts of the country, along its porous and mountainous border with Pakistan, particularly in cave complexes (built by mujahadeen fighters during the war against the Soviet Union in the 1980s) located at Tora Bora and Zawar Kili.

But by the end of 2001, the Americans had installed their own handpicked Afghan president Hamid Karzai and had near total control of the country. Dozens of top al-Qaeda fighters had been captured and would, within a month, be sent to a facility dubbed Camp X-Ray, in Guantanamo Bay, Cuba, where they would be held for interrogation.

The war should have ended right then and there. But it didn't.

"A DRAMATIC TURNING POINT"

There are several reasons why it didn't end. The first is the failure of the American military to capture bin Laden, who was last sighted with his al-Qaeda fighters in the Tora Bora cave complex at some point in January 2002. At the time, the Americans only had about 100 Special Forces troops on the scene, along with Northern Alliance fighters, but could have called in some 2,000 Army and Marine units stationed nearby to block the mountain passes in to Pakistan and press home the attack.

But, not certain that the intelligence of bin Laden's whereabouts was good, U.S. Army Central Commander General Tommy Franks and Secretary of Defense Donald Rumsfeld were unwilling to risk what might be serious American casualties in a pitched battle, just as victory seemed ensured to the American public. And so bin Laden escaped, probably to the wild border regions of Pakistan, and the Americans were left with an incomplete victory. Despite the fact that President Bush and other American officials now claimed that bin Laden was so isolated as to be completely impotent, he remained, even in hiding, an important rallying point for the forces of radical Islam.

Another reason why America failed in ending the war in Afghanistan in 2002 is that as early as November 2001, Bush had tasked Rumsfeld and Franks with working up attack plans for an invasion of Iraq. This shifted the focus of their work away from Afghanistan and toward Iraq and was, as a U.S. Senate Committee on Foreign Relations report later stated, "a dramatic turning point that allowed a sustained victory in Afghanistan to slip through our fingers." It was obvious to Rumsfeld and Franks that the president's chief focus—one that would drain thousands of troops—was on Iraq. Almost before it got started, the United States' effort in Afghanistan was on the back burner.

This did not mean the fighting in Afghanistan ended, of course. The invasion of Iraq did not begin until March 2003, and during that time the United States and its allies continued to fight. But the focus of the war now changed to one of anti-insurgency. No longer were Taliban forces rising to meet American troops—to be slaughtered by American firepower. Instead, they were fighting a tough guerilla war, keeping to bases in the remote southern and eastern parts of the country, and in Pakistan, and biding their time as more and more American forces were shifted to Iraq.

Finally, the Americans were beginning to lose the war that had started so promisingly because President Karzai was losing credibility. His government was rife with corruption, his armed forces still weak and dependent upon American aid and advisors, and he was unable to curb the power of the entrenched warlords who exerted regional control of the country. Most of all, he was unable to fully eradicate the Taliban, which, by 2005 and 2006, was staging a re-emergence. Taliban fighters infiltrated from Pakistan to join other Taliban in the southern part of Afghanistan and attack villages and mount offensives against U.S. and Afghan troops. The Taliban, formerly against the growing of poppies to produce opium, now controlled much of the opium production in the Helmand and Kandahar provinces and were thus able to fund their fight with drug money.

Finally, in 2006, Pakistan's president, Pervez Musharraf, signed a controversial peace agreement with seven militant groups calling themselves the "Pakistan Taliban," promising that his army would withdraw from border areas of Pakistan and leave the Taliban to govern itself, if they would agree not to infiltrate Afghanistan. The idea, from a Pakistani point of view, was to contain the Taliban, but, from the American point of view, the terrorists had just been handed a secure base of operations.

A TALL ORDER

After the successful "surge" in Iraq in 2007—the addition of new American troops in areas of heavy fighting—the security of the U.S.-backed government in Iraq was more assured and American attentions returned once again to Afghanistan, where the resurgent Taliban now controlled large portions of the country. With warnings from his military advisors, especially General Stanley A. McChrystal, former commander of American ground troops in Afghanistan, that the war there had become "a war of necessity" in order to stop global terrorism. The new U.S. president, Barack Obama, decided in 2009 to commit a total of 47,000 new American combat troops to Afghanistan in 2009, bringing the number of American troops in the country to more than 100,000, supported by their NATO allies.

American troops have in 2010 mounted major operations in Helmand province, which had become almost totally controlled by the Taliban. In February 2010, U.S. Marines battled with insurgents in Marja, a major poppy growing region in Helmand, and were able to drive them out after a sustained fight. More operations had been planned in Kandahar for the summer, and then the Americans were to have turned east to battle in the provinces of Paktia, and Khost. But as of this writing, the war has the promise of stretching on much longer, despite President Obama's promise to begin a troop draw-down in the summer of 2011. One reason for this is that the Taliban have learned from their terrorist counterparts in Iraq and have resorted to suicide bombings and the placement of improvised explosive devices along the roads; these tactics allow them to kill as many of the enemy, with as little risk to themselves, as possible.

Another reason why the war will go on a long time is because of the notoriously difficult Afghanistan landscape. No matter how sophisticated American spying capabilities are, they cannot find Taliban fighters hiding in mountainous border regions, just as they have not been able to find bin Laden or Omar. And if they are unable to do so, they will be unable to fully eradicate the Taliban.

Matters in Afghanistan became even more complex when an American team of geologists announced a startling find—nearly one trillion dollars worth of untapped mineral deposits (gold, iron, copper, lithium) that will make the country a rich prize for whoever wins the war. Added to the religious and ethnic tensions that the conflict is rife with is a startling profit motive, which may make all sides hold on even more aggressively.

Last, but perhaps most important, the Americans are now fighting a seesaw battle for the hearts and minds of the Afghan people. In 2001, the population, glad to be rid of the harsh yoke of the Taliban, for the most part welcomed the American attack. This is not quite the case in 2010. The government of Hamid Karzai is so corrupt that not only has it alienated many Afghanis, but it has left a vacuum of power in many remote regions that the Taliban have been only too happy to fill. In different parts of Helmand, Kandahar, and other provinces, the Taliban have their own "shadow" government—their own police force, mayors, press, radio stations. There are reports that the Taliban are now posing as the protectors of the poor people against an uncaring and devious Afghan government, and, especially, against foreign invaders who kill innocents with drone strikes and bomb attacks.

This is not to say American and allied forces cannot win in Afghanistan, but they must use force judiciously while winning over the population and helping rebuild the country's infrastructure. It's a tall order—and it will take a long time.

BIBLIOGRAPHY

CHAPTER 1:

Bradford, Ernle. *Thermopylae: The Battle for the West*. New York: Da Capo Press, 1980

Cummins, Joseph. *The War Chronicles: From Chariots to Flintlocks*. Beverly, MA: Fair Winds Press, 2008.

Green, Peter. *The Greco-Persian Wars*. Berkeley, CA: University of California Press, 1998.

Strauss, Barry. *The Battle of Salamis: The Naval Encounter that Saved Greece—and Western Civilization*. New York: Simon & Schuster, 2004.

CHAPTER 2:

Boatwright, Mary T., Daniel J. Gargola, and Richard J. A. Talbert. *The Romans: From Village to Empire*. New York: Oxford University Press, 2004.

Goldsworthy, Adrian. *The Fall of Carthage: The Punic Wars 265–146 BC*. London: Orion Books, Ltd., 2000.

Keegan, John. *A History of Warfare*. New York: Alfred A. Knopf, 1994.

Polybius. *The Histories*. New York: Twayne Publishers, 1966.

CHAPTER 3:

Cummins, Joseph. *History's Greatest Hits: Famous Events We Should All Know More About*. Sydney, Australia: Murdoch Books, 2007.

Curry, Anne. *The Hundred Years' War*. London: Osprey Publishing, 2002.

Seward, Desmond. *The Hundred Years' War: The English in France, 1337–1453*. New York: Atheneum, 1978.

CHAPTER 4:

Goodwin, Jason. *Lords of the Horizons: A History of the Ottoman Empire*. New York: Henry Holt & Co., 1998.

Kinross, Lord. *The Ottoman Centuries: The Rise and Fall of the Turkish Empire*. New York: HarperCollins, 2002.

O'Shea, Stephen. *Sea of Faith: Islam and Christianity in the Medieval Mediterranean World*. New York: Walker & Co., 2006.

CHAPTER 5:

Klingaman, William K. *The First Century: Emperors, Gods and Everyman*. New York: HarperCollins, 1986.

Lendering, Jona. "Wars between the Jews and Romans: The Subjugation of Judea (63 BCE)." www.livius.org/ja-jn/jewish_wars/jwar01.htm.

Rajak, Tessa. *Josephus: The Historian and His Society*. London: Duckworth Press, 2002.

Wasserstein, Abraham, ed. *Flavius Josephus: Selections from His Works*. New York: The Viking Press, 1974.

Williams, Derek. *The Reach of Rome: A History of the Roman Imperial Frontier 1st–5th Centuries AD*. New York: St. Martin's Press, 1996.

CHAPTER 6:

Coogan, Tim Pat. *The Troubles: Ireland's Ordeal and the Search for Peace*. Boulder, CO: Roberts Rinehart Publishers, 1996.

McKittrick, David, and David McVea. *Making Sense of the Troubles: The Story of the Conflict in Northern Ireland*. Chicago: New Amsterdam Books, 2002.

O'Connor, Ulick. *The Troubles: Ireland, 1912–1922*. New York: Bobbs-Merill Co., 1975.

CHAPTER 7:

Friedman, Thomas. *From Beirut to Jerusalem*. New York: Random House, 1990.

Herzog, Chaim. *The Arab-Israeli Wars: War and Peace in the Middle East*. New York: Random House, 1982.

Morris, Benny. *1948: The First Arab-Israeli War*. New Haven: Yale University Press, 2008.

Oren, Michael. *Six Days of War: June 1967 and the Making of the Modern Middle East*. New York: Oxford University Press, 2002.

Timerman, Jacobo. *The Longest War: Israel in Lebanon*. New York: Alfred A. Knopf, 1982.

CHAPTER 8:

Knetsch, Joe. *Florida's Seminole Wars, 1817–1858*. Charleston, SC: Arcadia Publishing, 2003.

Missall, John, and Mary Lou Missall. *The Seminole Wars: America's Longest Indian Conflict*. Gainesville, FL: The University Press of Florida, 2004.

Remini, Robert V. *The Life of Andrew Jackson*. New York: Harper & Row, 1988.

CHAPTER 9:

Loyn, David. *In Afghanistan: Two Hundred Years of British, Russian and American Occupation*. New York: St. Martin's Press, 2009.

Waller, John H. *Beyond the Khyber Pass: The Road to British Disaster in the First Afghan War*. New York: Random House, 1990.

CHAPTER 10:

Addington, Larry H. *America's War in Vietnam: A Short Narrative History*. Bloomington, IN: Indiana University Press, 2000.

Gettleman, Marvin, Jane Franklin, Marilyn B. Young, and H. Bruce Franklin, eds. *Vietnam and America: The Most Comprehensive Documented History of the Vietnam War*. New York: Grove Press, 1995.

Gibson, James William. *The Perfect War: Technowar in Vietnam*. New York: Atlantic Monthly Press, 1986.

Stanley, Karnow. *Vietnam: A History*. New York: Viking Penguin, 1991.

CHAPTER 11:

Brzezinski, Richard. *Polish Armies 1569–1696 (2)*. Oxford: Osprey, 1988.

Frost, Robert I. *The Northern Wars: War, State and Society in Northeastern Europe, 1558–1721*. Harlow, U.K.: Longman, 2000.

Kagan, Frederick W., and Robin Higham, eds. *The Military History of Tsarist Russia*. New York: Palgrave Macmillan, 2002.

Pennington, D. H. *Europe in the Seventeenth Century*. Second Edition. Harlow, U.K.: Longman, 1989.

Reddaway, W. F., J. H. Penson, O. Halecki, and R. Dyboski, eds. *The Cambridge History of Poland to 1696*. New York: Octagon Books, 1978.

Riasanovsky, Nicholas V. *A History of Russia*. Fifth Edition. New York: Oxford University Press, 1993.

CHAPTER 12:

Gerolymatos, André. *The Balkan Wars: Conquest, Revolution, and Retribution from the Ottoman Era to the Twentieth Century and Beyond*. New York: Basic Books, 2002.

Kaplan, Robert D. *Balkan Ghosts: A Journey Through History*. New York: St. Martin's Press, 1993.

Mazower, Mark. *The Balkans: A Short History*. New York: The Modern Library, 2000.

CHAPTER 13:

Grandin, Greg. *The Blood of Guatemala: A History of Race and Nation*. Durham, NC: Duke University Press, 2000.

Perera, Victor. *Unfinished Conquest: The Guatemalan Tragedy*. Berkeley, CA: University of California Press, 1995.

Sanford, Victoria. *Buried Secrets: Truth and Human Rights in Guatemala*. New York: Palgrave Macmillan, 2004.

Schlesinger, Stephen, and Stephen Kinzer. *Bitter Fruit: The Story of the American Coup in Guatemala*, Revised and Expanded. Cambridge, MA: David Rockefeller Center for Latin American Studies, 2005.

CHAPTER 14:

Deng, Francis Mading. *War of Visions: Conflicts of Identities in Sudan*. Washington, DC: Brookings Institution Press, 1995.

Flint, Julie. *Darfur: A New History of a Long War*. Second Edition. London: Zed Books, 2008.

Johnson, Douglas. *The Root Causes of Sudan's Civil Wars*. Bloomington, IN: Indiana University Press, 2003.

O'Ballance, Edgar. *Sudan, Civil War and Terrorism, 1976–1999*. New York: Palgrave Macmillan, 2000.

Poggo, Scopas S. *The First Sudanese Civil War: Africans, Arabs, and Israelis in the Southern Sudan, 1955–1972*. New York: Palgrave Macmillan, 2008.

U.S. Library of Congress, "Library of Congress Country Study: Sudan—Foreign Military Assistance." www.country-data.com/cgi-bin/query/r-13451.html.

ACKNOWLEDGMENTS

————————

Thanks to Will Kiester, Fair Winds Press publisher, and Cara Connors, editor, for their help with forming and writing this work. Also Karen Levy, for her great job copyediting; Tiffany Hill, for her uncanny organizational skills; and Sheila Hart, for her fine design work. I would also like to thank my brother, Mark Cummins, whose voluminous knowledge of lengthy mayhem I was able to tap into.

ABOUT THE AUTHOR

————————

Joseph Cummins is the author of *The World's Bloodiest History*, *War Chronicles: From Chariots to Flintlocks*, *War Chronicles: From Flintlocks to Machine Guns*, *History's Greatest Untold Stories*, *Great Rivals in History: When Politics Get Personal*, *President Obama and a New Birth of Freedom*, and *Anything for a Vote: Dirty Tricks, Cheap Shots, and October Surprises in U.S. Presidential Campaigns*. He has also written a novel, *The Snow Train*. He lives in Maplewood, New Jersey.

INDEX

275